KU-460-472

Acquiring a Conception of Mind:
A Review of Psychological Research and Theory

Peter Mitchell
School of Psychology
University of Birmingham, UK

Psychology Press
An imprint of Erlbaum (UK) Taylor & Francis

Copyright © 1996 by Psychology Press
an imprint of Erlbaum (UK) Taylor & Francis Ltd.
   All rights reserved. No part of this book may be reproduced in any form,
   by photostat, microform, retrieval system, or any other means without the
   prior written permission of the publisher.

Psychology Press, Publishers
27 Church Road
Hove
East Sussex, BN3 2FA
UK

British Library Cataloguing in Publication Data

A catalogue record for this book is available from the British Library

   ISBN 0-86377-736-8 (Hbk)
   ISBN 0-86377-737-6 (Pbk)

Printed and bound in the United Kingdom by Biddles Ltd., Guildford and King's Lynn

10016834606

For my son, Andrew —
the light of my life

Contents

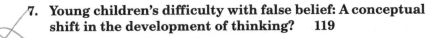

**7. Young children's difficulty with false belief: A conceptual
    shift in the development of thinking?   119**

**8. The reality masking hypothesis: The idea of a smooth
    developmental progression   135**

Acknowledgements

If it had not been for my friend and colleague Elizabeth Robinson I would not have had much to say in this book. Most of my own research that I report was either conducted in collaboration with Elizabeth or at the very least in consultation with her. Apart from that, she has made detailed comments on the first draft that have resulted in very substantial improvements to the final version. Norman Freeman and Peter Hobson, plus an anonymous reviewer appointed by the publisher, made invaluable comments. My friend and ex-student Rebecca Saltmarsh also made comments on the whole of the first draft. She too has contributed in an important way to the body of research that I report. My other ex-student, Emma Steverson, influenced the direction of my thinking, both with her ideas and the findings she obtained. My present student, Laura Taylor, has also offered valuable input with her findings to date, even though her PhD is still at an early stage. Robert W. Mitchell (no relation) made very detailed comments on the first draft of Chapter 2, which helped strengthen it substantially. I am grateful to Judy Dunn and Alan Leslie, who both provided encouragement and guidance in the planning stage. Having written the first draft, I read aloud the whole thing, chapter by chapter, to my wife Rita and son Andrew. Both made invaluable comments that helped improve the presentation of the final version. The bulk of research I was involved in personally was supported by three ESRC project grants. Elizabeth Robinson was co-director of these and Donald Peterson and Kevin Riggs were involved in one of them.

CHAPTER ONE

Understanding minds

INTRODUCTION

The purpose of this first chapter is to introduce the topic and then provide an overview of the rest of the book. The aim of the book is to present a comprehensive and up-to-date review of research into the development of what is widely known as "theory of mind". This is not referring to the theory held formally by a researcher, but rather to the notion or insights that ordinary people have about the mind. The human understanding of mind appears at times to be so sophisticated that it seems appropriate to say metaphorically that we all (or nearly all of us) possess our own informal theory of what the mind is. This form of intelligence (for that is what it is) has profound functional benefits that permit interpersonal understanding and social coordination. Humans live in complex social groups, and the degree to which any individual can thrive and prosper will be determined by the extent to which the individual can function smoothly in a social context. We require the skills of empathy, diplomacy, and guile if we are to be held in high esteem; without such esteem, we stand little chance of enjoying the privileges that will be experienced by those who have greater interpersonal insight. In order to investigate this intriguing and tantalising aspect of human psychology, it is valuable to explore the origin of the social intellect and how it develops. Hence, the topic forms a branch of developmental psychology.

The book contains a critical review of a wide variety of research that is organised by theme under several major subheadings, and these form the chapters of the book. The aim was to provide a description and evaluation of the research, in conjunction with a synthesis of the myriad findings and conflicting theories propounded by different psychologists. In doing this, I have expressed a particular point of view that is both supported and driven by the research I have been engaged in personally over the past decade. In other words, the book does not just reflect and summarise what is to be found in frontline journal articles, but the aim is to take our understanding a step further. In writing the book, I have assumed that the reader will already be familiar with the conventions of a psychological monograph, whilst at the same time I have striven to ensure that the book is highly readable. Given the level of detail and specialism, the book is probably most suited to people who are taking a final-year undergraduate course on the topic, people taking a postgraduate degree, and researchers who work in this field of investigation. It will also be of interest to practitioners in clinical psychology who specialise in autism; in particular the final two chapters. I shall set the scene by very briefly placing the development of an understanding of mind in its broadest context, both with respect to the history of our species and the history of the research tradition in developmental psychology.

TECHNOLOGICAL OR SOCIAL INTELLECT?

Several million years ago our ancestor Homo habillis inhabited this planet. The creature was so named because fossil evidence implicated a newly evolved ability to make and use tools. The arrival of our handyman ancestor seemed to herald the birth of technical and technological intelligence that we take as the precursor of our own scientific and mathematical competence. Presumably, without such competence the industrial revolution would never have occurred, though obviously sociological processes featured prominently in contributing to the unfolding of our history. Although there are negative ramifications of the fruits of our technological prowess, it is sometimes difficult not to celebrate and admire the achievements. We have conquered the sea and the air and have even ventured into space. It seems that the existence of a technological intellect over several millennia has contributed substantially to the industrial and scientific revolution that we now experience.

However, we should not lose sight of the fact that an ability to exert substantial change on our physical environment is something that has emerged very recently in the history of our species. Our species prospered for many tens of thousands of years prior to the advent of the technological revolution. It is thus tempting to suggest that, paradoxically, our technological prowess might actually be a by-product of an intelligence that evolved outside the technological arena. Indeed, the giant human intellect evolved in the context of a hunter-gatherer social milieu. Perhaps the evolutionary challenge that stimulated the ballooning of our brain and mind was the increasing complexity of the social rather than the physical environment.

In the late 20th century, perhaps it is not surprising that those who have sought to measure individual differences in intellectual ability have devised tests that are, generally speaking, of a mathematical character. People who can hold in mind lots of information all at once, and who can manipulate that information without losing the thread, are likely to be the people who do well on such tests. People who can mentally rotate figures, and abstract parts from larger patterns, will get a high score. People who have an aptitude for chess and grappling with computer programs would also probably fare well. Suppose we could identify a person whose intellectual profile matches the characteristics we assume are necessary to achieve a high score on a test of intelligence; this person might have charm, be skilful in handling people, and have lots of faithful and supportive friends. Sadly, though, it is also highly likely that the person with the fine mathematical intellectual profile is something of a loner, awkward with others, and not well liked. What are we to make of this? Are social skill, tact, sensitivity, and general intuition where people are concerned qualities that do not require much intelligence? Alternatively, do they require a different kind of cognitive activity that falls beyond the scope of a standard test of intelligence? If the latter, what is its origin? How important is its development in children?

SOCIAL INTELLECT IN APES

Nicholas Humphrey (1992) ventured to the African rainforests in search of the origin of human intelligence, with the aim of observing apes in their natural habitat. He expected to find the glimmer of a primitive mathematical and technological competence, which would be suggested by the inkling of an embryo capacity to use tools for the construction of shelters as protection against the elements. Additionally, weapons might be devised to ward off predators. Meanwhile, systematic and logical thought might be in evidence in the planning of strategies of how to forage most efficiently for food. Contrary to Humphrey's expectations, the apes he observed in the heart of the forest apparently were not using their intellect—certainly not for the things he had anticipated. The apes were not inventive in making tools and they seemed to face no intellectually taxing challenge where food and predators were concerned.

It gradually became apparent that the apes faced a nonobvious intellectual challenge of such proportions that their cognitive abilities were pushed to their limit. The apes lived in a social group, which formed a kind of mini-society in terms of its hierarchical structure. Some were dominant and some submissive. Some were popular and some not so popular. Individuals apparently do not necessarily hold a fixed position, to which they are born, in the social order. To prosper and hold influence over others in this context seems to require very substantial intellectual ability to understand the psychology of one's acquaintances. Esteem and survival depend critically on the ability to wield social psychological skills, which in turn presumably depend on having good insight into others. These skills would determine the individual's prospects in reproduction, including the extent to which the reproduction was successful and profusive. According to this criterion, the successful apes were not necessarily the ones who were good at foraging, skilful with tools, or aggressive toward predators.

Accordingly, ever since Premack and Woodruff (1978) asked whether chimpanzees possess a "theory of mind" in their seminal article, the study of the ape's social intellect has aroused great interest. It seems that chimpanzees might have some understanding of deception, be capable of empathy in a primitive sense, and possess what could qualify as a rudimentary understanding of knowledge and belief (see Povinelli, 1993, for a review), though considerable caution is required when attributing sophisticated intellectual abilities to apes (Heyes, 1993). Having said that, it is not surprising to find that the ape's understanding of mind is far less developed than that of the human (e.g. Povinelli & Eddy, in press; Savage-Rumbaugh et al., 1993).

Having speculated very briefly on the history of interpersonal understanding, the way is prepared for considering the richness of human development in an understanding of mind. The obvious starting point is Piaget, since his writings not only dominate research into cognitive development in general, but also have a great deal to say about the development of understanding intersubjectivity. In other words, Piaget had a substantial interest in children's emerging understanding that different people hold different visual and conceptual perspectives. Without such a conception, interpersonal understanding would be impossible.

PIAGET'S CONTRIBUTION

Briefly, among Piaget's many remarkable insights was that we have to overcome inadequacies in our intellect that will allow us to achieve a mathematical and technical competence, with the consequence that our understanding of other people will improve also. He thus forged a link between rational thought and social behaviour. Thanks to this, we can regard Piaget as a pioneer of the cognitive approach to the origin of social understanding. Piaget suggested that in the "preoperational stage" children are egocentric, meaning that they have serious difficulty in conceiving of anybody else's cognitive or even visual perspective. A classic example is 6- and 7-year-old children's difficulty with the three mountains task. In this, the child is shown a model of three mountains side by side, each with a distinctive feature at the summit. The child is initially allowed to navigate right the way round the model, taking in how it looks from the various vantage points. Finally, the child stands at one particular point and is asked how the mountains look to another person situated on the opposite side of the model. To make a response, children are offered a selection of photos that show the model from the various perspectives. Children of this age wrongly tend to select a photo showing their own view in preference to one showing the array in left-right reversal.

Piaget's interpretation was roughly as follows. The children have an intellect that is dominated by immediate appearances. Consequently, they seem to assume that their current view of the array is the only one. A bizarre implication is that effectively children are behaving as though the array undergoes radical changes in its physical structure as the child wanders around it. This is not to say that the child is ignorant of the *permanence* of reality but rather of the underlying objective essence and substance of reality that is non-person-specific. The child therefore cannot conceive of how a person standing in one position will have a visual experience of the array that is different from a person situated in another position. The child is thus trapped in his or her own subjective experience of the world and is hence said to be egocentric.

Piaget noticed that children of the same age show a related difficulty in making judgements about moral misdemeanours, which require an understanding of the intent behind the act rather than the extent of damage caused. For example, they judge the naughtiness of a protagonist according to the seriousness of the damage he caused rather than according to whether he was well or badly intentioned. The children thus seem to concentrate on the salient physical damage in preference to the hidden psychological motive. Being egocentric seems to prevent children from conceptual as well as perceptual role-taking.

Piaget reports that slightly older children are seemingly able to contrast their own view with another's and are able to consider intent when making moral judgements. Although he stressed that chronological age is only indirectly related with more sophisticated judgements, nonetheless the age of success in clinically normal children seldom deviated greatly from approximately 7 years. This age norm, coupled with Piaget's assumptions about the way in which knowledge is constructed, seems to have persuaded him that these children's intellects had undergone a cognitive restructuring—they profited from a radical conceptual shift that allowed them to shed their immature egocentrism.

Piaget's theory and methodology has been subjected to severe criticism (e.g. Donaldson, 1978), and in consequence there is reason to suppose that he underestimated children's abilities. Additionally, Piaget seems to have underestimated the social and cultural contribution to development. Nonetheless, a remaining legacy of his work is the idea that children might start out with little capacity for understanding other people's conceptual perspectives. Additionally, many researchers are attached to the idea that development of such understanding progresses through stages involving radical conceptual shifts in thought processes. In other words, we are asking questions about the character of developmental history that allows people to realise their intellectual potential to understand minds. An understanding of mind stands at the heart of the human intellect: What can we say about its development?

DEFINING A CONCEPTION OF MIND

Examples of things associated with mind are purpose, desire, imagination, daydreams, thoughts, communication, and deception. It is virtually impossible to state categorically what does and does not qualify as an understanding of mind. Nonetheless, this has not deterred brave theoreticians from making a good attempt. Premack and Woodruff (1978) define a "theory of mind" as an ability to impute mental states to others and to self. They specifically investigated the ape's ability to understand purpose and desire. Success was defined as the ape's ability to link the apparent intention of a protagonist with an appropriate goal or outcome. This is something their participant achieved, which led the authors to claim that apes probably do have a primitive theory of mind. The conclusion aroused considerable controversy, which stimulated something of a rethink on what qualifies as a theory of mind.

Perhaps the most influential reaction to Premack and Woodruff's (1978) controversial argument was to be found in the commentary by Dennett (1978). He suggested that to qualify as holding an understanding of the mind as a representational organ, the individual should be able to acknowledge that people hold beliefs which govern their behaviour. Note that we would not say that a rat trained in a Skinner box exhibits behaviour that is governed by its beliefs. Rather the behaviour can be described as the product of the prior reinforcement history. However, we can say that people conceive of such and such being true and act accordingly. Sometimes, this leads to curious acts. For example, certain people might come to believe that a spiritual entity is beckoning them, tragically leading to a mass communal suicide. It is very difficult indeed to imagine how that behaviour is the product of reinforcement history, but we are able to explain it once we know that the hapless individuals who met their doom had acquired bizarre and dangerous beliefs, which caused them to commit a fatal act.

At the risk of taking this depressing theme a stage further, jealous lovers have been known to commit what they consider to be hideous acts of revenge on someone they perceive to be pursuing their partner. If we knew that the recipient of the lover's wrath was guilty, then the vengeance would make some kind of sense. If the recipient was actually entirely innocent, then superficially the injury inflicted upon him might seem puzzling. Why should he be the victim of an attack if he is innocent? The story begins to fall into place when we recognise that the explanation lies not in the reality of the person's guilt or innocence, but in what the angry lover believes about the guilt or innocence.

One of the vital things we need to know about people is that their actions are governed not just by externally observable contingencies, but also by their beliefs. If we are to thrive and prosper in a social group, we need to be able to predict and explain the behaviour of those around us. Making accurate predictions depends on making accurate diagnoses of belief. On a more sophisticated but sinister level, we can say that anyone who is skilled in manipulating the content of other people's beliefs is equipped to control the behaviour of others—perhaps to suit their own ends. This is, of course, the stuff of good literature. Shakespeare's plays are full of the intrigue of the struggle for power over other people. The unprincipled characters in those stories wield their psychological skills to manipulate information to mislead others. This reveals not only a dark human skill, but also shows the intrigue we find in such machinations, given the continuing popularity of Shakespeare and his imitators over the centuries. Additionally, propaganda and commercial advertising campaigns are premised on the assumption that to influence the content of belief is to influence the overt behaviour. It might be possible to coerce people to behave in a certain way, but it is a good deal more satisfactory for the despot or profiteer if he can get people to behave in the same way whilst thinking that they are doing so out of their own volition!

In this context, it seems to make sense to say that an understanding that people hold beliefs should be a core criterion for judging whether or not an individual possesses an understanding of mind. The problem falls within the province of experimental psychology when we ask what kind of test would be appropriate for assessing this capacity. Suppose children witnessed a scene in which John left his ball in the box before going out to play. Subsequently, we are told that John is going to return to play with his ball again. The observing children participants are then asked where John thinks his ball is or where he will look for his ball, and they would probably respond correctly by gesturing to the box. Hence, the children would correctly have answered a question asking about another person's belief, and apparently understand how that would govern his behaviour. However, Dennett (1978) urges us not to be seduced by this correct judgement into thinking that the child really does understand anything about mind. Although the children were asked about belief, and they responded correctly, that does not guarantee that they understand anything about mind. Rather, the children could know virtually nothing about mind but make their best attempt at an answer to the question by responding as though they had been asked "Where is the ball?", in place of "Where will he look?" or "Where does he think it is?"

We require a test that is capable of showing that the children answer correctly for the right reason. Essentially, we need a test of understanding false belief. Suppose John's ball was moved, unknown to him, from the box to the cupboard in his absence. A correct judgement is still that he will look for his ball in the box, or that he thinks it is in there, because that is where he last saw it. However, if children interpreted the question effectively to mean "Where is the ball?", then they would now respond by gesturing to the cupboard. Wimmer and Perner (1983) put Dennett's (1978) suggestion to the test on young children, and found that those aged around 5 years and above judged that the protagonist would look in the place he last saw the item and not where it currently is. They felt entitled to claim that children aged 5 years have a theory of mind, but that the younger children they tested, who reported current reality when asked about belief, did not . Wimmer and Perner also noted a sharp age trend, and on the strength of this concluded that children's acquisition of a representational under-standing of mind is achieved in a radical conceptual shift in thought.

Although the age is different, their conclusion seemed to fit with the Piagetian notion of egocentrism in early childhood, which is shed when thought undergoes restructuring. Having said that, recent research suggests that preschoolers' lack of insight into mind is best not described as egocentrism in the sense that Piaget intended. The research surrounding this is explored thoroughly in Chapters 7 and 8.

UNDERSTANDING MIND BEFORE 4 YEARS OF AGE

Wimmer and Perner (1983) would have us believe that, prior to age 4, children do not have a representational understanding of mind. However, very young children certainly know something about mind. Wellman (1990) reports that 2- and 3-year-olds at least understand that the properties of physically real things are distinct from those of thoughts, as we will see in Chapter 3. They judged correctly that a real cookie is publicly accessible and enduring (so long as it was not eaten!). In contrast, they acknowledged that a thought of a cookie could not be given to a friend and could not be saved until the next day. They also recognised that it is possible to do things with thoughts that are impossible with real objects. For example, it is possible to elongate a thought of a balloon just by thinking about out it, but impossible to do the same with a real balloon just by thinking about it. Wellman also reports that 2- and 3-year-olds have considerable insight into desires. Apparently, they understand that knowing a protagonist's desire can help us predict his behaviour. Children are also accurate in stating precisely when desires are or are not satisfied and are able to recall prior unsatisfied desires (Gopnik & Slaughter, 1991). This led Wellman to argue that initially children are just desire psychologists but subsequently they develop into belief-desire psychologists.

Another relevant characteristic of 2-year-old children is their capacity for pretence or symbolic play (see Chapter 2). Leslie (1987) argued persuasively that the very existence of pretence in young children implies that they have an up-and-running understanding of mind. The central tenet of his argument hinges around the claim that the ability to pretend implicates an ability to handle referential opacity. Quine (1961) introduced this term in linguistic contexts. He pointed out that the statement

"Jane believes the Prime Minister lives at Number 10"

does not mean the same as

"Jane believes John Major lives at Number 10".

At the time of writing, it so happens that the Prime Minister and John Major are one and the same person. However, we cannot be sure of the equivalence of these two statements, because that would depend on whether Jane's belief is true or false. Additionally, consider the statement

"Jane believes Clinton lives at Number 10."

If we are asked if this is true or false, impulsively we might be tempted to say "false" on the grounds that Clinton actually lives in the White House. However, that could be incorrect, because however silly, it might be the case that Jane believes Clinton lives at Number 10. In these contexts, to evaluate statements with respect to belief is to handle referential opacity. In other words, handling referential opacity and understanding about belief could reduce to the same thing. So anyone who can handle opacity can handle belief, and so should be credited with an understanding of the representational character of mind.

According to Leslie (1987), symbolic pretence (beginning at age 18 months) would not be possible without a working understanding of referential opacity (see Chapter 2 for his justification). He argues that the emergence of pretence, rather than ability to acknowledge false belief, is therefore the appropriate criterion for saying that the child has an understanding of mind. Pretence developmentally predates ability to acknowledge false belief by a couple of years, so Leslie suggests that an understanding of mind is very primitive indeed and is probably innate. A further implication of this account is that there is no radical restructuring of thought at age 4 years that equips the child with an understanding of mind—he or she has one already. This claim has aroused healthy controversy, which is reviewed in Chapter 2.

APPLYING AN UNDERSTANDING OF MIND

An understanding of mind could be deployed against others competitively or it could be used cooperatively to share with others and learn from them. An obvious example of the former is deception. Since an understanding of mind almost certainly owes its existence to whatever utilitarian value it can confer, then the place to look for the earliest understanding of mind is in the context of the child applying his or her knowledge to advantage. This was a view adopted by Chandler,

Fritz, and Hala (1989), reviewed in Chapter 4. They report that even children as young as 2 years seem to understand something about fabricating misinformation in order to mislead a competitor about the location of a prize, a prize that the child actually wants to retain for him or herself. It seems difficult to explain this ability without crediting the child with some insight into beliefs. Their actions seemed designed to manipulate the content of belief, which implies that they have some understanding of the existence of mind. However, the research involving 2- and 3-year-old children has aroused controversy. On balance, the evidence does point toward understanding of mind in preschoolers, but the claims are disputed.

A uniquely human application of an understanding of mind falls within the province of verbal communication (see Chapters 5 and 6). Knowing the meaning of words and understanding grammar is sometimes insufficient to understand what the speaker means. Often, we also need to know something about what the speaker is thinking (independently of the content of the message) in order to decipher what is said. In its simplest form, the nucleus of this ability might be apparent in the 18-month-old child who is rapidly acquiring a vocabulary. In some circumstances, the infant and adult are fixated on different things when the adult utters a novel word. For example, suppose the mother says "dog" when she is looking at the family pet while the infant is actually gazing at the chair. Would the infant call the chair a dog thereafter? The seminal work of Dare Baldwin (e.g. Baldwin & Moses, 1994) suggests that they do not. When infants hear their mother speak, they promptly check their mother's face to establish her direction of gaze and then focus on the object of the *mother's* attention. Effectively, they are behaving as though meaning is the privilege of the person articulating the message, which this example suggests is essential for vocabulary to expand rapidly. Exactly what infants understand about mind is unclear, but at least they have some insight into the relation between visual attention and reference.

Although an understanding of mind benefits understanding of meaning in the context of verbal communication, the debt is repaid with dividends. Once we are fluent in communication, then a particularly direct channel of access to other minds becomes available. What people think is implicit in what they say, and we can assume an affinity between the language of speech and the language of thought. When people speak to us, there is a sense in which we hear their thoughts, allowing us to picture the psychology of people around us in a detail and lucidity that surely would be impossible if we were without language. This idea is explored in Chapter 6.

IS THE CHILD'S CONCEPTION OF MIND A THEORY?

The child's conception of mind has been compared to a theory for two primary reasons (see Chapter 7). First, some claim that the child's ability to acknowledge false belief is sudden, making its first appearance at about the age of 4 years. It appears that the child aged 4 or 5 years is not just like a preschooler equipped with additional knowledge. Rather, the 4–5-year-old is claimed to have a different *quality* of thought. The ability to acknowledge belief seems like a categorical thing. Surely, either you take into account someone's belief or you do not. Many claim that a sharp increase in correct judgements emerges between 3 and 4 years of age. This phenomenon seems to lend itself to the claim that the child has suddenly acquired a new concept. In turn, the possibility that a new concept is suddenly acquired resembles the revolutions in thinking that take place when there is a shift from one conceptual paradigm to another in natural science. *the evidence for new theory (or against current one) Build up until you feel have to change theory*.

Another characteristic of scientific theories is that a principle stands at the core, which explains diverse phenomena in a parsimonious manner and is able to make testable predictions. The principle at the heart of the child's "theory" of mind was held by Wimmer, Hogrefe, and Perner (1988) to be a rule that links informational access with belief: They suggest that children construct the rule "seeing is believing; not seeing is not believing (or not knowing)". Hence, children would not impute false beliefs to others if they did not realise that it is necessary to see in order to know; they might suppose it is possible to know without seeing. However, this suggestion now seems untenable. Gopnik and Astington (1988) found that children had just as much difficulty in recalling their own prior but outdated belief as in predicting another person's false belief. The children did not need to make any link between seeing and believing to recall their own belief, but simply accessed their memory and called up an old belief resident in there. Whatever the cause of young children's difficulty with false belief, it is more general than could be accounted for by suggesting they lack a rule linking seeing with believing in the sense that Wimmer et al. intended, as we shall see in Chapter 7.

The research reviewed in Chapter 8 proposes an alternative to the view that children possess an informal theory of what the mind is. A novel way of looking at the problem is to see children as appealing to one of two potential criteria when judging about belief. They can either report reality (usually current reality) or they can report a particular hypothetical reality that they themselves actually believe is untrue. Physical reality may hold an attentional magnetism for young children. It may be that when judging belief they report reality not by default on lacking understanding of belief, but because reality holds an attentional bias for them. The appeal of reality could seduce children into making a wrong judgement. What changes with age might not be the acquisition of a sudden insight into belief, but a gradual fading of a reality bias. Supporting evidence shows that a reality bias is still present in older children and even in adults in some circumstances. On the other side of the coin, it seems that young children, whom we would normally expect to give a realist judgement, can succeed in acknowledging false belief if their attention is diverted away from current reality. It seems that an understanding of mind is not theory-like, and that its development does not involve a conceptual revolution. Instead, it might be that an understanding of mind is based on an ability to simulate mentally another individual's conceptual perspective. This suggestion carries far-reaching implications for the structure of human knowledge and the character of perception, which are discussed in Chapter 8. These implications concern not just the development of understanding about mind, but extend also into the province of adult social cognition.

AUTISM

The basis of an understanding of mind is a gift donated to us by our evolutionary history. Just as gifts can be granted, so they can be denied. Having an understanding of mind is so much part of the human condition that it is very difficult to imagine what it would feel like without one. Indeed it is hard to conceive of how we might go about recognising an unfortunate individual who lacked this faculty. The evidence reviewed in Chapter 9 suggests that people with autism could be seriously lacking in an understanding of mind. Wing and Gould (1979) characterise autism as a triad of impairments, these being in the domains of imagination, communication, and socialisation. If an individual did lack an understanding of mind, then he or she probably would not engage in pretend play, since this could only be generated by a capacity that stands at the core of an understanding of mind, according to Leslie (1987). When Wing and Gould suggest that children with autism lack imagination, apart from other things, they mean that they do not engage in pretend play. To say that a child does not engage in pretence in itself is perhaps tantamount to saying that they lack an understanding of mind.

As for communication, there is a variety of reasons why this should be linked in principle with an understanding of mind. As Baldwin's (e.g. Baldwin & Moses, 1994) work suggests, to acquire vocabulary rapidly depends on a working understanding that meaning is the prerogative of another mind. If the child did not have this working understanding, then vocabulary acquisition and general linguistic development would be tardy. This is precisely what we find in autism. However, there is a double jeopardy here. If the individual is poor at communication, then they will be denied access to other minds through the medium of communication. As discussed in Chapter 10, speech provides a window on the mind, so an individual who was unable to profit from this due to impaired communicative abilities presumably would also be pretty much left in the dark where the unique psychology of those around them is concerned. A feature of autism is that the child shows severe impairments in language and communication. Language development can be delayed by several years. When the child is able to converse, this is characteristically abnormal. The frustrated parent and teacher will be able to exchange words with the child, yet there will be an intangible feeling of failure to share information or achieve any kind of interpersonal connectedness through speech.

If the child lacks imaginative capacities and communicative abilities, the account presented here suggests that he or she would effectively be lacking an understanding of mind, which in turn would be manifest as defective social behaviour. Hence, children with autism would show impairments in socialisation. This completes Wing's triad of impairments, showing an irresistible link between the signs of autism and the lack of an understanding of mind. Having said that, autism seems to amount to more than just deficiency in understanding mind. Children with autism show abnormalities in basic affective contact, which seems difficult to explain purely by reference to impaired understanding of mind. Additionally, people with autism show rigidity in their behaviour, coupled with a stimulus-driven impulsiveness that might account for some of their difficulties in understanding mind but that also engenders more general cognitive deficiencies.*

Chapter 10 offers a speculative attempt to make further links between communication and understanding mind. The account is the culmination of the picture emanating from the rest of the book, but, being speculative, seeks to take the story a step further. The idea being advanced is that ultimately, linguistic communication is the most powerful process supporting the development of an understanding of mind. The structured symbolism that language offers as a tool of thought might assist the child to contemplate representations of things detached from their primary iconic (visually faithful) image. The child is then liberated from exclusive focus on current reality, and would be equipped to think about the content of mind as something substantive and distinct from reality. Both Leslie (1987) and Harris and Kavanaugh (1993) ascribed such properties to pretence, but surely the system would be a good deal more powerful and flexible if it were supported by a lexicon of words that serve as labels for objects once removed from reality, that stand in an arbitrary relation to reality. Because the relation is inherently arbitrary it allows labels to be easily redefined, so what is X for me can be redefined as Y for John. I think X and John thinks Y. To illustrate, consider the following. It so happens that I believe the content of a particular Smarties tube to be pencils, but I can simulate and notate John's false belief that it contains Smarties by saying that what is pencils for me is Smarties for John. Utilising the arbitrary relation between things and labels in this way allows me to keep track of John's false belief that stands in distinction from my own. This is a particular use of language as a tool of thought.

Individuals who have impaired or nonexistent linguistic abilities, then, would find it hard to detach themselves from current reality, which would be a serious impediment to contemplating mind. In this light, it might be no coincidence that humans are uniquely linguistic creatures and have an impressive understanding of mind. Also, it might be no coincidence that children with autism have both impaired linguistic-communicative capacities and lack insight into mind. Indeed, as I said earlier, actually being able to communicate with language offers a further priceless benefit in understanding the psychology of people around us, because when we hear people talk we effectively hear their thought; so speech opens a window on the minds of our acquaintances.

The rest of this book details evidence that points to the character of the human understanding of mind. I describe and assess various theories that compete to interpret the evidence and seek to explain how development progresses. The book concludes with a novel vision of how an understanding of mind can be possible, coupled with suggestions on the main influences in its development. There are implications inherent in this for future directions in research, to explore both normal and autistic development.

CHAPTER TWO

Children's pretence

Being able to understand about mind depends on a symbolic faculty in the sense that the mind cannot be perceived directly. Whatever we understand about mind must therefore exist in the ether of mental space as a construction or symbolism. Pretence is overtly symbolic given that the child might impose an exotic identity on a mundane household object. Evidently, the child has formulated a sphere of existence that the object inhabits that is detached from the sensory input that is experienced. A world of make-believe is thus enshrined in symbolism; if the experience is not sensory then it is symbolic. If symbolism is a common denominator, we should expect a very strong link between being able to engage in pretence and having an understanding of mind. A remarkable feature of a typical 18–24-month-old toddler is his or her proficiency in two main domains of symbolism. One is that the infant uses verbal symbols to stand in for objects and uses these in effective if somewhat limited communication. Putting it plainly, the infant will have acquired a vocabulary of words that allows him or her to make assertions or exclamations about things, to refer to things and to request things. The second domain of symbolism is pretend play; for example, pretending that a banana is a telephone by holding it to the head and speaking to it with an appropriate telephone manner. Aspects of these two kinds of symbolic activity can be unified by an underlying linguistically based concept known as "referential opacity". Referential opacity is a product of symbolic activity and is embedded in symbolism.

If one lacked a symbolic capacity, then it would make no sense to say that the individual possessed a concept of referential opacity. There is an asymmetry, however, in that having a symbolic capacity is not sufficient for possession of the concept of referential opacity. In this chapter, I shall define "referential opacity" and spell out its relevance to the possession of an understanding of mind. We shall examine whether pretence, as one form of symbolic activity, implies a conception of referential opacity and ultimately the rudiment of an understanding of mind.

PRETENCE AND REFERENTIAL OPACITY

The seminal work outlining the link between early pretence and understanding of mind was formulated by Alan Leslie (1987). The claim that pretence is a sign of an underlying understanding of mind has an obvious intuitive appeal. The strength of Leslie's thesis is that it attached a cogent theoretical framework involving the concept of referential opacity to the existing intuitive link between pretence and understanding of mind. First we shall consider the intuitive aspect of pretence.

If a child lacked the imagination to conceive of a mind, then that same lack of imagination could be manifest in other ways. A profound lack of imagination would mean that the child would be exclusively immersed in the current stream of events and entirely unable to conceive of how things might have seemed in the past, how they might seem in the future, and of course how anybody else might see them. The child might be able to recall past physical events, but that would just be retrieval of traces laid down in memory by sensory experiences. However, given that the child engages in pretence, he or she is patently liberated from the here and now thanks to imagination. For example, consider the child who pretends that a banana is a telephone. Evidently, the child is able to consider an alternative (make-believe) world in which this fruit has been invested with the properties of an electronic artefact of long-distance communication (i.e. a telephone). It is then tempting to suppose that, since the child can conjure up a world in which a banana is a telephone, so he or she could conceive of a world in which a person (anyone—somebody else) would have a different perspective or views. If a child can conceive of the latter then he or she should be credited with an understanding of mind.

Not only is pretence a symptom of a capability to detach oneself from one's immediate experiences and sensations, it could actually serve as a tool for reasoning about other minds. Harris (1991) suggests that a child might make judgements about what other people think and feel by simulating through pretence how oneself might feel in a different state of informedness or emotion. For example, the child might be able to pretend that he or she was in possession of a desirable and coveted toy. Engaging in this pretence could alert the child to the possibility that one would experience a feeling of pride and joy that would accompany having such a prized object. From this, the child could extrapolate that anyone who owned a highly attractive toy would probably experience a feeling of happiness. In this way, pretence might allow the child to simulate through role playing the mental states of those around him or her.

However, there are at least two points of controversy surrounding the claim that pretence implies a capacity to understand mind through simulation. The first is that a simulation account seems to make the tacit assumption that children have a predetermined understanding of their own mind and all they have to do to make judgements about other people's feelings and beliefs is to introspect and simulate. If it turned out that the child were unable to reflect on his or her own state of mind, then he or she could hardly be expected to use this as a basis for judging about others. There is a body of existing evidence showing that young children have just as much difficulty acknowledging that they themselves have beliefs as they do in acknowledging others' beliefs (e.g. Gopnik & Astington, 1988). This finding suggests that young children might generally lack understanding of belief (but this will be challenged in Chapter 8), in which case they could not utilise knowledge of their own mental states as a basis for simulating the mental states of others. The second point of controversy is the competing evidence suggesting that children employ simple rules for inferring other people's feelings and beliefs. For example, the child might apply the rule that if John has not looked in the box then he does not know what is inside. Applying such a rule obviates the need to imagine how oneself would feel or think in a different circumstance, and instead it might be possible to hold a rule-based understanding of mind that does not involve mental simulation. We shall explore these issues more thoroughly in subsequent chapters but at this point we shall persevere with our investigation of the link between pretence and understanding mind.

Leslie (1987) argues (as does Perner, 1988) that the concept underlying an understanding of mind is what Quine (1961) called "referential opacity". Quine was a philosopher interested in analysing the logical implications that follow from the use of certain expressions. In particular, he was interested in the effect on the meaning of a sentence caused by verbs of propositional attitude. These verbs include mental state terms, such as *think, believe, desire*, and, Leslie would argue, *pretend*. In the absence of a verb of propositional attitude, sentences can be paraphrased without risk of changing the meaning of the sentence. For example, if it were true that the President lived at the

White House, then it would also be true that Clinton lived at the White House (at the time of writing). This follows in the sense that one aspect of the principal inhabitant of the White House is "President" and another aspect is "Clinton". If we placed the same sentence in the context of a verb of propositional attitude (e.g. "think"), then paraphrasing the sentence as before could jeopardise the meaning (where a change in meaning is tested by checking the truth or falsity of the sentence). For example, if it were true that *Jane thinks* that the President lived at the White House, it would not necessarily be true that Jane thinks that Clinton lived at the White House. It might be that Jane is naïve where US administration is concerned and assumes that Bush is President and therefore the inhabitant of the White House. Jane might not have an accurate conception of the principal inhabitant of the White House in its (his) various aspects.

In other words, we can make a judgement on the truth of simple sentences like "Clinton lives at the White House." by using what we know of reality as a yardstick criterion. We ask ourselves whether or not it is true that Clinton lives at the White House, and it so happens that it is true. However, it is not so easy to make a judgement on the truth of a simple sentence like "Jane thinks Bush lives at the White House." Impulsively, we might be tempted to say the sentence is false by applying our knowledge of reality as a criterion: Although Bush used to live in the White House, he does not do so now. However, on reflection we might be willing to concede that Jane has an unusual informational history, causing her to think something untrue about who is the occupant of the White House. In other words, we must assess the truth of the sentence in relation to Jane's distinctive belief framework and suppress our own impinging knowledge of what holds true in reality. Metaphorically, we should place any statement following on from "Jane thinks" in quotation marks to abstract it from the truth conditions that would normally apply. Within the mental world Jane inhabits, it might be held as true that Bush lives at the White House. "Bush" and "President" might be different aspects of one and the same thing as far as Jane is concerned. To use Leslie's phraseology, we could say that we *decouple* the statement from what we know of reality when assessing whether or not it is correct. That is, we confine the statement "Bush lives in the White House" to epistemic quarantine to avoid confusing it with what we know or presume maintains in reality.

If we have a working understanding of the construction Quine (1961) termed *referential opacity*, then we have a fundamental basis for an understanding of mind as an organ that interprets and represents reality. No longer would we be restricted to thinking just about reality, and our thinking could be once removed, allowing us to think of propositions about reality. We will understand that propositions are held about reality, yet grasp that those very propositions are not isomorphic with reality but independent of it. Hence, we will understand that people have propositions about reality swimming round in their minds, and these propositions could be unique to individuals and maybe different from reality. It might be (but might not) a small further step to understand how desires link with beliefs to govern behaviour, at which time we should credit the individual with an elementary belief-desire conception of mind according to Wellman's (1990) definition.

If a young child can be shown to possess the concept of referential opacity, then we have a very sound reason for suspecting that the child could have an understanding of mind. That is one reason why a focus on early pretence has rightly assumed a central position in this field of investigation: Leslie (1987) argued that an analogue of the linguistically based version of referential opacity is an essential and even a defining feature of pretence. Pretence shares properties with referential opacity in at least two important respects: (1) nonsubstitution by coreferential terms; (2) nonentailment of truth. We shall consider these two criteria in turn.

Nonsubstitution by coreferential terms

As mentioned earlier, if we are told that Jane believes the President lives at the White House, we are not entitled to exchange "Clinton" for "President" without risking loss of meaning. Leslie (1987) suggests that if the child pretends to communicate with a distant imaginary person with the aid of a banana, we are not entitled to substitute "banana" for "comical tropical fruit with slippery yellow skin". If we elaborate upon the standard definition of what a banana is, this will offer no insight at all into the child's pretence, and may even be misleading in this respect. For example, we can predict that under normal circumstances, bananas are something one would eat. However, this knowledge is unhelpful in predicting the child's sequence of actions in a pretend episode. Indeed, it is most unlikely that the child would eat the banana whilst pretending it was a phone. The child's pretence is concerned with telephones, and the details of a banana are incidental to this, other than that the shape lends itself to pretence about the handset of a phone. Hence, we must evaluate the child's behaviour relating to the banana in terms of the child's distinctive attitude of pretence and not in relation to our own knowledge of what bananas are really about.

According to Leslie, the child not only engages in pretence, but he or she understands about pretence. He argues this on two counts. First, the child evidently distinguishes between pretence and reality. If the child confuses the two, then he or she might expect to hear a physically real voice emanating from within the banana when pretending that it is a phone; apparently, children hold no such expectation and show no puzzlement on the sustained silence of the banana. Another example is when a young child pretends that a playing brick is a cookie. The child will gladly pretend to feed toy animals with this object and pretend to have a feast on it him or herself, but will never try to eat the brick in earnest! Young children clearly do not confuse pretence with reality and in this respect they stand in contrast to adults suffering from certain forms of mental illness who might be described as being detached from reality. Second, young children recognise pretence for what it is in other people. This point was demonstrated by Flavell, Flavell, and Green (1987), who issued an assistant with a candle that had been moulded and coloured to look like an apple. This person proceeded to take a pretend bite of the apple-candle. Observing children had no difficulty acknowledging that the person was pretending that the object was an apple but that really it was a candle. In other words, the children's knowledge of the object's true identity posed no obstacle to their accurate report of the confederate's pretence.

Nonentailment of truth

In the case of referential opacity, it is inappropriate to assess the truth of a statement by relating it to what we know of reality. Although we know that Clinton is President (at least at the time of writing!), it might be that Jane thinks Bush is President. It would be inappropriate to say the latter statement is false on the grounds that Bush is not President because the statement has to be evaluated in relation to Jane's distinctive belief framework. Putting it another way, we cannot be entirely certain what is the true state of affairs (supposing we were ignorant of who is President) from the information stating who Jane believes is President. The same applies in pretence. We cannot be sure what the true state of affairs is just from information pertaining to the child's pretence. For example, if we are told that a child is pretending that a tea cup is empty (and we cannot see whether or not it is), we cannot make any inference from this about whether the cup is actually full or empty.

This is a point that has aroused controversy, since Perner (1988) claims that we can evaluate the true state of affairs from pretence. He argues that pretence implies that something is not true. In the tea cup example, this would mean that we can infer that the cup must be full if the child is bothering to pretend that it is empty. This may seem like rather trivial nit-picking, but it is not because Perner suggests that if pretence can be shown not to have the properties of referential opacity, then an ability to pretend should not be taken as a sign that the child holds much of an understanding of mind. To relate the point to everyday situations, we might wish to say the following. Judging what people think or feel usually depends on evaluating a link between that person's mind and some aspect of reality. For example, the person's belief is held in relation to the real world rather than in relation to some fantasy world, and therefore is implicitly held as being true (even though we might know it is false). In contrast, because pretence is about a fantasy world, it would appear implicitly not to relate to what is held to maintain in the real world. Therefore, Perner argues, we can say that pretence must be about something that is not true—otherwise it would not be pretence.

Perner's (1988) argument is actually fallacious, as demonstrated by Leslie and Frith (1990). They report the case of a 2-year-old child pretending that her tea cup is full and then pretending to drink all the tea that it holds. At that moment, the child is effectively pretending that an empty cup is empty. Hence, it is possible for a child to pretend something is true when it is true, and this is after all a feature of belief that is shared with pretence, contrary to Perner (1988).

HOW MUCH DO TODDLERS UNDERSTAND ABOUT PRETENCE?

Leslie has been effective in arguing that engaging in pretence rests upon a process that has the properties of referential opacity. He has also been effective in arguing that young children can recognise pretence for what it is in others. However, Lillard (1993a,b) questions whether the child's understanding of pretence is actually reflective. If it is not, she argues, then perhaps the child does not understand pretence as a state of mind. If the child does not understand pretence as a state of mind, perhaps this is a sign that the child does not understand states of mind per se. Lillard makes a distinction, then, between understanding that someone has a pretence state of mind and that someone is acting as if such and such were the case. For example, when we consider Mother speaking to a banana, she has a pretence state of mind to the effect that the banana is a telephone, and related with this is her distinctive behaviour, about which we can say she is acting as if the banana is a telephone. Perhaps children's understanding of pretence is confined to the behavioural manifestation and does not extend to the accompanying state of mind.

This view is amplified by Jarrold, Carruthers, Smith, and Boucher (1994a). They argue that pretence could only be a sign of a conception of mind if the child held an associated attitude that pretence is make-believe. In other words, the child must understand that the pretence relates to a make-believe world for the child's behaviour to be coded as genuinely symbolic. On the face of things it might seem self-evident that the child understands his or her pretence, or any one else's pretence, to be make-believe. However, that need not be the case. If a kitten acts as if a ball of wool is prey, we might say that the kitten is playing and we might even be tempted to say that the kitten is pretending, but it would be going a bit too far to say that the kitten has a conception of mind. So what is the difference between the kitten's activity with the ball of wool and the toddler's pretending that a banana is a phone? It seems that Jarrold et al.'s view is that there is no difference and the same stance is adopted by Lillard (1993a,b). In other words, these authors are claiming that, although young children might be able to act as if such and such is the case, it need not imply that they have any conception of a distinctive attitude of pretence as a mental state.

Lillard (1993b) conducted a study to support her claim that merely engaging in pretence does not entail understanding of pretence. Children aged 4 and 5 years were introduced to a Troll doll called Moe. The experimenter explained that he was from a different world in which there were no birds, that Moe does not know what a bird is and has never seen a bird or heard of one. The experimenter then stretched out Moe's arms such that they resembled a bird spreading its wings, and proceeded to move Moe around in sweeping and graceful movements, but always with feet on the ground. The experimenter asked the observing child if Moe knows what a bird is and children readily judged that he did not. Then the experimenter asked if Moe was pretending he was a bird. To this, a considerable majority of children in both age groups judged (wrongly) that he was pretending to be a bird.

Lillard's (1993b) procedure creates a dissociation between pretending as a state of mind and the behaviour that accompanies pretence. She achieved this by having a protagonist behaving in a way that could be described as being like that of a bird, but without entertaining a pretence attitude in connection with the behaviour. If children understand "pretence" to mean specifically that one can be described as "behaving as if", and have no idea that it can mean that the pretender has conjured up a make-believe world, then the child would attribute pretence purely according to a behavioural criterion. This is precisely what the children did who were tested by Lillard. In other words, the children seemed to define "pretence" as shorthand for saying "the behaviour I am observing resembles that of such and such". Apparently, they did not conceive of pretence as having anything to do with make-believe, symbolising, or imagination, since they attributed pretence to an individual who they acknowledged had no such state of mind.

The possibility that young children lack understanding of the mentalistic quality of pretence is supported by findings reported by Perner, Baker, and Hutton (1994). They presented a story to children enacted with dolls, about a protagonist who was putting food in her pet rabbit's hutch. The observing children were alerted to the fact that actually the rabbit was not in the hutch. Under one condition of testing, the protagonist doing the feeding was portrayed as being privy to the rabbit's absence whereas under another condition she was depicted as being ignorant of this fact. In the latter condition, we could explain the protagonist's behaviour by saying that she was acting on a false and out-dated assumption (that the rabbit was present when in fact it was absent). Children were then asked if the protagonist really thought the rabbit was at home or whether she was just pretending. Perner et al. assumed that it was correct to judge that the protagonist really thought the rabbit was at home if she was depicted as being ignorant but that she was just pretending if she was depicted as being informed about the rabbit's absence.

The findings from this study were that children who were approach-ing their fifth birthday generally seemed able to differentiate between pretence and belief. They appropriately ascribed pretence to a protagonist who knew the rabbit was absent and ascribed a false belief to explain the aberrant behaviour of the protagonist depicted as being in a state of ignorance. In contrast, younger children tended to ascribe pretence whether the actor was depicted as knowing or not knowing the rabbit was in its hutch. Perner et al. (1994) interpreted this bias as children's construing the situation globally as one of pretence, unlike older children who were content to ascribe belief when appropriate.

This finding is largely consistent with Lillard's (1993a,b) and also Jarrold et al.'s (1994a) suggestion that young children lack a mentalistic understanding of pretence. Instead, they seemed to understand "pretence" to mean "acting as if" in the sense of "the protagonist is acting as if she is feeding her rabbit". This possibility is reinforced by the findings from a control condition Perner et al. included in their study. In that, the rabbit was in fact in the hutch and the protagonist was portrayed as knowing this fact. Yet young children persisted in judging that the protagonist was pretending to feed the rabbit even under this condition. This is further evidence to the effect that the young children were understanding "pretence" to refer to a behavioural description, whatever the mental state of the protagonist and whatever actually maintains in reality.

In that case, we are led into questioning the motivation behind the child's appetite for pretence. Perhaps pretence is nothing more than an expression of what the child is learning about social roles and routines, or what we might call "scripts". When the child pretends that a banana is a phone, perhaps he or she is simply enacting a script. Obviously practising this script would best be done with a real telephone but any suitably shaped object (e.g. a banana) would suffice. In sum, we can say that if the child's behaviour is nothing more than a reflection of a stereotyped routine, then there are no grounds for claiming that the child has any insight into pretence as a distinctive attitude. We would only be entitled to argue this if the child showed creativity or deviation from a social script when engaging in pretence.

The possibility that young children only understand pretence as a social script is supported by the findings of Howes, Unger, and Matheson (1992). They report that prior to approximately two-and-a-half years of age, children do not modify their pretence to accord with the pretence of those around them. Children seem to run through their social script irrespective of what others are doing, much like a machine running through its programmed sequence. Only older children adapted their pretence in accordance with others' behaviour, thus showing that they were not at the mercy of a stereotyped routine.

In sum, these findings seem to suggest that Leslie (1987) over-interpreted the significance of pretence in relation to the child's early understanding of mind. Although the child might engage in pretence, he or she seems to lack much of a reflective grasp of this as a mental state. Perhaps this lack of understanding forms part of a more general lack of insight into mind during early childhood.

However, it might be that, rather than Leslie (1987) overestimating young children, other researchers have underestimated them. At the very least, it might be that young children's actual competence lies somewhere in between the two polarised views. Let us take another look at Lillard's study. Because children used the word "pretend" in a situation where behaviour was not accompanied by an appropriate mental state of pretence, this does not necessarily mean that the child lacks an understanding of the mentalistic properties of pretence. Rather, the child might just have an overinclusive definition of "pretence" that could be used with reference to a certain mental attitude but also to a whole lot more. After all, ordinary adults set a poor example for children. They typically do not apply the rigorous definition Lillard advocates, given that they seem entirely comfortable in saying that the cat is pretending that a ball of wool is a mouse (when strictly, the cat is "behaving as if" the wool is a mouse). If children picked up this "bad" practice of adults, it would then be possible to put a different interpretation on the results reported by Perner et al. (1994a). Children judged that a protagonist was pretending to feed the rabbit when in fact he really was feeding the rabbit. It might be that at a young age children have an overinclusive definition of pretence, just as they have overinclusive definitions of other things. Sometimes young children call the moon a ball, but it is most unlikely that this is a sign of deep conceptual confusion about the moon as a plaything.

The point can be explained further by analogy from the results of a study conducted by Russell (1987). He told a group of children aged 5 and 6 years a story about a person called George who had his watch stolen by a man with curly red hair. Observing children knew the identity of the thief but George did not because he was asleep at the time of the theft. George awoke to find his watch missing. Observing children were asked if George was thinking that he must find the man with curly red hair who stole his watch. Many of them judged that he was thinking that, which strictly speaking is a wrong judgement because George was actually oblivious to the appearance of the thief on account of his slumber. If we interpreted this result according to Lillard's logic, we would deny the children any understanding of the concept of belief. In this case, children credited George with a thought that he could not have possessed, suggesting that children were confusing George's search for the thief (who we know has curly red hair) with his thoughts about the appearance of a specific person (a thief with curly red hair).

However, Russell (1987) demonstrated that the children did understand the concept of belief on the grounds that they could acknowledge false beliefs. The children were easily able to predict that a person holding a false belief about the location of a desired item would search in the wrong place. What the child had difficulty with was using words to describe the content of George's belief. Similarly, we might say that Lillard's (1993b) children had difficulty in using words to describe the mental content of a protagonist's pretence. The common denominator is that children used the behaviour as a guide for describing the pretence or the belief. Moreover, perhaps it is no coincidence that the children making this kind of error in the two studies were approximately the same age. Hence, just as Russell's data do not imply that children aged about 5 years lack a mentalistic understanding of belief, so perhaps Lillard's data do not imply that children of the same age lack a mentalistic understanding of pretence. I am not saying that the children were linguistically incompetent, because as Lillard argues persuasively, children of the age she tested show considerable linguistic sophistication in many respects.

However, to judge correctly in the tasks devised by both Lillard and Russell would imply a level of linguistic sophistication that qualifies as *intensionality*. This concerns not just the understanding of a person's mental state, but the appropriate use of language to characterise that mental state. For example, George does not know that a man with curly red hair stole his watch. Nonetheless, George is looking for the man with curly red hair (though he doesn't know it) who stole his watch. Yet we cannot say that George is thinking, "I must find the man with curly red hair who stole my watch." Hence, although it is true that George is looking for a man with certain identity as described, that identity cannot form any part of George's thoughts owing to his ignorance. To make the distinction captured in the previous sentence is to grasp the concept of intensionality. According to Russell, it is something that is acquired at about 6 or 7 years of age. I am suggesting that intensionality is entailed in Lillard's task and so two things follow: (1) it is not surprising that her young children experienced difficulties with the task; (2) the difficulties children had with the task are not a sign of failure to understand the mentalistic features of the task. That is, it is possible to understand about belief and pretence without understanding about intensionality.

This analysis of Lillard's (1993b) results helps to bring into focus a related problem with Perner et al.'s (1994a) study. Again, children were being asked to judge the content of a protagonist's mental state, though this time they were faced with a forced choice of attributing pretence or belief. As reported easrlier, the children did not make appropriate discriminations between pretence and belief, which only tells us that they have difficulty in assigning verbal labels to the contents of mental states. The data are not strong enough, though, to argue that young children lack a mentalistic understanding of pretence. Even so, we might question why the children performed better in Perner et al.'s than in Lillard's study: Four-year-olds succeeded in the former but not the latter. Differences in subject populations aside, the forced-choice wording may have assisted children in Perner et al., whereas the open-ended question employed by Lillard might have posed more of a problem. Altogether, Lillard's and Perner's results can be interpreted within a single framework, which need not imply that young children lack a mentalistic understanding of pretence.

It is one thing to criticise Perner et al. (1994a) and Lillard (1993b), but it is quite another to find evidence showing positively that young children do have a mentalistic understanding of pretence. Fortunately, the work of Harris and Kavanaugh (1993) satisfies the requirement. The aim of their study was to establish more clearly what we can infer about the child's mentalistic understanding from his or her pretence. They focused on children's ability to relate to the pretence instigated by another person.

CREATIVITY IN PRETENCE

In Harris and Kavanaugh's (1993) study, a villainous teddy bear was determined to spoil the pretend scenario created by the experimenter. The experimenter was playing with the child and a toy pig, whereupon Naughty Teddy appeared holding a cup of pretend tea. Teddy pretend spilled the tea all over either the pig or the floor and the experimenter asked the 2-year-old child involved in the game to clean the pretend spillage with a pretend cloth. Children readily complied with this request and calibrated their clean-up operation appropriately to the location of the pretend spillage.

This might seen like a typical pretend episode involving a child of 2 years but it has the potential to offer vital clarification on precisely what the child understands about pretence. As mentioned earlier, one way of construing early pretence is to suppose that the child is not so much involved in a creatively formulated world of make-believe, but that in fact the child is enacting scripts of various familiar social situations. An example is the familiar routine of afternoon tea, which involves an invariant sequence of actions in conjunction with props such as plates, cups, teapot, and so on. It might have been that children's pretence was merely a practice run of familiar social routines, and if so, it would be consistent with children's conception of pretence being behaviourally based—acting as if. However, Harris and Kavanaugh (1993) demonstrated that children were able to keep track of the novel pretence environment stipulated by the experimenter as demonstrated by the child's capacity to deviate from ordinary social routines. The child might know about the social routine of serving tea, but he or she is unlikely to be familiar with the antics of a delinquent teddy bear. Moreover, the child evidently was engaged in the specific pretend episode created by the experimenter because he or she mopped up the "spillage" in the place one might calculate that Naughty Teddy would have slopped the mess had the cup actually contained tea. At the very least, the children had no difficulty invoking and combining a tea script with a mop-up script. As regards the latter, the novel experience of the teddy was sufficient to trigger the mop-up script, suggesting they were capable of considerable insight and flexibility, much more so than we might have expected if they were relying on stereotyped routines.

Not only were the children able to carry out actions appropriate to the pretend situation, but they were able to reflect on the sequence of events sufficiently to offer an explicit verbal commentary on what was happening. For example, when asked to describe the effect Teddy had on his victim, children answered that he had become soggy. If Teddy had squeezed pretend toothpaste over the toy pig, then they judged that the pig had become toothpasty. Under another condition, Teddy poured imaginary tea over imaginary chocolate. The latter was actually a child's playing brick. When asked to described this object in the aftermath of Teddy's wicked deed, they did so entirely in terms of pretend identities, that the chocolate was made soggy by the tea. Hence, the children were able to use such creative language to describe an event that was far removed from their experience of the real world, suggesting that their pretence involves a great deal more than enacting frequently observed and well-rehearsed social scripts, even to the point of introducing specially created language (e.g. "toothpasty").

This account brings us very nearly full circle back to Leslie's (1987) suggestion that a capacity for pretence entails a capacity for referential opacity. The latter engenders an understanding of the nonliteral use of language. For example, if we are told that Jane believes Bush is President, we should not interpret this literally, or transparently, to mean that Bush really is President. If one had no capacity for interpreting a sentence nonliterally, then one could not possess the concept of referential opacity. If one is able to interpret nonliterally, then one has made an important step along the road to understanding opacity and thereby holding the concept of mind. Returning to pretence, the finding that children are able to use nonliteral language in reporting a sequence of pretend events shows that they have one of the necessary prerequisites for a full-blown conception of mind. The example also serves to illustrate that pretence offers a forum in which the child can become acquainted with nonliteral language. Hence, we see yet another facet of the affinity between pretence and referential opacity.

Earlier, we considered Leslie's (1987) account of the implications of pretence. He argued that pretend identities of objects are placed in mental quotation marks, which highlights them from their background default identity. The two identities of the same object are then preserved and prevented from being confused. If they were not decoupled in this way, then Leslie suggests rather colourfully that the child would be indulging in "representational abuse", in which the represented identity of the object would become unstable (Is this thing really a banana or a telephone?). Leslie feels entitled to call the designated identity of the object a metarepresentation, which means that it is a representation of a representation rather than a representation of something in reality. The child's representation of banana as a telephone is actually twice removed from reality because it is conceived as a representation (telephone) of a representation (banana) of something out there in reality (a yellow skinned tropical fruit of comical appearance).

Harris and Kavanaugh (1993) disagree with Leslie (1987) on this point, and so do Jarrold et al. (1994a). Let us take a look at the latter objection first. Jarrold et al. claim that representing a representation is not sufficient in itself to qualify as a metarepresentation. They make the argument on the following grounds of *reductio ad absurdum*, using an example conceived by Perner (1991). If an artist paints a portrait from a photo, then the resulting painting will be of the subject per se and not of the photo of the subject. This can be shown to be the case, so these authors might claim, in the sense that anyone seeing the painting would assume that it was of the subject and not of a photo of the subject.

However, there is a problem with this argument. Strictly, photos do not represent anything but simply register a trace of a previous reality in the form of what we would call a photographic image. Only intentional organisms (and maybe machines one day!) can represent, which means that not only do we hold a proposition in mind but we also have an attitude toward it. That is not true of photos and neither is it true of paintings. Hence, the painting itself is not a metarepresentation—it is not a representation of a representation. But that is trivial. What is important is that the painting is an overt expression of a metarepresentation. The artist knows that the painting is based on a mere image of reality rather than reality itself, so in this respect the artist might be construing his or her painting as twice removed from reality and accordingly hold a metarepresentational stance with respect to the painting. A consequence might be that if the artist were to meet the subject of the painting face-to-face, and find that this person does not quite have the expected appearance, this would not necessarily come as a surprise. Being merely an image of reality, the photo might have imperfections which the artist unwittingly captured in the painting, thereby showing that the artist has a distorted conception of the subject. The main point to come from this is that although children habitually take their representation of a banana to be a yellow tropical fruit, on some occasions they can take this to a level one step further removed from reality (as a "phone"). At this moment we can say that the banana (reality) is represented as a yellow tropical fruit, and is metarepresented as a telephone. The argument about paintings from photos does not weaken this claim. Crucially, according to Leslie (1987), the child holds not just a representation of a representation, but also entertains the accompanying attitude of pretence that allows the child to avoid confusion between what is pretended and what is reality. It is this special attitude in relation to the representation that is crucial, and it is that which means pretence qualifies as a metarepresentation.

However, Harris and Kavanaugh (1993) suggest that children might be able to keep track of pretend identities without the need to hold an explicit distinction between the primary and the secondary representation of an object. If they are right, then pretence would not be evidence of a metarepresentational capacity. They suggest that the child marks the pretend identity of an object with a kind of mental flag, which is somewhat similar to Leslie's (1987) suggestion of mental quotation marks. Harris and Kavanaugh argue that the child is able to substitute one identity of an object for another with the aid of mental flags and that in doing so it is unnecessary to posit that the child holds a representation of a representation when engaging in pretence. To illustrate their point, these authors suggest a similarity between engaging in pretence and comprehending a narrative. Such comprehension entails an understanding that general concept words, such as "fish", denote a specific case within a given narrative. For example, "Sharky" might be interchanged with "the fish", and we can assume that the child will know that we mean "Sharky" when we say "the fish". Indeed, if the child did not understand that "the fish" means "Sharky", then it would be impossible for the child even to begin comprehending stories. Within this narrative episode, the child will have erected a mental flag next to "the fish" which means "Sharky". Crucially, when "the fish" is mentioned in the narrative, the child will think of Sharky and not of the more general concept of "fish". Temporarily and within a specific context, "the fish" will have assumed a specific meaning, and the child need not juggle with this and the more general meaning at one and the same time.

Once the narrative has ended, the mental flag will vanish and no longer intrude when somebody makes reference to a fish. For example, if Father says that we are having fish for dinner, the child would not assume we were about to devour Sharky! Again, we see the relevance of the concept of referential opacity. In listening to a dialogue, we should assume that although what is said might be held as true by the person uttering it, it is not necessarily true of reality. Just as an understanding of nonliteral language is necessary for comprehending fiction, so it is necessary for understanding referential opacity. As mentioned earlier, Leslie (1987) views the concept of referential opacity as being at the heart of a capacity for pretence, which adds weight to Harris and Kavanaugh's (1993) comparison between understanding pretence and comprehending narratives.

We can say that Harris and Kavanaugh (1993) assume that understanding pretence boils down to identifying what is fictional and what is not fictional. For example, the child will mark his or her concept of "banana" with a flag that denotes it as a telephone. When the child relates to the banana in his or her pretence, he or she will be thinking of it as a telephone. The chief difference between Harris and Kavanaugh on one hand and Leslie (1987) on the other is that the former authors seem to regard the child's handling of the dual identities of the yellow tropical fruit in a sequential fashion, with the consequence that the concept of the item as a telephone need not be a metarepresentation of that item as a banana. In contrast, Leslie seems to assume that the child juggles with the two identities simultaneously, which he supposes necessarily implies a metarepresentational competence. In sum, whether or not pretence entails metarepresentation remains unclear. However, it seems reasonable to argue that pretence, like comprehending narrative, does require some working grasp of referential opacity.

It would be easy to lose sight of the young child's understanding of mind when we become entangled in these rather esoteric debates. Perhaps we can say that Harris and Kavanaugh (1993) are claiming that a capacity for pretence requires an ability to differentiate between the fictional and the nonfictional. In this respect, perhaps a capacity for pretence need not imply much about understanding other minds as organs that represent reality. In contrast, Leslie's view is that, insofar as pretence entails representing a representation (telephone as banana) without confusion over what is reality, it shows that the child has the ability to conceive of mental states as such. The child should thus understand both *pretence* and presumably *belief* as attitudes of mind about propositions. For example, that Jane believes (attitude) that Bush is President (proposition).

Even if Leslie were to concede that pretence need not imply any metarepresentational competence, we could still conclude from Harris and Kavanaugh's (1993) account that the child grasps the difference between what is real and what might be proclaimed in fiction. Hence, the child understands that the world could be described in various ways, only one of which is true. Surely such an understanding provides the foundations for understanding that people might entertain as their beliefs what are really only fictions about the world. If so, the child has made a substantial inroad into understanding the difference between reality and mind. What we require at this point is evidence of a more direct nature, showing that early pretence is linked with an early understanding of mind and abilities in communication.

PRETENCE, COMMUNICATION, AND SOCIAL COMPETENCE

We can see from the work of Harris and Kavanaugh (1993) that there should be a link between pretence and interpreting communications from others. Evidence for this link is reported by Dunn (1994) and colleagues. Dunn observed that a great deal of children's talk with siblings and other children occurs in the context of joint pretence. She suggests that it is in this context that much of the child's early verbal communication skills first emerge and develop (and presumably their more general understanding of mind becomes refined). Because we might suppose there is a three-way relation between pretence, linguistic communication, and conception of mind, so we might expect to find intercorrelations between these abilities. Dunn reports that children who have a proclivity for role-enactment in their pretence are the ones who also show most aptitude in judging about other people's mental states. In particular, they are especially skilled in explaining the futile search of another person by suggesting that the person in question holds a mistaken belief. This finding is consistent with the possibility that pretend play with others offers a forum in which the child can practise simulating other people's mental states, with the consequence that the child becomes more finely attuned to the minds of others in real life. This forum is richly verbal and communicative in its character, which is not surprising if we suppose that pretence and communication are based on a single or at least two highly related underlying competencies.

There is independent evidence suggesting that a capacity for pretence is linked with an understanding of mind. Connolly and Doyle (1984) observed the pretend play of children aged between 2:11 years and 5:9 years. The pretence took the form of adopting pretend roles in which, for example, they spontaneously called themselves "Mother" and their partner "Baby". Additionally, children spontaneously assigned fantasy identities to otherwise mundane objects. For example, they pretended that a wooden playing brick was a gun and then pursued another child in a game of cops and robbers. The researchers also assessed the complexity of pretence, noting how many pretend identities were conferred upon objects within a single episode of pretence. The other component of the study involved assessing children's social competence. A battery of measures included the teacher's rating of each child's social competence, the teacher's rating of each child's popularity with peers, and each child's ability to select an appropriate gift from a set of alternatives (toy truck, doll, purse, tie) for various people (mother, father, teacher, opposite sex peer). Additionally the researchers observed children's spontaneous interaction with peers and made a special note of the verbal quality of social exchanges each child was involved in.

The results showed a strong relation between the quantity and quality of a child's pretence and the child's social competence according to the measures identified earlier. In particular, the children who engaged in an abundance of pretence tended to be the ones who were especially verbally competent in their social interactions. In this respect, the findings were highly consistent with those of Dunn (1994), mentioned earlier. Before contemplating the theoretical significance of Connolly and Doyle's (1984) findings, we should consider the possibility that this relation was due incidentally to a third variable of no theoretical interest. For example, it might be that intelligence is responsible for both pretence and social competence, and the latter two correlate with each other purely by virtue of their shared correlation with intelligence. Fortunately, Connolly and Doyle took the precaution of measuring children's IQ, and were able to confirm that pretence and social competence still correlated substantially even when the variance associated with intelligence was subtracted. Although it is likely that verbal ability is highly intercorrelated with IQ, the relation between pretence and social competence must have been strong enough to shine through even when intelligence was partialled out. Further findings arising from the same techniques of analysis were that age and gender also appeared not to be responsible for the correlation between pretence and social competence.

The findings reported by Connolly and Doyle (1984) support the view that a capacity for pretence specifically has a strong link with verbally based social competence, and vice versa. More generally, the results suggest that we should consider the tripartite relation between pretence, verbal communication, and social competence, where we might regard the latter as the triumph of a functioning understanding of mind. As mentioned earlier, pretence and verbal communication can be united by the underlying concept of referential opacity, and the relation between these two forms of symbolism reported by Connolly and Doyle offers empirical support to that effect.

In conclusion, it seems that early pretence signifies a cognition well prepared for the task of conceiving of other minds. This is apparent in at least two respects. First, the child shows a mastery of fiction in his or her pretence, a competence that can be applied to the task of hypothesising about other minds. Second, a capacity for pretence provides a tool for simulating, through role play, what others might think and feel. On these grounds, it seems that the views of Lillard (1993a,b), Perner et al. (1994) and Jarrold et al. (1994) were overly pessimistic. The naturalistic data reported by Connolly and Doyle (1984) and also by Dunn (1994) suggest that in practice, as well as in principle, a capacity for pretence is linked with an up-and-running understanding of mind that confers a social competence upon the child.

CHAPTER THREE

Children's awareness of mental phenomena

Children's early pretence is both revealing in what they know about mind and also frustrating in that the evidence is circumstantial. We might be able to argue that if the child engages in pretence, then the child has the necessary cognitive equipment for conceiving of the mind, but there is no direct evidence demonstrating the latter arising from the research into early pretence. It would be desirable, therefore, to obtain more explicit evidence concerning the child's understanding of mental activity. Pretence can perhaps be defined as a capacity to venture into the world of imagination. In this chapter, we shall explore what children understand about the imagination (as distinct from the ability to imagine). That is, perhaps from an early age, children not only engage in imagination but they are able to make explicit judgements about imagination, and especially how it contrasts with reality. The work of Henry Wellman (e.g. 1990) and colleagues has made a substantial contribution in this field of inquiry. Wellman has researched what young children understand about thoughts, especially with respect to how these govern behaviour and how they relate to motivation, emotions, and desires.

Lillard (1993a) suggests colourfully that children's early pretence might be a "fool's gold" in the sense that it seems to signify a potential for insight into mind and yet ultimately amounts to very little. If that were the case, then we might say that young children are mind behaviourists. If young children were "mind-blind", then they would share something in common with the approach to psychology adopted by the radical behaviourist John Watson, and deny that mental phenomena exist. Obviously it would not make sense to ask a young child directly about his or her views on mental life, but effectively a young child would be denying the existence of the mental if he or she did not acknowledge that mental phenomena have special properties that distinguish them from the physical world.

THE NONPHYSICAL QUALITY OF THOUGHTS

Wellman and Estes (1986) took the first step along the route of investigating what young children understand about the special qualities of mental phenomena. They told children aged 3, 4, and 5 years a story about two different protagonists, both of whom were hungry. One was given a cookie by his mother while the other's hunger pangs stimulated him to think about a cookie. Children were asked a series of questions about these two boys: Which boy can see the cookie? Which boy can't touch the cookie? Which boy can eat the cookie? Which boy can let his friend eat the cookie? Which boy can save the cookie to eat tomorrow? The motivation behind this series of questions was as follows. Thoughts cannot be seen or touched and generally are not amenable to public scrutiny and cannot be acted upon. Physical objects contrast with thoughts in all these respects and additionally have a consistent existence. For example, they can be saved until tomorrow. If children understand properties of thoughts, and thus are not behaviourists, then they would answer the questions differently according to whether a real object or a thought was at issue. Particularly, children would acknowledge that thoughts are nontangible and offer no accessibility to the senses. The results were that 72% of 3-year-olds, 86% of 4-year-olds, and 92% of 5-year-olds made the appropriate distinction between physical and imaginary objects in their answers to this series of questions.

These results were supported by a second test presented to children by Wellman and Estes (1986). They introduced two boxes, one labelled as the "real box" and the other as the "not real box". The child was instructed to sort items according to their membership of the real or not real class by pointing to the appropriate box. For example, the child was told about one boy with a cookie and another boy just thinking about a cookie. A child who sorted correctly would point to the not real box for the thought about a cookie and the real box for the real cookie.

Eighty-three percent of children aged 3 years had no difficulty with this task, again demonstrating a good understanding about the classificatory difference between objects and thoughts about objects.

Consistent findings were reported by Flavell, Green, and Flavell (1995). Young 3-year-olds were introduced to a second experimenter (Ellie) who was blindfolded. They were asked various questions about what Ellie could and could not do and think. Approximately three-quarters of the sample of children judged correctly that Ellie was able to think about an object, but that she could not see it. They were able to make these judgements independently of whether the object in question was present or absent. In a further study, young 3-year-olds demonstrated their insight into thinking in another respect. Ellie was asked who she would like to send a postcard to, and she then appeared to ponder on this, as suggested by the classic signs of putting her chin in her hands, tilting her head and wearing a pensive expression. The observing children were asked to say what she was doing. Most of the children responded blankly to this question, but when prompted by the question, "Is she thinking?" the great majority agreed that she was. This was not just a "yes" bias, because they judged correctly that Ellie was not talking about, touching, or looking at the card (her gaze was averted from it).

The results reported by Wellman and Estes (1986) and also Flavell et al. (1995) give a strong impression that children aged 3 years generally have a good understanding about mental life. They apparently know enough about thoughts to appreciate that they lack some of the properties of physical objects. They also understand something of the cues and context that suggest someone is thinking, and that this activity is different from seeing, talking, and touching.

However, all this actually tells us little of what children do understand about thoughts themselves. Indeed, if children understood nothing of thoughts, or more precisely, understood thoughts as nothing, then perhaps they would answer the same way in the reported studies. To be explicit about this, if children construe a thought as being nothing, and effectively they reinterpret the questions to be about having a cookie against not having a cookie, then they would have answered according to the same pattern in the studies by Wellman and Estes. In the Flavell et al. study, when children say that Ellie is thinking they actually mean that she is doing nothing. However, thoughts do positively have qualities that real objects lack. For example, one can manipulate the content of a thought just by thinking about it, whereas one cannot manipulate a real object just by thinking about it. Table 3.1 provides a summary of the various studies, suggesting that most children aged 3 years know a good deal about the quality of thoughts.

TABLE 3.1

**A summary of studies showing that most children aged 3 years understand a
considerable amount about the quality of thoughts**

Authors	Demonstrated competence
Wellman & Estes (1986)	Understanding that imaginary objects lack physical properties
Wellman & Estes (1986)	Classification of physical and imaginary objects
Flavell et al. (1995)	Acknowledging that Ellie could think of something she could not see
Flavell et al. (1995)	Judging that Ellie was thinking of something when she assumed a pensive attitude
Estes et al. (1989)	Acknowledging that imaginary (but not real) objects can be transformed just by thinking about them

SPECIAL QUALITIES OF THOUGHTS

To check whether young children understand about the substantive
existence of thoughts, Estes, Wellman, and Woolley (1989) assessed
children's awareness of their positive characteristics. They presented
three kinds of scenario to children. Two of these involved real objects
(balloons), one in which the balloon was visible and another in which it
was hidden. The third scenario concerned a boy thinking about a
balloon. Children were then asked a series of questions as posed by
Wellman and Estes (1986) about whether the respective balloons could
be seen or touched. Estes et al. also introduced a further question asking
if the boy could transform the balloon into a sausage shape just by
thinking about it.

Children's judgements about the two scenarios involving physical
objects differed in predictable ways. They judged that a hidden object
could not be seen, touched, or transformed just by thinking about it. In
contrast, they judged that an unhidden balloon could be seen and could
be touched, though they conceded that it could not be made into a
sausage shape just by thinking about it. In contrast, children judged in
a distinctly different way when asked about the imaginary balloon. Like
the hidden balloon, they judged that it could not be seen or touched.
However, unlike both the hidden and unhidden real balloons, they
judged that it would be possible to transform the shape of an imaginary
balloon into a sausage just by thinking about it. Children aged 3 years
judge according to the described pattern just as much as children aged
5 years. Evidently, the children had a good understanding of properties
of thoughts in a positive as well as a negative sense. On one hand they
understood that you can do things with real objects that you cannot do

with thoughts, but on the other hand they also recognised that you can do other things with thoughts that you cannot do with real objects.

Another property of thoughts is that they need not be contingent upon sensory input. In plain language, we can daydream, in which we conjure up mental images that are not evoked by seeing and indeed could be entirely fictitious. For example, we can imagine in our mind's eye a unicorn. Well, we have seen depictions of unicorns previously and one might object that what we are imagining is actually an image from some depiction presented to us previously. However, we can also imagine our own unique creations. For example, we could create an image in our mind's eye of a man who had a television set on his shoulders instead of a head. This image is of a thing that is impossible in real life. If young children understand about imagination, they should acknowledge that one can imagine things without sensory input and that the things imagined correspond with nothing in the real world. That is, imagining an object is not sufficient for that object to have any existence in reality.

CONFUSING IMAGINATION WITH REALITY

Research by Harris, Brown, Marriott, Whittall, and Harmer (1991) suggests that children aged 4 and 6 years do not have an understanding of imagined objects as substantive and distinct from reality. They showed children a box and asked them to imagine either that there was a puppy inside or that there was a monster inside. They then noted children's willingness to approach the box or put their finger in through the partially opened lid, when requested to do so. The children showed eagerness to approach the box and venture to put their fingers inside after imagining that it contained a puppy, but showed considerable reluctance after imagining that it contained a monster. A further finding was that when the experimenter left the children alone in the room for a short period, many ventured over and fingered it—perhaps nervously if they had been instructed to imagine that it contained a monster. On the face of things, it seems hard to account for children's apparent intrigue over the box if they had not begun to believe that its content had been altered by their imagination. These findings are consistent with the possibility that children conflate what they imagine to be true with what is really true. If that interpretation is correct, then it would seem that young children's grasp of imagination as substantive and distinct from reality is severely limited.

However, there is a way of explaining children's behaviour in Harris et al.'s (1991) study without conceding that they have a concept of imagination. The imagined items in their study had powerful emotional valences. Presumably, the emotion associated with a puppy is very positive for young children whereas the emotion associated with a monster is profoundly negative. Merely imagining these objects in the target box could have been sufficient to contaminate the box with the emotion associated with the imagined object, from the child's point of view. If so, this study might not tell us anything distinctive about children, and what they actually observed could be a natural human reaction. Indeed, Rozin, Millman, and Nemeroff (1986) report a related finding in adults. Participants watched the experimenter pour an identical sugar solution into two bottles and then asked subjects to label one of these as "sugar" and the other as "cyanide". Subsequently, participants were invited to drink from the bottles, and there was a rather mysterious reluctance in the participants to imbibe from the bottle marked "cyanide"! Presumably, the negative emotion associated with this lethal chemical was sufficient to make the contents of the bottle aversive to the adults participating in the study.

A similar interpretation can be placed on children's size scaling in their drawings of nice or nasty things. This was demonstrated by Thomas and colleagues (Fox & Thomas, 1989; Thomas, Chaigne, & Fox, 1989), who asked children to draw a picture of a nasty person, such as a witch, and to draw a picture of a nice person. Their drawings of the nice person tended to be substantially larger than their drawings of a nasty person. Moreover, children who said they were very scared of witches drew smaller pictures of witches than children who said they were not so scared. These authors argued that things (e.g. drawings) that are associated with something anxiety-provoking will themselves give rise to anxiety by proxy. Hence children do small drawings of such things to reduce the saliency of the aversive stimulus and thus reduce the anxiety: A little witch is less terrifying than a big witch, and the same applies with drawings.

Returning to Harris et al. (1991), it might be that what these researchers observed was the consequence of an anxiety aroused by thinking of monsters, but that need not imply that children assume what is imagined necessarily exists in reality. Admittedly, it still seems odd that children ventured to the box in the experimenter's absence, as though they expected to find something tangible in there. However, it would not be surprising if adults showed a similar orientation to a bottle of water to which they had just attached a cyanide label. Sometimes people's imaginations are externalised, perhaps inadvertently, in terms of overt fragments of speech or truncated actions, but that is not necessarily a sign that they have lost sight of the distinction between imagination and reality. Presumably the adult participants would have no difficulty reporting explicitly what was reality and what was nonreality if asked directly about the content of the bottle of water marked "cyanide". As yet, there are no good reasons for supposing that children are any different.

What is required is a study probing the young child's grasp of imagination that is emotionally neutral. This was the aim expressed by Woolley and Wellman (1993), who tested children aged from 2:11 to 5:2. Children were shown an empty box and asked if they could imagine two kinds of object inside. One was purely fictional, such as a purple turtle, and another was an ordinary object such as a crayon. Even the youngest children judged that they could imagine both kinds of object in the box and, furthermore, judged that really the box was empty and that purple turtles do not really exist anywhere.

In another part of the study, the same children were told stories about two different protagonists. One protagonist was said to remember that there was a red furry teddy inside a box. In the other story, children were told that a protagonist did not know what was in the box but imagined that there might be a red furry teddy inside. Observing child participants were then asked if each protagonist thought there really was a red furry teddy inside. Again, even the youngest children tended to judge that the protagonist remembering a red teddy thought this really was inside, but that a protagonist just imagining a teddy really thought there was no such thing inside.

In a second experiment, Woolley and Wellman (1993) asked children aged 3 years to look in a box under two conditions. Under one condition, they saw a crayon inside. Under another condition, they looked inside and saw that the box was empty, but were then asked to imagine that there was a crayon inside. Finally, children tested under both conditions were asked if there really was a crayon in the box. All of those who saw the real crayon correctly judged that there was a crayon inside, whereas only 46% of those asked to imagine a crayon judged that there really was such an object inside.

Perhaps it is this second study that is most relevant to that conducted by Harris et al. (1991). On a group basis, the young children tested by Woolley and Wellman (1993) showed very clearly that they discriminated between real and imagined objects in terms of their actual existence in reality. Nonetheless, many children did judge that an imagined object actually existed when it did not. This might be a sign that some children confuse imagination with reality, but there is a whole variety of artefactual reasons why they might answer wrongly. They might have a "yes bias", misunderstand the question (to mean "what is the case in your imagination"), or even assume that the experimenter has acted to make the imagined thing appear. For example, adults sometimes ask young children to articulate their wishes for Christmas, and then, as if by magic, the adult suddenly produces the imagined(?) items. It might be best to focus on the significant group contrast in children's judgements between real and imagined objects. When we do so, it seems reasonable to conclude that generally young children do have considerable insight into imagination. They accept that they can imagine things without perceptual input, and even acknowledge explicitly that they can imagine totally fictitious things, such as purple turtles. They also understand that they themselves, as well as others, do not regard their imaginings as being true of reality. At least they acknowledge that people are more likely to hold things as true that they have seen or remembered than that they just imagine to be the case. Hence, young children's early understanding of mind provides them with a comprehensive grasp of what imagination is.

THE SUBJECTIVE QUALITY OF THOUGHT

It is one thing to understand some of the properties of thoughts and imagination but it is quite another to understand how different thoughts are held by different people, each with a unique mentalistic framework interlinking thoughts, desires, emotions, motivations, and behaviour. If the young child grasped a few of the properties of thoughts but no more, then we would hardly have grounds for crediting the child with an impressive understanding of mind. We now turn to the question of what young children understand about the specific thoughts held by individual people.

A ground-breaking study on this was conducted by Wellman and Bartsch (1988). They told children a story about a boy called Sam who wanted to find his puppy. His puppy, the observing children were told, might be under the porch or in the garage, but Sam thinks it is in the garage. Children were then asked where Sam will look for his puppy. Seventy-seven percent of children aged 3 years and 79% aged 4 years judged that Sam would look for the puppy in the place where he thinks it is. In making these correct judgements, children were demonstrating an understanding of a linkage between desire, belief, and behaviour that is unique to the individual—in this case, Sam. Children apparently understood that Sam's desire will motivate his search, the specifics of which will be determined by his belief. In this respect, it would appear that young children have an understanding of mind that allows them to predict other people's behaviour by taking into account the mentalistic states of desire and belief.

Perhaps we are overestimating the children. Perhaps they have little understanding of mind but solved the task presented by Wellman and

Bartsch (1988) according to some noninsightful strategy. If the children had no insight into mind but were being cajoled into responding anyway, perhaps they would simply echo the location mentioned last by the experimenter. Coincidentally, this was the location that happened to be mentioned in connection with Sam's thought: "Sam thinks his puppy is under the porch." To eliminate this possibility, Wellman and Bartsch included a control condition in which children were told that Sam thinks his puppy is *not* in the garage. If they mindlessly echo the last mentioned location, they would say he will search in the garage. However, 90% of 3-year-olds and the same percentage of 4-year-olds correctly judged that Sam would search under the porch.

Another reductive explanation for children's success is that they actually have no insight into Sam's mind but simply report that Sam will look for the puppy where the observing child participant thinks it is. To eliminate this possibility, Wellman and Bartsch (1988) presented a further control condition in which they took the precaution of gauging the observing child participant's own belief before announcing Sam's belief. This allowed the experimenter to assert that Sam's belief was discrepant with the child participant's. For example, having stated that Sam wants to find his puppy, and that it might be in the garage or under the porch, children were asked to guess where it was. If the child responded with "garage", then the experimenter explained that Sam thought it was under the porch. Children were asked to predict, as usual, where Sam would look for his puppy and 83% of 3-year-olds and 79% of 4-year-olds replied with "porch". In other words, it seems that the children recognised that Sam's belief would determine where he would search, rather than the child's own belief/guess, which was contrived to be different. It thus seems that children's apparent insight into the link between desire, belief, and behaviour, amounting to the fundamentals of a conception of mind, cannot be explained reductively by experimental artefact. Table 3.2 summarises the principal findings reported by Wellman and Bartsch.

A drawback of the research conducted by Wellman and Bartsch (1988) is that it still involves an indirectness of approach. What we really want to know is what young children understand about the mental phenomena swimming around in the ether of people's minds. Wellman and Bartsch asked children not about thoughts but about actions. Children's judgements suggest indirectly that they do take into account the mental phenomena of desires and beliefs but the whole research enterprise would be more satisfactory if we could investigate directly what young children understand about such things as thoughts. The difficulty such an endeavour presents is that thoughts, by their very nature, are invisible and not amenable to direct perceptual access.

TABLE 3.2

Principal findings reported by Wellman and Bartsch (1988), investigating young children's ability to link thoughts with actions

Description	Percentage correct 3-year-olds	Percentage correct 4-year-olds
The puppy could be in the garage or under the porch. Sam thinks it is under the porch.	77	79
Sam thinks his puppy is *not* in the garage.	90	90
Sam thinks his puppy is *not* where the participating child thinks it is.	83	79

Success is defined as children's judgement that Sam will look for his puppy in the place he thinks it is.

Indeed, it is for that reason that we need a special cognitive process for inferring mental states that amounts to a conception of mind. If others' thoughts were directly accessible, there would be no need for such a conception of mind.

THOUGHT BUBBLES

Wellman, Hollander, and Schult (1995) circumvented the problem of thoughts being invisible by taking the rather bold step of presenting them to children visually encapsulated within thought bubbles. A disadvantage of this approach is that a thought bubble is an artefact, and not something that occurs naturally. Therefore, it might seem odd to use such a patently artificial device as a tool for investigating the child's natural understanding of mind. However, if it turned out that children were easily and readily able to interpret thought bubbles in an intelligent and insightful manner, it would be difficult to conclude anything other than that the child came to the task already equipped with an understanding of thought. We would have to conclude that the child's pre-existing conception endowed him or her with a framework within which to interpret the thought bubbles.

Wellman et al. (1995) began by showing children a picture of a person escorting his dog on the end of a lead. The person also had a thought bubble that showed a picture of a toy wagon. The observing child participants, who were aged between 2:11 and 4:11, were asked what the person was thinking and what he was doing. Nearly all children, including the youngest members of the sample, judged that the person was thinking about a wagon but was taking his dog for a walk. Moreover, when children were asked about the real object, they usually responded by articulating an action verb, for example that he is *taking* the dog for a walk. In contrast, when judging what he was thinking, children never used an action verb and instead used the prepositions *of* and *about*. For example, they judged that the protagonist was thinking of or about a wagon. Hence, not only did children discriminate appropriately between actions and thoughts according to specific content, but they also showed sensitivity to the same in their choice of grammar for reporting mental and physical phenomena. Incidentally, this finding seems to provide further evidence against Lillard's (1993a) supposition (presented in the previous chapter) that young children confuse thinking with acting in the domain of pretence.

These findings are consistent with results reported by Flavell, Green, and Flavell (1993). They showed children aged 3 and 4 years a picture of a character riding a trike with a thought bubble suspended above her head containing an image of her kicking a football. Observing children were asked what the character was doing and what she was thinking. Three-year-olds were correct 80% of the time in judging that the character was thinking about kicking a football but that she was actually riding a trike. Children aged 4 years were correct 90% of the time. This finding was replicated by Flavell et al. (1995), which led them to conclude that although we cannot be sure from these data alone what 3-year-olds think thinking is, at least we can be sure of what they think it is not. At least young children do not confuse thinking with physical action.

One of the features of thoughts is that they can be person-specific or idiosyncratic. Hence two people can have different thoughts about a single aspect of reality. If children had only a partial understanding of thoughts, they might not grasp that thoughts are subjective, personal, and possibly even unique in some circumstances. Wellman et al. (1995) conducted a further test on 3- and 4-year-olds with thought bubbles to investigate this issue. They showed children two protagonists who each looked into a box in turn. Previously, the observing child participant had been informed that the box contained just a single item, but they were not able to see what it was yet. After each of the protagonists looked in the mystery box, they were shown to have a thought bubble over their respective heads. In one, there was an image of a doll, whereas the thought bubble belonging to the other protagonist had an image of a teddy. All 3-year-olds correctly ascribed the thought to the protagonists that corresponded with their respective thought bubbles. When questioned further, the children acknowledged explicitly that each protagonist had a different thought about the content of the same box and explicitly acknowledged that the box had just one item inside.

Hence, the child unequivocally acknowledged that two people could have different thoughts about one and the same thing.

Thoughts have a representational quality, meaning that they can depict some aspect of reality—they can be about reality and thus possess the quality of "aboutness". This allows us to learn about reality indirectly, as when somebody articulates their thoughts and knowledge of a subject. We need not always have first-hand experience to achieve a state of wisdom but can learn vicariously from the knowledge of others. This kind of learning can only be of benefit to us if we accept that the knowledge being passed on faithfully portrays some aspect of reality. What do young children know about this characteristic of representations, and how can thought bubbles serve as a tool of investigation? Wellman et al. (1995) answered these questions by effecting a small adaptation to their procedure in which children witness a protagonist looking into a box. This time only one protagonist was involved and children were asked a different question. They were not asked what the protagonist thinks but instead were asked what they themselves thought was in the box. Would the children use the protagonist's thought bubble as a clue to this? If so, they would be demonstrating an understanding of the affinity between thoughts and things in the world—an affinity that would amount to an understanding of a representational relationship.

Nearly all children aged 3 years judged that the box contained a teddy, which was the image shown in the protagonist's thought bubble. To avoid being hasty in concluding that young children do understand something of the "aboutness" of thoughts, we need to eliminate an alternative explanation for children's correct judgements. In fact, children had no other means of guessing the content of the box other than to refer to the thought bubble. Perhaps children would have accepted any suggestion made to them in this context, irrespective of whether it appeared within the confines of a thought bubble. To find out, Wellman et al. (1995) presented a control condition in which the protagonist began looking at a book after peering into the box. In the book was a conspicuous picture of a teddy, just as salient as the image of the same shown in the thought bubble condition. If children were just using any pictorially presented clue to guess what was in the box, they would also have judged that the box contained a teddy under this control condition that did not involve a thought bubble. However, children seldom did so. Their judgements that the box contained a teddy were confined to the thought bubble condition.

A sceptic would be forgiven for having lingering doubts about whether the children really did regard the thought bubbles in anything like the way one might understand actual thoughts. Wellman and Estes (1986) investigated children's understanding of thoughts as being unseeable and untouchable, as described earlier. Wellman et al. (1995) applied the same technique to establish whether children accept thought bubbles as thoughts according to the same criteria. They found that children judged that the contents of a thought bubble could neither be seen nor touched. In contrast, they judged in a control condition that a physical picture of the same thing could be seen and touched. It would thus seem that children do relate to thought bubbles as thoughts.

However, there is still a residual problem with applying what children know about thought bubbles to what they know about thoughts themselves. Ultimately, thought bubbles are an artefact, and as mentioned earlier, it seems odd to use them to investigate the child's natural understanding of actual thoughts. Perhaps children's judgements are restricted to what they understand in the domain of children's fiction, in which thought bubbles are used as a literary device. Although children might have a fine understanding of thought in this domain, perhaps they do not fully relate this to real people's thoughts. Even if this possibility were the case, note that we might be compelled to argue that one way children learn about mind is through the enculturation they experience when exposed to works of fiction.

In fact, it turned out that children had not gleaned much of an understanding of thought bubbles from fiction. In an informal survey of 200 children's books, Wellman et al. (1995) found only 4 that contained thought bubbles. Moreover, when children were shown a picture of a protagonist and asked to describe what the thought bubble was, nearly all remained silent and wore a blank expression. In all of the studies conducted by Wellman et al., the researchers had to present a preamble instructing the children that the thought bubbles were showing what the protagonist was thinking. Little elaboration was required for the child to grasp what was being explained, but nonetheless this warm-up phase proved to be necessary. This suggests that children's understanding of thought bubbles was not arising directly from their familiarity with these from children's books. Rather it seems that children were applying their cognitive framework of thoughts to make sense of the thought bubbles: Their competence in interpreting thought bubbles implies that they had a pre-existing conception of real thought.

Up to this point, we have looked at what children understand about thoughts from their interpretations of thought bubbles. A study by Flavell et al. (1993) tackled the problem from a different angle. They investigated children's judgements of the content of a protagonist's thought (bubbles) on the basis of the protagonist's activity. Children watched a protagonist who was doing one of three things: she was looking at something, she was engaged in problem solving, or she was looking blankly at nothing and wearing an expressionless visage. Children were presented with the task of selecting either a full or an empty thought bubble to match the protagonist in these three states of mental activity or inactivity. Seventy percent of children aged 3 years appropriately chose full thought bubbles when the protagonist was engaged in problem solving or surveying a picture and an empty one when she was staring blankly. It seems that children of this age not only read thoughts as such from thought bubbles but also understand the implications for thought (bubbles) that arise from various states of mental activity or inactivity.

It seems from this series of investigations that young children have considerable insight into thoughts. They understand that thoughts are specific to individuals such that two people can have different thoughts about one and the same thing. They also understand that thoughts depict aspects of reality and indeed are prepared to be informed about reality when told about someone's thought. Children understand that thoughts are ephemeral and intangible, and not amenable to sensory scrutiny. Children read people's thoughts from their thought bubbles in perhaps the same way that they would read people's thoughts from various clues that might be available in a natural environment. The real-world equivalent to thought bubbles might be what people say—they say what they think most of the time. It might be that children are already acquainted with thought bubbles via their experience, metaphorically, of speech bubbles. What people say is revealing of what they think. This early familiarity with speech and its connection with thought might provide the framework within which children can make sense of thought bubbles. We shall explore that issue later in the book (especially Chapters 5, 6, and 10), but now we shall turn our attention to another aspect of understanding of thoughts in young children. Namely, what they understand about the link between thoughts and emotions. So far, we have looked largely at the link between desire, belief, and behaviour. Next we shall add *emotion* to the trilogy.

THOUGHT AND EMOTION

Wellman and Bartsch (1988) reasoned that beliefs and desires are associated with distinctly different states of emotion. Desire is associated with the emotional continuum of happiness and sadness: If a desire is satisfied, as when we receive a coveted gift, then generally we experience happiness; if a desire is thwarted, as when failing to achieve a goal, then generally we experience sadness. In contrast, belief, as in expectations or assumptions, is associated with the emotion of surprise. If we have low expectations about the bonuses we might receive, then it will come as a pleasant surprise if we unexpectedly receive something a good deal more hefty.

To assess 3-year-olds' understanding of the emotions associated with the mental state of desire, Wellman and Bartsch (1988) told children a story about Mary, who either wanted orange juice or did not want orange with her lunch. Under one condition, the children were told that Mary actually got orange juice and under another condition they were told that she was given another kind of juice. The children where then invited to judge whether Mary feels happy, unhappy, or just okay. In other words, there were four permutations of wanting versus not wanting and receiving versus not receiving. The children's pattern of judging showed that they had a good insight into the connection between desire and the associated emotion of happiness. When the wanting and not wanting were matched with getting and not getting, respectively, children tended to judge that Mary was happy. In contrast, when the wanting and not wanting were mismatched with getting and not getting, then they tended to judge that Mary was unhappy.

To assess children's understanding of the link between belief and surprise, Wellman and Bartsch (1988) told children about a protagonist called Lisa, who (so they were told) thought it was or was not going to rain, depending on the experimental condition. Children were then told either that it did or did not rain. As in the case of the desire story, the four permutations of expectation and outcome were presented to children in various experimental conditions. The ideal pattern of responding would be to judge that Lisa was surprised when her expectation was mismatched with the outcome, and this is precisely what Wellman and Bartsch found. In contrast, when Lisa's expectation was depicted as proving true, then children were inclined to judge that she was not surprised.

Evidently, children aged 3 years have a good grasp of the link between mental states like belief and desire and their associated emotions of surprise and happiness. Yet there is even more to the young child's understanding of mind, specifically in relation to desire. Desire is linked not just with a particular emotion but also with a motivational state. If one desires something, then one will be motivated to satisfy that desire, which will be apparent in the individual's behaviour. This aspect of an understanding of desire was investigated by Wellman and Woolley (1990). They note that if one has a desire, then one is likely to persist in appropriate action until it is satisfied. In contrast, the action will cease once that desire is satisfied. If children show good insight into how desire relates to behaviour in this respect, then we will have grounds for claiming that children also understand the mediating role of motivation, that desire gives rise to motivation that can be quenched by appropriate action.

Wellman and Woolley (1990) told children aged 2 years a story about a boy who wanted to find his pet rabbit. The boy looked in the garage and, under one condition, found the rabbit in there, but under another condition found nothing. Observing child participants were asked whether the boy would look somewhere else. If told that the boy found nothing, the children judged that he would search further, but if he found the rabbit, they judged that his search would cease. Before we conclude that children do understand about motivation linking desire with behaviour, we should note that there is a reductionistic explanation for children's judgements that the protagonist would look no further on finding the rabbit. Perhaps children lacked any specific understanding of desire and motivation, but assumed that anyone who finds something attractive, such as a rabbit but also anything else attractive, would stop looking. To eliminate this possibility, Wellman and Woolley included a control condition in which the protagonist was searching for his rabbit but found his puppy in the garage instead. Presumably, a puppy is about as attractive as a rabbit, so if children were simply judging that the protagonist was searching until he found something attractive, they would have judged that his search would terminate in this scenario as well. However, unlike the condition in which the protagonist found his rabbit, children frequently judged that he would look somewhere else when he found the puppy. Children were also asked to predict the protagonist's associated emotion, and they judged that he would feel happy on finding the rabbit but sad (or at least not so happy) on finding either nothing or the puppy. Hence, even children as young as 2 years understand something about the network of connections between desire, motivation, action, and emotion. Unequivocally, they have a very sophisticated understanding of mind.

LATER DEVELOPMENTS IN CHILDREN'S UNDERSTANDING OF THOUGHT

It is impressive how much young children understand about thought. However, it would be astonishing if they did not still have a lot to learn. From the research of Flavell et al. (1995), it seems that between the ages of 5 and 8 years children learn a great deal about inferring the specific content of a person's thought. Looking at it the other way, the findings suggest that it is quite surprising how ignorant younger children are about the kinds of thoughts people have and even the character of thought as an unstoppable stream of consciousness. For example,

Flavell et al. (1995) told children aged 4 to 7 years a story about a boy who was waiting to visit the doctor for an injection. The boy, so it was explained, was very nervous about this. Observing child participants were asked to say what the protagonist might be thinking about during the wait. Surprisingly, 4- and 5-year-olds tended to judge that the protagonist was thinking about nothing, whereas older participants were more likely to say that he would be thinking about the injection.

In a further study, the cues were very gross in indicating the content of thought. In the company of the observing child participant, the experimenter asked Ellie (a confederate) to say how a shirt presented to her had become so dirty. Ellie gave the classic cues of pondering by saying "That's a difficult one", rubbing her chin, wearing a pensive expression, touching the shirt periodically and starring at it. Both 4- and 5-year-olds judged correctly that Ellie was thinking. When asked what she was thinking about, three-quarters of the 4-year-olds said that she was thinking about the shirt and nearly all 5-year-olds did so. When asked if she was also thinking about a distracter object, about half the 4-year-olds said that she was not, whereas about three-quarters of the 5-year-olds judged this way. Presumably, adults would judge that Ellie was totally absorbed with the dirty shirt, given all the available cues, but the children, especially the younger ones, did not always seem to grasp this. Generally, the children were biased against judging that the protagonist was thinking about something, and when they judged that she was, they did not seem to have much insight into what that thought process would be like.

Another limitation in young children's understanding of thought arises in the context of introspection. Flavell et al. (1995) showed 5-year-olds some magic tricks and other intriguing phenomena, and then asked them either immediately or after a delay what they were or had been thinking about. Presumably, they had been thinking about how the trick was done and whether magic was actually involved. Very often, the children judged that they were thinking about something other than the puzzling stimuli presented to them. Sometimes they judged that they were thinking about nothing and sometimes they judged that they were thinking about something totally unrelated. In contrast, 7–8-year-olds were likely to judge correctly in the expected way, that they were thinking about the magic trick.

It might be that the young children's judgements were accurate, and that they really were thinking about something irrelevant. However, that seems unlikely given the attention-capturing nature of the magic tricks, coupled with the children's mystified expressions. It is a good deal more likely that the children were thinking about the magic tricks but were not able introspectively to reflect on these thoughts. In general, then, it might be that younger children are not skilled in inferring the content of thought and have little insight into thought as forming the unstoppable stream of consciousness. This is evident from their inclination to judge that physically passive people are thinking nothing and their failure to introspect on their own thought as an on-line reflection of what is going on.

CONCLUSION

Children aged around 3 years know a remarkable amount about mental phenomena, despite the fact that they still have a lot to learn. Why should it be useful for them to know something of the rudiments of mind at this young age? One obvious utility is that the individual who understands the role of mind in governing behaviour is well positioned to manipulate information another person receives in order to manipulate the content of that person's mind in order to manipulate his or her behaviour. Presumably, early insight into mind is not just an incidental and largely superfluous luxury. Rather, it is likely that early insights into mind serve a valuable function.

We should now turn our attention to young children's ability to utilise their insights into mind. An obvious starting place is the ability to deceive. In nature generally, guile and deception allow the individual to survive and thrive. Presumably, the same is true in humans in particular. Successful deception allows you to enjoy a benefit without incurring any associated cost. Are young children skilled in executing acts of deception, given that they have a sophisticated understanding of thought, desire, motivation, and so on?

Another utility of an understanding of mind is that it enables us to interpret other people's speech. If we lacked an understanding of mind, then interpreting other people via their speech would be very difficult indeed—because we would not grasp that there is a meaning that resides behind the literal words of the message. Moreover, the relation between speech and understanding mind is two-directional—if we interpret speech, then we are interpreting another mind: Speech opens a window into the minds of those around us, and therefore enriches our understanding of mind generally. If we had no language, then we would have a severely impoverished understanding of mind. Apart from all this, we learned from the chapter on pretence that an understanding of mind and an understanding of speech might be unified by the underlying concept of referential opacity. In the following chapters, we shall explore children's early communication and their early ability to deceive, to explore the functional benefits of having a conception of mind.

CHAPTER FOUR

Children's deception

I have stressed that an insight into mind has a utilitarian value. It is something that is functional rather than a superfluous luxury. We have already briefly explored the possibility that an understanding of mind confers social competence on the individual, by examining the relation between pretence and various measures of social functioning, especially communicative. Now we shall turn our attention to the darker side of the utility of having an understanding of mind. Although mutual altruism and honesty generally make for a stress-free and satisfying passage through life, occasionally people are tempted to short-cut the route to realising their goals by Machiavellian means. Machiavellianism usually involves manipulating the information presented to others such that they have a distorted or completely untrue belief of what maintains in reality. For example, when selling our old car we might wish to give the misleading impression that it is in much better condition than it really is. Prospective buyers usually check the mileage gauge to estimate how likely it is that the car is mechanically worn out. On realising this, if we were Machiavellian, we could be tempted to tamper with the mileage gauge to give the false impression that the car has been used little and therefore is likely to offer further good service for a long time to come. If an understanding of mind owes its very existence to such a utilitarian value, then we might expect to find early evidence of a functioning insight into mind in the form of the young child's capacity for deception.

FALSE TRAILS

A seminal study by Chandler et al. (1989) was based on precisely this assumption. They tested a group of children aged 2, 3, and 4 years and introduced them to a doll carrying a basket full of treasure. The doll was going to navigate towards one of four miniature dustbins in which she would deposit her loot, and her aim in doing so was to conceal the treasure from a second experimenter who was absent from the room at the time of the concealment. Unfortunately for the doll, her attempt to hide the treasure was thwarted by the existence of a series of tell-tale footprints left in her wake, leading to the baited bin. This occurred on account of the doll setting out from an ink pad, causing the soles of her feet to absorb the dye and hence leave the damning physical evidence. The ink was in fact washable, allowing the footprints to be wiped away with a cloth issued to the children. In a warm-up phase, the experimenter demonstrated to the child how it was possible to erase footprints with the cloth.

The experimenter reminded the children that the aim was to prevent the second experimenter finding the treasure, pointed to the footprints leading to one of the four bins, and asked if the child could think of doing anything to obstruct the second experimenter. In response, very many of the children, including 2-year-olds, promptly took the cloth and proceeded to erase the footprints. Children were then asked if they could think of anything else to prevent the second experimenter finding the treasure. Many children grasped the doll and walked her from the ink pad to an empty bin, thus laying spurious clues. Some of the children who did not wipe away the initial trail to the baited bin nonetheless laid a false trail to an empty one. Following this episode, the second experimenter returned and asked the child directly where the treasure was hidden. Nearly all refrained from indicating, verbally or otherwise, the baited bin, and could be described as withholding evidence. In preference, many indicated a false location.

The results Chandler et al. (1989) report are precisely what we might expect if one force driving the onset and development of an understanding of mind is its Machiavellian utility. If we take a broader perspective on the whole issue, then it makes good sense to amalgamate the evidence documented on children's understanding of mental phenomena and their capacity for pretence and their ability to deceive. In other words, it seems highly plausible to suppose that children marshall what they understand about mind to their own advantage in figuring out how to implant misinformation in another person's mind.

However, not everybody is impressed by the evidence reported by Chandler et al. (1989). Those most vigorously critical are Sodian, Taylor,

Harris, and Perner (1991), who asked two related questions of Chandler et al.'s methodology. First, how can we be sure that children's manipulation of evidence was actually motivated by an understanding that it would be possible to implant misinformation in the second experimenter's mind? Hence, would children tamper with evidence even if they were supposed to be assisting a benign second experimenter to find the treasure? If so, then apparently they have a general tendency to wipe away old footprints and lay new ones, not to deceive but just because they cannot think of anything else to do when prompted to do something in connection with the footprints; or perhaps the children just regard wiping away the footprints as good fun. The second question posed by Sodian et al. is that, if explicitly asked where the second experimenter thinks the treasure is, will children indicate the location implicated by the misleading clues? If they laid false trails in order to deceive, then presumably children would judge that the second experimenter would think something contrary to the truth. In contrast, if children were wiping away existing trails and laying new ones just because it is a fun thing to do, without explicitly considering the ramifications for what the second experimenter would think, then presumably they might not acknowledge that the second experimenter would be misinformed. At the very most, children would be seen to have a working understanding of mind on the behavioural level, but one that is not sufficiently formulated to be articulated explicitly in language.

Sodian et al. (1991) conducted the following study with children aged 2–4 years to clarify matters. They began by checking whether children would explicitly acknowledge that the second experimenter would be misled by the false trails. In a procedure analogous to that of Chandler et al. (1989), children were introduced to a toy truck with a driver who was trying to hide from the second experimenter. The truck set out from its base and then navigated across sand to one of five cups. On arrival at the destination, the driver dismounted and was deposited under the adjacent cup. The truck was then removed, but tell-tale tracks in the sand remained. To ensure that children had first-hand experience of the significance of these tracks, in a warm-up phase they themselves had to guess where the driver was, just on the basis of the tyre marks in the sand. All children successfully negotiated this part of the procedure.

In the test phase, after the driver was hidden and the truck removed, children received a succession of prompts designed to encourage them to erase the tyre marks. The results were different from those reported by Chandler et al. (1989). To begin with, the 2- and 3-year-olds required very explicit and heavy prompting before they raked the sand to remove the tell-tale tracks. In this respect, they differed from the 4-year-olds who required virtually no prompting to do the same. After children were cajoled into erasing the old tracks and laying false trails to a new empty location, they were questioned on where the second experimenter would think the treasure was. The 4-year-olds acknowledged that the second experimenter would be misled but the younger ones judged that the second experimenter would think the treasure was where it really was; the younger ones seemed to be oblivious to the informational implications of erasing existing evidence and fabricating misleading evidence. Chandler could say in his defence that he was concerned only to reveal a working behavioural understanding of deception in 3-year-olds, an understanding that perhaps does not extend to a verbally explicit level of cognitive access. Nonetheless, the possibility that children's understanding is only apparent on one level of cognitive access would weaken the impact of Chandler's enterprise.

In a second experiment, Sodian et al. (1991) explored whether young children tailored their tampering with evidence to suit the situation, either to help an accomplice or to hinder a competitor. The modification to the procedure was that the driver was replaced by a doll who walked to one of five cups whereupon he deposited treasure, leaving a trail of inky footprints in the process, as in Chandler et al. (1989). Additionally, a doll replaced the second experimenter, and appeared in one of two guises. In one, the doll was a benign king who was going to help the child. If the king found the treasure, then he would relay it to the child as a reward for being nice. In another guise, the doll was a burglar who was going to steal the treasure and keep it for himself. If the child could prevent the burglar finding the treasure, then the child was entitled to keep the treasure for him or herself. In a warm-up phase, the child learned about strengthening the trail of footprints by drawing a line with a marker pen, parallel to the path of the footprints. This would be useful for assisting the king. The child was also shown that the footprints could be erased altogether with the aid of a cloth, which would be useful for impeding the burglar.

The results of this study were that very many children aged both 3 and 4 years erased the footprints. In this respect, the results were consistent with Chandler et al. (1989). However, another aspect of the results suggested that Chandler et al. overinterpreted their data. Children aged 3 years erased the footprints nonsystematically, apparently overlooking whether they were trying to help the king or hinder the burglar. Moreover, they laid false trails indiscriminately. In contrast, the children aged 4 years restricted their erasing of footprints to the condition involving the burglar, and likewise with laying false trails. This suggests that the younger children erased the tell-tale footprints not with a view to manipulating another person's information, but simply because such young children find it a fun thing to fiddle with the apparatus, which incidentally leads them to wipe away footprints.

The trouble with Sodian et al.'s (1991) finding is that it does not really tell us much. It tells us that young children apparently derived pleasure from wiping away footprints just for fun, and as such it undermines Chandler et al.'s (1989) evidence. However, the results do not tell us directly that the children lack an understanding of how manipulating information has an impact on the content of a recipient's thought. Children may have wiped away the trails just because it was fun, yet still understand about the relation between information and thought content. What we require is independent evidence to show that the young children genuinely were motivated to obstruct the burglar but assist the king. If we could demonstrate that, and children still failed to manipulate information appropriately, it would suggest that the relation between information and thought content is a difficult one for the children to grasp.

Sodian (1991) devised a condition that had scope to disentangle the child's motivation to assist or obstruct as required, and their understanding of the significance of manipulating information. She tested children aged 3 and 4 years in a procedure that involved a box containing treasure, and the child was encouraged either to help a benign person in a cooperative condition or hinder a nasty person in a competitive condition. Under one condition, the child was issued with a key and was able to lock the box. Under another condition, the child was not issued with a key and the box remained unlocked, but the child was informed that if he or she told the other person that it was locked, then the other person would accept the information in good faith and proceed no further. In other words, under one condition the child could sabotage the other's plight by locking the box, whereas under another condition the child could effect the same outcome by telling a lie. The results showed that both the 3- and 4-year-olds were easily able to engage in sabotage specifically where appropriate (to hinder a competitor), in the form of locking the box. In contrast, children failed to tell lies as a vehicle for obstructing a competitor. These results suggest that children were trying to play the game in such a way as to help the benign person and obstruct the nasty person, and would engage in sabotage to these ends. The results suggest that when it came to manipulating information the other person was to receive, children were unable to proceed effectively. Apparently, they could not grasp the implications of misinforming a competitor.

Further evidence suggesting young children's difficulty with understanding the informational implications of deception is given by Ruffman, Olson, Ash, and Keenan (1993). They tested children aged 3 and 4 years who witnessed a miscreant puppet called John not only steal some treasure but have the nerve to frame an innocent and unsuspecting Katy (another protagonist), by wearing her shoes! It so happened that John was a small person with small feet, whereas Katy was a very large person with large feet. Having donned Katy's large shoes, John crept to the location of the treasure, leaving behind a trail of footprints that were distinctly from Katy's shoes. After John had completed his despicable deed, an authority puppet arrived who was alarmed at finding the treasure stolen and wished to identify the culprit. Observing child participants were asked who the authority puppet thought did the stealing. Ruffman et al. observed an age trend to the effect that the 3-year-olds they tested judged that the authority doll would think John stole the treasure, whereas the older children apparently more insightfully judged that the authority doll would think the treasure was stolen by Katy. These results are entirely consistent with those reported by Sodian et al., suggesting that children aged around 3 years have little grasp of the informational implications of misleading evidence.

The accumulation of findings relating to 3-year-olds is presenting a picture of inability to utilise an insight into mind that is apparent in other domains such as pretence and aptitude for making judgements about thoughts. The evidence to this effect is compounded by a study conducted by Sodian and Schneider (1991). Children aged between 4 and 6 years were introduced to a model village consisting of 10 houses. Each was to be inhabited by a person with a familiar kind of profession, for example a doctor, a policeman, and a soccer player. The child participant was asked to assign each house to a person by placing a sticker on the front door signifying the identity of the occupant: for example, a syringe, a police car, and a football. They were then introduced to a couple of puppets who were trying to find each occupant in turn. One of these was a benign king and the other was a nasty burglar. The children were under instruction to assist the king but obstruct the burglar. These two puppets left the scene, and in their absence, children had to place the various professionals in houses at the child's own choice. The researchers' assumption was that if one wanted to assist a nice person (the king), then one would place the professional in the house designated by the appropriate cue. For example, the policeman should be deposited in the house with a picture of a police car on the front door. In contrast, if one wished to obstruct a nasty person, then one would be wise to place the policeman in a different house, such as the one with a picture of a football on the front door.

The children aged 6 years performed well in this task, in that they placed the various professionals in houses with the appropriate revealing stickers specifically under the cooperative condition in which a king was to appear and search. Meanwhile, they placed the various professionals in houses discrepant with the sticker proclaiming the occupant on the front door under the condition involving the nasty burglar. In contrast, the children aged 4 and 5 years tended either to place the professional in a discrepant house in both the cooperative and competitive condition, or to place them in a house consistent with the information displayed in the sticker in both conditions. The authors concluded that the children aged around 4 and 5 years do not understand how people use clues, such as stickers on front doors, in forming educated guesses about such things as the occupant of a house. Flavell et al. (1995) interpret this finding along with their own results (summarised in the previous chapter) as suggesting that until they are as old as 7 or 8 years, children have little insight into how one thought leads to another—in this case, how the thought of a distinctive sticker on the front door might lead to a thought of who occupies the house. Thought forms a stream of consciousness, and this stream is generated by one thought or input cueing another. This limitation in understanding thought could prevent children from grasping how one might manipulate clues in order to influence the informational content of another person's mind. If this view is correct, it would suggest that despite children's competence in pretence and making judgements about the character of thoughts in other respects, they are still severely limited in their understanding of the temporal dimension of thought.

We need to reconcile children's difficulty with the cueing task devised by Sodian and Schneider (1991), with their apparent ease in manipulating cues in Chandler et al.'s (1989) task.

In the latter, children's judgements related to whether another person knew or did not know a fact. In Sodian and Schneider's task, the judgement to be made concerned how a specific cue was linked with a specific belief. There is nothing absolute about a sticker on a front door. It is merely a clue that a person would probably utilise in guessing the whereabouts of a target protagonist. As Flavell et al. (1995) suggest, it seems to require more of an understanding of how one thought is likely to lead to another. More generally, a picture is beginning to emerge in which an understanding of mind cannot be said to have been acquired at any given point, as defined by the results of any given test. Rather, there are many facets to an understanding of mind, facets which are not necessarily acquired as a single unit.

GESTURING TO A NONTARGET LOCATION

Further evidence suggesting that 3-year-olds have little insight into deception is reported by Russell, Mauthner, Sharpe, and Tidswell (1991), who devised what they called the "windows task". During an introductory phase, children aged 3 and 4 years were trained to point at one of two boxes, and learned from this experience that the second experimenter reliably searched in the indicated location. Children also came to discover that one of the boxes was baited with chocolate, which the second experimenter retained if it so happened that the box she searched in (as indicated by the child) was the baited one. If not, then the child was entitled to search in the other box, find the chocolate and devour it. In other words, children were effectively being rewarded with chocolate if they gestured to the empty location. However, during this phase of the procedure, children were helpless to misinform the second experimenter in any proactive sense because they themselves did not actually know in which box the chocolate was stored.

During the experimental phase, there was a small modification to the boxes in that the previously opaque sides facing the child were now transparent. Meanwhile, the sides facing the second experimenter, who was situated on the opposite side of the boxes, remained opaque. Hence the child, but not the second experimenter, could see which of the boxes was baited with chocolate. Would the child now systematically misinform the second experimenter by gesturing to the empty box, to secure the chocolate for him or herself? The results showed just the opposite in the case of 3-year-olds. Of the 17 3-year-olds tested, 16 pointed to the baited box on the first experimental trial, thus denying themselves the chocolate reward. A further 11 children persisted in gesturing to the baited box on all of the subsequent 19 trials of the same task. In contrast, children aged 4 years were different. Only 6 of the 16 children gestured to the baited box on the first trial and none of them persevered in doing so on the subsequent 19 trials.

A similar kind of study was conducted by Peskin (1992), who tested 3-, 4-, and 5-year-olds. The children were shown three stickers, one of which they would be allowed to keep eventually. One was glittery silver and gold, another showed scenes from Care Bears and Ducktales, and a third showed "olde worlde" scenes in sepia hues. Children had to place the stickers in rank order of preference, and most did so according to the sequence just presented, with the glitter ranked most preferred and the sepias ranked as least preferred. Children were then introduced to a pair of puppets who were also to choose from the stickers, one of whom (called dark blue) was benign and, the children were told, would refrain from choosing the child's preferred sticker. The other (light blue) was nasty and would choose the child's preferred sticker for himself. The nice dark blue puppet arrived first and asked which sticker the child wanted. He proceeded to choose for himself the sticker about which the child expressed intermediate preference (Ducktales and Care Bears). This left the least and most preferred stickers for the nasty light blue puppet to choose between. He arrived and demanded of the child which he or she preferred. Would children try to conceal their preference or even actively misinform this nasty puppet?

The results showed marked differences between the children aged 3 years and the older participants in the study. Not only did the 3-year-olds consistently reveal their preference to the nice puppet, but they also tended to do so to the nasty puppet, thus effectively denying themselves their preferred reward. As in Russell et al.'s (1991) study, they persisted in the same pattern of responding over a succession of trials. In contrast, the older children concealed their preference specifically when appropriate; namely, they refused to inform or even went as far as misinforming the nasty puppet. However, the 3-year-olds did actively try to obstruct the nasty puppet by, for example, shielding their preferred sticker. This was less common in the older children. This aspect of the results resembles a finding reported by Sodian (1991), described earlier. Sodian found that 3-year-olds were effective and willing to engage in sabotage, taking the form of locking a treasure box to obstruct a nasty puppet from gaining access. It seems that young children are well-versed in manipulating the physical situation to retain a reward for themselves, but far less effective in manipulating information to achieve the same end.

In another respect, the youngest children tested by Peskin (1992) showed their sensitivity to the contrasting personalities of the puppets. In this there was just a two-way choice involving the child's most preferred and least preferred sticker. This time, the child's task was to choose one of the puppets to have first choice of sticker. The 3-year-olds reliably choose the nice dark blue puppet, and in this respect performed just as well as the older children.

It seems peculiar that young children should know so much about the mind, yet be unable to deploy this knowledge as a tactic either for preventing a competitor acquiring a coveted treat or for the child obtaining that prize for him or herself. We can assume that an understanding of mind is not just a superfluous auxiliary aspect of cognition, but actually functions to serve a useful purpose in the child's own interest. How, then, can we explain the discrepancy between their competence in pretence and judging about thoughts on one hand, but their inability to perform well in carrying out deception on the other?

There are several ways that the discrepancy could be reconciled. One is that really young children are severely lacking in their conception of mind. Specifically, perhaps the criteria for crediting the child with a conception of mind in the previous two chapters (pretence and acknowledging mental phenomena) are far too lax. According to Perner (1991), the essential criterion is that one should be able to acknowledge that people hold their beliefs to be true of reality. Because people hold their beliefs to be true, so they will behave accordingly and act on them. This is a stricter criterion than merely acknowledging that thoughts exist. It is an understanding that people not only have thoughts but have a particular attitude toward them that will have special consequences for the person's behaviour. So people will have a great corpus of thoughts, some of which they will regard as daydreams and some of which they will regard as serious and accurately representing reality. If children understood this latter point, then presumably they would grasp that if we could implant a thought in someone's mind that the person will take seriously and hold as true (due to our skilful deception), then the person might be fooled into acting in a way that thwarts his or her aim. For example, if we tell an adversary that a prize is in location A, then if he takes it seriously he will believe as true that the prize is there. He will proceed to look there but be disappointed on finding the location empty. In sum, perhaps the essence of a functional understanding of mind is an understanding that people can hold false beliefs whilst paradoxically maintaining an attitude that they are true (Perner, 1991).

An alternative explanation is that early pretence and understanding of thoughts does signify a comprehensive understanding of mind, but the child is unable to deploy this competence in performing effective acts of deception. It might be that however much the child knows about the mind, he or she is delayed in coming to terms with the idea that this understanding can be used to one's own ends by misleading other people. If this is the correct explanation, it would no longer be necessary to claim, as Perner (1991) does, that the young child's difficulty is in grasping the attitude people hold toward their own thoughts, whether to take them as seriously representing reality or just as fanciful products of the imagination. A compromise view would be that children have an understanding of mind sufficiently elaborated to ensure success on some tasks but not others. For example, although it might be that the child's understanding of the effect of misinformation is sufficiently explicit to allow an enactment of behavioural deception (e.g. laying false trails in some contexts), it may not be sufficiently explicit to allow the child deliberately to articulate a nontruth.

We shall proceed via two routes. One is to put the spotlight on the child's difficulty in acknowledging false beliefs, with a view to investigating whether some other factor can account for this phenomenon (i.e. other than that the child fails to take into account the attitudes people hold toward their thoughts). This is the province of Chapters 7 and 8. Another way of proceeding is to challenge the evidence suggesting that children have difficulty with even the simplest forms of deception. This is a matter we shall explore in the remainder of the present chapter.

HAVE CHILDREN BEEN UNDERESTIMATED?

In addition to the study by Chandler et al. (1989), there are several other studies to date that suggest that young children do have an understanding of deception. The first we shall consider is another conducted by Chandler's team (Hala, Chandler, & Fritz, 1991), which was motivated by an attempt to introduce the controls suggested and deployed by Sodian et al. (1991). Although the results of Sodian et al.'s study suggested that young children actually do not have much insight into deception, the results reported by Hala et al. (1991) suggest otherwise. Children were 3 and 4 years old. As in Chandler et al. (1989), a doll left a trail of tell-tale inky footprints leading to a plastic bin. Children became acquainted with the informative value of these footprints in a warm-up phase, when they left the room while the doll hid the treasure, and children then returned and were able to search correctly by using the footprints as clues. Children had no difficulty with this inferential task. The main part of the study concerned children's erasing of existing footprints and laying false trails. The results were that 90% of children aged 3 years carried out this kind of deceptive act. Moreover, 70% of the young 3s and 80% of the old 3s correctly predicted that the second experimenter would search in the empty location signified by the false trail. The latter stands in direct contradiction to the results reported by Sodian et al. (1991). Sodian et al. found that although young children laid false trails when prompted, they seemed not to grasp the informational implications of these: They frequently judged that another person, whose only source of information was the false trails, nonetheless would think the treasure was where it really was.

In a second experiment, children were given the task either of preventing a nasty second experimenter finding the treasure, or the task of helping a nice experimenter to succeed in finding it. The former condition was identical to that employed in the first experiment, while in the latter the puppet left no trail. The results replicated and extended those of the first experiment. Under the deceptive condition, nearly all the 3-year-olds tested either wiped away the old trail or laid a new one(s) or both. As before, they predicted that the second experimenter would search in the wrong location. In contrast, under the cooperative condition, nearly all children made just a single trail of footprints to the container housing the treasure, and predicted that the second experimenter would look in the correct place. In a third experiment, this finding was supplemented by children answering a "think" question appropriately. They judged that an experimenter seeing misleading trails would think the treasure was somewhere other than where it really was, and that an experimenter seeing a single trail leading to the correct location would think it was there.

It is difficult to reconcile these results with those reported by Sodian et al. (1991). There are small differences in procedure, such as that the cooperative condition in Sodian et al. required the child to strengthen an existing faint trail to the correct location if the child was to be recorded as performing correctly. In Hala et al. (1991), in contrast, there was no trail at all initially, so any trail the child laid would be the sole one. It might be that children understand the difference in the informative value of a trail versus no trail, as in Hala et al., but do not understand the difference in informative value of a weak trail versus a strong one, as in Sodian et al. If that does account for the difference in results, it would seem appropriate to conclude that young children understand about deception in the sense that they lay trails to an empty location when trying to deceive, but to the correct location when trying to inform. However, there is no obvious explanation for the discrepancy between the two studies in children's explicit judgements of where another person would search or where the other person thinks the treasure is.

If the only studies to suggest that young children are capable of insightful deception were those conducted by Chandler's team, then we might still be left with the impression that young children do not have much aptitude for deception, given the collection of studies implicating difficulties for young children. However, there is also doubt hanging over the claim that young children have difficulty in engaging in deception in the windows task. Samuels, Brooks, and Frye (1996) presented a procedure to children which replicated that devised by Russell et al. (1991) and additionally introduced variations that, a priori, the researchers had assumed would make the task easier. For example, Russell et al. asked the children to point to a box to tell his opponent to look so that the opponent does not get the prize. Samuels et al. asked children to give (or point out) a box to the opponent so that the children themselves get the prize. It turned out that, irrespective of question wording, the 3-year-olds had little difficulty in pointing to the empty box. Any who did have difficulty on the first trial very rapidly learned to point to the empty box. Again, it is difficult to reconcile this positive result with the negative result reported in the study originally conducted by Russell et al.

Now we shall consider two novel procedures that further highlight children's competence in deception. The first of these was conducted by Sullivan and Winner (1993), who tested children aged 3 and 4 years. The children were shown various boxes whose contents were proclaimed by familiar packaging, such as a Smarties tube. Children were encouraged to remove the usual content and replace it with something atypical (pencils), with the aim of tricking the second experimenter. Children were then asked to judge what the second experimenter (who was absent when the box was tampered with) would think was in the box, and 9 out of 13 3-year-olds and 10 out of 13 4-year-olds correctly judged that the second experimenter would think there were Smarties inside. In contrast, children were less likely to acknowledge the second experimenter's false belief when the test was modified slightly. In this, the child was shown that the tube contained a pencil all along, and then judged what the second experimenter would think was inside. In this control condition there was no aura of trickery, and children very often failed to acknowledge the second experimenter's false belief. These results suggest that in a "straight" procedure designed to assess what young children understand of false belief, many fail. In contrast, when they are actively involved in trickery, they seem able to succeed.

A highly consistent finding is reported by Chandler and Hala (1994), and this is the second of the novel procedures mentioned. They tested children aged 3 years. The children were shown a cookies box, whose familiar content was proclaimed by the picture on the exterior. The experimenter then ostensibly entered into a conspiracy with the child to trick the second experimenter. This involved exchanging the expected content of cookies for something unfamiliar and surprising. It was a disgusting rubber spider purchased from a joke shop, that presumably would give the second experimenter a nasty shock when she opened the cookies box. After the spider was placed in the box, children were asked what the second experimenter would think was in there and around 80% correctly acknowledged the second experimenter's false belief by judging "cookies".

Under another very similar condition, children did not perform well in acknowledging the second experimenter's false belief. The first experimenter again stated that the aim was to trick the second experimenter, but denied the child an active role in this enterprise. The first experimenter was the one who did the swap while the child was a passive observer. Under this condition, only about 40% of those aged 3 years correctly judged that the second experimenter would be fooled into thinking there were cookies in the box. The rest judged that the second experimenter would think there was a spider in the box.

Not only did children show a grasp of deception when actively involved, the result also confirms that they were able to dissociate thought from reality, contrary to Harris et al.'s (1991) study described in the previous chapter. Recall that Harris et al. argued that young children confuse a thought about the content of a box with its real content. In Chandler and Hala's (1994) study, children showed no such confusion. They were comfortable judging that another person's thought (cookies) and the real content (a spider) were different.

Chandler and Hala (1994) concluded that what helps reveal competence in young children in these tasks is a motivation to deceive coupled with an opportunity for them to be instrumental in that deception. Similarly, the study by Sullivan and Winner (1993) involved children actively manipulating the materials so that another person would be misled by them. It might be that generally, young children are actually effective in engaging in deception and understand the consequences for another person's belief state, so long as they are allowed to play an active role. It might be that studies reporting that children have difficulty with deception (such as that by Sodian et al., 1991, and by Russell et al., 1991) inadvertently denied children much of an active role, whereas the studies by Chandler et al. (1989) and by Hala et al. (1991) encouraged children to be more actively involved. Such differences were not apparent from the descriptions of the procedures for these studies, but nonetheless, the interaction style of the experimenter could have been a crucial but hitherto unrecognised factor.

DECEPTION AS A SOCIAL SKILL

If children are more effective in engaging in deception when they are actively involved, then we might expect their competence to be revealed in procedures that begin to approximate real life. Many of the studies reviewed so far are unashamedly contrived, and such procedures are not necessarily suited to revealing children's early competence. Additionally, many procedures have been designed to identify explicitly what young children understand about the consequences of deception on a recipient's informational state. If we return to the basic theme introduced at the beginning of this chapter, the question concerns whether or not young children can engage in deception effectively. We might expect that they would be able to if they have an understanding of mind, since one function of such an understanding is that it confers special advantages upon the child in terms of his or her dealings with others. When we present the issue in this way, a study by Lewis, Stanger, and Sullivan (1989) comes into focus.

Lewis et al. (1989) observed a group of young children, most of whom were just under 3 years of age. The experimenter introduced an attractive toy animal zoo that was covered by a cloth. She explained that the child could play with it shortly but was not allowed to look until she (the experimenter) returned in a few moments. The experimenter then departed, leaving the child, who continued to be observed surreptitiously via a hidden camera, alone in the test room. Twenty-nine of the 33 children tested disobeyed the experimenter by peeping under the cloth at the toy zoo. The experimenter returned and directly asked the children if they had peeped. If the children had no insight into other people's ignorance and if they did not understand that lies and deception can mislead others, then they would see no point in uttering anything other than the truth to this question. However, nearly two-thirds of the children who peeped apparently attempted to deceive the experimenter. Either they remained mute, even when the experimenter repeated her question (24% of those who peeped), or they blatantly lied by saying that they had not peeped when they had (38% of those who peeped). Evidently, many of these very young children were willing and able to engage in deception.

It is one thing to engage in deception, but it is quite another to do it skilfully. One of the great strengths of the study by Lewis et al. (1989) was that it allowed an examination of how convincing children appeared when they were telling lies. This is an important functional issue, since being able to deceive would only have a utilitarian value if one were able to tell a lie as though it were the truth. If one told lies in such a way that it was obvious they were lies, then this would be worse than useless. Not only would the recipient not be deceived, but the recipient might impose unpleasant sanctions. Having the children's lies recorded on video allowed Lewis et al. to show the resulting footage to adult raters who were ignorant of the details of the study and who observed the children without sound. The panel of adults was unable to discriminate between children who falsely claimed they had not peeped and those who truthfully claimed they had not peeped. Hence, the children who told lies did so in a convincing manner. In contrast, the children who failed to respond were identified by the adults as appearing suspicious.

Lewis et al. (1989) proceeded to analyse the facial expressions in some detail in an attempt to identify what distinguished those who peeped and lied from those who peeped and did not own up to their misdeed by remaining silent. The children who told lies smiled as they did so and maintained a relaxed expression. In contrast, the children who remained silent wore an unsmiling face that was unrelaxed. These children were perceived by the adult judges as wearing their guilt on their faces. In summary, then, it seems that many children who are not yet 3 years old are capable of either withholding information or giving false information, and those capable of the latter can do so in convincing style.

Although the evidence for early skill in deception presented by Lewis et al. (1989) is largely compelling, there is a way of interpreting children's behaviour without ascribing much insight into mind. It might be that the children engaged in general denial, not just to the experimenter but for their own benefit as well. They knew that they were engaging in a forbidden deed, which may have caused feelings of guilt. Accordingly, they may have attempted to re-invent history by denying (to themselves as well as others) that they actually carried out the act. If so, then children would deny that they peeped even if they did so as the experimenter watched. It is likely that Lewis et al.'s interpretation is correct, but it will be even more convincing when this vital control is added to their design.

It would not be surprising if individuals who are skilful in deception show mastery over other aspects of interpersonal dealings. This is what we would expect if deception serves a functional purpose of conferring advantages on the individual in his or her interactions with others. Precisely this view was adopted by Keating and Heltman (1994) in their study of the relation between deception and dominance. These authors assumed that individuals who are masterful and dominant possess what ordinary people might see as leadership qualities. They supposed that such individuals succeed in being dominant because they have skill in manipulating others, sometimes perhaps through acts of deception, which led Keating and Heltman to pose the following provocative question as part of the title of their article: "Are leaders the best misleaders?"

Keating and Heltman (1994) asked children aged between 3 and 6 years to taste two drinks of orange juice. When they did so, they discovered that one tasted sweet and pleasant, while the other tasted sour and nasty. The children were unanimous in their verdict of the differing palatability of the two drinks. Subsequently, the children were persuaded to convince the experimenter's assistant, who arrived late on the scene, that both drinks were nice tasting. A film was made of the children doing this, which was later shown to adult judges minus the soundtrack. These judges were fully informed about the details of the study, except that they did not know which of the drinks really tasted nasty. Their job was to infer the identity of the nasty drink from any nonverbal clues present in the children's communication with the assistant. In other words, the adults were trying to diagnose when the children were telling lies from nonverbal aspects of their behaviour. Meanwhile, children were observed during free play to determine who was dominant and who was submissive. Dominant children were identified as such if their behavioural profile conformed to three criteria: (1) physical assertion in the form of pulling, hitting and chasing other children; (2) dominance gestures in the form of staring and pointing at others; (3) verbal assertion in the form of teasing and ridiculing others.

A highlight of the results was an intriguing relation between (1) the ability to carry off a convincing act of deception that fooled adults and (2) dominance of peers; those who were most skilled at deception were also the most dominant. Before we consider the ramifications of this finding, we should pause to eliminate some theoretically uninteresting reasons for the relation. One possibility is that the most dominant children tended to be the older ones, and also the best at deception, raising the possibility that maturity is responsible both for dominance and skilled deception, and that the latter two are related with each other only trivially in so far as they are both related with age. To check this possibility, Keating and Heltman (1994) statistically subtracted age as a variable from the relation between deception and dominance. They found that age was correlated with dominance (older children were more dominant than younger ones) but age was not correlated with skill in deception. Consequently, the relation between dominance and deception survived the statistical partialling of age as a variable. Although the primary purpose of this analysis was to eliminate the role of age in the relation between dominance and deception, incidentally the results support the view that competence in deception is not something that develops rapidly between 3 and 5 years of age, contrary to Sodian et al. (1991) and other researchers of the same genre.

Another trivial explanation for the relation between dominance and deception is that dominant children tend to be socially confident, a confidence that is manifest also in their communication about the taste of the drinks. If so, adult raters were mistaking social confidence for honesty, and on the other side of the coin were assuming that the submissive children who were lacking confidence appeared furtive and dishonest. To eliminate this possibility, Keating and Heltman (1994) statistically subtracted the raters' judgements of how convincing the children seemed when they were actually telling the truth from the relation between deception and dominance. The results showed that the skill of the dominant children in telling a convincing lie could not be accounted for by more general aspects of their confident style of interaction; their ability to tell a convincing lie extended beyond their generally confident demeanour.

Keating and Heltman (1994) proceeded to conduct a more detailed analysis of precisely which aspects of the children's nonverbal behaviour adults found especially convincing. The findings turned out to be highly consistent with those reported by Lewis et al. (1989). Namely, the children who were skilful in deceiving were able to assert that the drink was nice tasting whilst wearing a smile. These children happened to be the socially dominant ones. Lewis et al. also found that the children most skilful in telling lies were able to do so with a smiling face. The implications of these results are as follows. A way of using an understanding of mind is to manipulate others. One example of this is deception and another is domination. It might be that deception and domination go hand in hand as symptoms of a more general proclivity to deploy an understanding of mind against others. A rather dark ramification is that among the characteristics associated with leadership is dominance and deception to suit the leader's own interests. Having said that, there is probably an asymmetry here. Whereas it is likely that dominant individuals have a well-developed understanding of mind that they are willing to use in effective deception, it would not necessarily follow that people with an impressive understanding of mind would automatically use this against other people in an act of dominance. Such factors as temperament would also have to be taken into consideration.

If it is the case that there is a reliable association between dominance and deception, we would expect to find that the relation maintains in adults also. To find out, Keating and Heltman (1994) repeated their study with adult participants. Obviously a different measure was required to assess dominance, and this was achieved by organising the participants into groups of six composed of same-sex members. Each group was given the task of working out the problem of winter survival in a hypothetical situation in which the participants were supposedly stranded in the Arctic wilderness. Following this session, participants ranked each member of the group, including themselves, according to dominance. Subsequently, the participants communicated to a camera that a nasty tasting drink was nice. Like the children, the most dominant adults were the ones capable of telling the most convincing lies. In this case, those who were effective at deceiving maintained an unsmiling and "sincere" expression whilst holding a steady gaze at the camera. Those identified as telling lies tended to grin and shift their gaze. Although the technique for telling convincing lies differed between child and adult, the two populations were united in the sense that a tendency to dominate coincided with skill in deceiving.

CONCLUSION

There is some evidence to suggest that young children can utilise what they know about mind to their advantage by engaging in deception. There is also evidence arising from these studies suggesting that young children experience considerable difficulty in acknowledging false belief. It seems that young children can overcome their difficulty with false belief in some cases and are able to deceive as a consequence. We are left, then, with the substantive issue of how to construe children's difficulty with false belief. It seems there are two prominent explanations. One is that young children do not know anything of the attitude people adopt toward their own beliefs. For example, we adults assume that people take their own simple factual beliefs seriously and take them to reflect reality accurately and truthfully. For this reason, they can be seen to act as though their beliefs are true even when, in fact, they are false. This is a view adopted forcefully by Perner (e.g. 1991). Another explanation is that when beliefs are discrepant with reality, young children cannot but help attend to reality, making it hard for them to acknowledge false belief. Although young children may have an implicit and working understanding of mind that allows them to deceive in some contexts, this understanding might not yet be sufficiently formulated to allow the child to make an explicit contrast between belief and reality. If this is so, then there is no need to suppose young children have any difficulty with the attitudes people hold about their own beliefs. These competing explanations will be explored in depth in Chapters 7 and 8. Although at this point the difference between the two competing explanations may seem purely academic, we shall see that they have very substantial ramifications in terms of how we should construe not only the child's understanding of mind, but the adult's too. The debate also touches on how we should view development in what the child understands about mind. Before we turn to that, we shall examine the link between what children know about mind and their early communication. One utility of an understanding of mind is that it provides a motivation for communication and assists the child to interpret the speech of others. This is the province of the next two chapters.

CHAPTER FIVE

Children's early language and communication

A young child must have some understanding of mind, however primitive, in order to learn language and use it appropriately in communication. I will say more about this shortly. Having a primitive understanding of mind is to the benefit of a developing linguistic proficiency, but this favour is soon repaid in the sense that an understanding of mind will be enriched by the knowledge of other minds that one derives from communicating with them. The latter point is a very simple and self-evident truth. It is that in principle the most direct route to another person's thoughts is via what they say. There is an affinity between the language of thought and the language of speech such that what people say provides a window on their underlying thought processes. It is a window that is metaphorically glazed with panes of frosted glass, though, because what is said will not always be a replica of what one is thinking. For a start, people do not habitually go round blurting out all that they are thinking at any given moment, so what people say is but a sample of what they think. Apart from this, people exert voluntary control over what they say and are thereby not compelled to report exactly what they think. They might systematically withhold information or even report misinformation (something they think is not true).

Despite these qualifications, linguistic communication nonetheless offers the most accurate insight into mind. If we want to know what somebody thinks, usually we would ask them in words and they would answer in words. In the aftermath of this exchange, we would feel enlightened on what was in the other person's mind, and quite rightly so in nearly all cases. This is the assumption that resides behind interviewing and questionnaires. In appointing a new person to a company, it is likely that a substantial amount of weight will be given to what the candidate says about him or herself at interview. From a brief meeting, the appointing committee will infer whether or not the candidate is intelligent, reliable, competent, qualified, has integrity, is punctual, and so on. This impression will be based largely on what the person says, in which case the appointing committee will feel (rightly or wrongly) that it has appraised the psychology of the candidate. That impression rests upon an assumption that the contents of the candidate's mind can be accessed through a question–answer session; in other words, through the medium of speech. A similar assumption is made about personality questionnaires, though here the questions are usually read and the responses presented in writing (or more commonly in a simple forced choice). Assumptions are made that an individual's unique personality profile and character can be diagnosed by what the person says about him or herself.

These examples show that we tacitly and routinely assume that we can access the minds or the psychology of other people by allowing ourselves to be informed by what they say—and generally we are right to make this assumption. Granted that sometimes bad appointments are made on the basis of an interview and granted that sometimes questionnaires turn out to be unreliable or invalid; nevertheless, it is difficult to imagine how we could gain quick access to an unfamiliar person's mind by other means. Although speech offers only a fuzzy vision of the underlying mind, it still remains the best available method of access. Later, we shall explore systematically how a proficiency in speech, with the riches of accompanying verbal exchanges, promotes an understanding of mind. First, we shall examine why some rudimentary grasp of mind is a necessary precursor of linguistic development.

JOINT ATTENTION

The starting point is not verbal but nonverbal communication, especially involving what babies infer from the direction of gaze. This could lay the foundations for subsequent verbal reference made by another person to things in the outside world. Butterworth and colleagues (e.g. Butterworth & Cochran, 1980; Butterworth & Jarrett, 1991) investigated babies' understanding of the mother's reference to something in the outside world on the basis of her gaze. Babies were propped up facing their mother, who was under instruction to establish eye contact with the baby and then fix her gaze on a predetermined location. By 18 months of age most babies respond by rapidly fixating on the location that has become the object of the mother's gaze, even when that location falls outside the baby's immediate field of view, as when the mother locks on to a location in space that is behind the baby.

A common-sense interpretation of this intriguing phenomenon is that infants are aware of various perspectives upon reality. Perhaps infants understand on some level, however primitive, that their current perspective on reality is but a sample of all that is out there. Taking note and tracing the trajectory of the mother's gaze seems difficult to explain without supposing that the infant is expecting to see an object not previously in the field of view.

An alternative reductive explanation is offered by Moore and Corkum (1994), who suggest that at least the behaviour of a baby aged 12 months or less can be explained entirely in the behavioural terms of stimulus–response–reinforcement. They put forward as the defining condition of joint attention that there should be a joint attention triangle that involves the object of attention as one of its vertices. Acting upon the mother's gaze per se is not sufficient for these authors; the infant must also show some insight into the possibility of an object of the mother's gaze, an object that they will also see if they look to the same point in space. According to Moore and Corkum, it might be that infants have no insight into the part of the world currently not visible to them, but potentially accessible to another mind, since they could succeed in Butterworth's task (so they claim, but see below) purely according to a stimulus–response contingency. The infants learn to imitate the mother's head turn without insight, because when they do so this is usually reinforced by seeing an interesting object (coincidentally, the one that the mother happened to be looking at). Apart from being possible to explain the infant's apparent joint-attention skills in this way, Moore and Corkum suggest that to do so allows them to advance an account consistent with Perner's (1991) view that infants are capable of entertaining only a single model of reality. In other words, the infant assumes that reality is as it appears and it is impossible to consider any alternative, either real or fictional.

It so happens that the 18-month-olds tested by Butterworth and Jarrett (1991) meet Moore and Corkum's (1994) requirement with respect to the conceptually richer interpretation of their behaviour. Butterworth and Jarrett had already considered the possibility that perhaps the babies were not grasping that the mother was looking at an *object out of view* that they should seek to detect, but that they were merely imitating the mother's head turning. They were able to eliminate this reductive explanation by having the mother fixate on an empty space and then calculate whether the baby's gaze bisected the same imaginary target. In fact, it turned out that the babies' gaze was highly calibrated to the mothers', suggesting that they were able to calculate the coordinates geometrically to identify the same location in space whether or not there was a salient object there. Under another condition the mother shifted her gaze from the infant to a predetermined space just by moving her eyes. Babies still shifted their gaze appropriately, which is independent evidence to the effect that they were not just imitating the mother's head turn. Calculating the geometry of the gaze surely suggests that we should consider more than imitation and stimulus–response. Rather, the babies seemed to be looking for a *particular* object fixated by the mother, which existed in a particular space.

Apart from this evidence being inconsistent with Moore and Corkum's (1994) thesis, their argument does not apply to older infants in principle. They suppose that younger infants have a one-dimensional conception of reality that is incompatible with the claim that they can consider alternative perspectives. However, we are concerned with 18-month-old infants, who have reached an age at which they can be expected to imagine alternative realities. This has been acknowledged since the time of Piaget's writings in the 1920s about the development of the object concept, where it is documented that at about 15 to 18 months infants begin to imagine the covert displacement of a hidden toy. Perner's (1991) account is entirely consistent with this. Additionally, infants show the first signs of pretence at 18 months, which also implies the ability to conceive of alternative models. Moore and Corkum's argument is only contentious if we wish to argue that below age 18 months infants understand about joint attention; but we do not wish to argue that.

Although Moore and Corkum's (1994) argument about the timetable of early competence is entirely compatible with other accounts, such as Butterworth's, their account has additional features that are contentious. Their aim is not just to explain very early apparent joint attention reductively, but also to begin to offer a learning account of the genesis of an understanding of mind. They suggest that from initial stimulus–response relations, infants proceed to map meaning onto early behaviour when a capacity for considering multiple models eventually develops. In arguing this, Moore and Corkum do not regard the early stimulus–response experience as causal in stimulating the growth of a capacity for multiple models; rather, they seem to assume that it is purely maturational. However, this does not seem to be a useful way of looking at things. If infants perform so well on the basis of stimulus–response associations, so much so that their behaviour appears insightful, then where would the motivation come from to represent other perspectives or minds in this context? Indeed, one could actually go as far as explaining all human phenomena that we take to be signs of an understanding of mind, as being reducible to stimulus–response behaviour, but that does not offer a useful framework for investigation.

Apparently, then, 18-month-old babies have a working understanding that information about the world available to another mind can be accessed by carefully tracing the source of that information. Babies also have a working understanding of other kinds of information that can be imparted by other minds. When venturing into an unfamiliar environment, the baby should proceed with caution in case danger is lurking. If the baby is receptive to advice from the parent, then he or she is unlikely to get into trouble. In fact, not only are babies from about 12 months receptive, but they actually seek their mother's guidance. This was demonstrated by Sorce, Emde, Campos, and Klinnert (1985), who placed babies aged around 12 months at the edge of a piece of apparatus known as the visual cliff. This is a glass platform suspended several feet in height above the ground. Would the babies move over the apparent precipice, or would they stay put? In fact, whether or not the babies were adventurous in this respect depended largely on the facial expression their mother was wearing. If the mother was cringing with paroxysms of horror, then the babies remained motionless, whereas if the mother presented a placid and cheerful expression the babies happily ventured over the precipice. In sum, the babies sought information from their mothers, apparently to gauge the danger in the situation, and acted accordingly after reading the mother's facial expression. In doing so, the babies were behaving as though their mothers were better informed than themselves, and hence were effectively sensitive to differences between their own knowledge (or ignorance) and their mother's. Moore and Corkum (1994) also try to explain this phenomenon by reference to stimulus–response relations, and in this case their argument carries a little more force because we are concerned with 12- rather than 18-month-olds.

It seems likely, then, that infants are attuned to the rich source of information that is available to them from other people (usually the mother). This is a tacit acknowledgement by babies that information held by others is different from their own information, which in turn seems to form the basis for an understanding of mind. This sensitivity to other's information and reference is vital if the infant is to learn language. This point is highlighted in the work of Baldwin (1991, 1993a,b; Baldwin & Moses, 1994). Mothers informally teach vocabulary to their babies by saying the names of objects. However, mothers are sometimes remiss in failing to check that their baby is looking at the thing they are naming. In some cases, the baby is looking at something quite different. For example, suppose the baby is looking at the family dog when the mother is looking at a cup and she articulates "cup". Would this result in the baby saying "cup" on next encountering the dog? If so, language acquisition would be terribly tardy, and perhaps even impossible.

Baldwin (1993a) found that when infants hear their mothers utter a word, they typically shift their gaze from whatever they are attending to and look at the mother, apparently to assess what she is focusing on. Then they identify what the mother is looking at and attend to the same, thus allowing them to learn the new word in relation to the object of the mother's attention rather than in relation to the object of their own attention. If children were learning vocabulary by simple association, in which they pair a word with a salient object, they would not bother to check the direction of the mother's gaze. Because they do check their mother's gaze in this context, it facilitates the growth of correct vocabulary. Additionally, it seems that the babies have a preconception about verbal communication, specifically that reference is the prerogative of the person who utters the message, with the implication that it is partly the listener's responsibility to figure out what the speaker means. This provides a framework for understanding that verbal communication has a potential to transmit information from one person, or one mind, to another. Hence, being able to communicate effectively rests upon a working understanding of mind, however primitive. Such understanding of mind allows vocabulary to develop rapidly.

CHILDREN'S EARLY CONVERSATION

As mentioned previously, we know from Butterworth's research that babies aged 18 months have the motivation and the means to achieve joint visual focus with their mother (Butterworth, 1994, for a summary). The same motivation is apparent in infants of the same age with respect to topics of conversation. Shatz (1994) reports as much in her descriptions of the conversational abilities of her grandson, Ricky, at the age of 17 months. Shatz was speaking to Ricky on the phone when he uttered the word "house". Ricky was at the one-word stage of language development, and did not have the necessary linguistic skill to elaborate and clarify his meaning. Shatz tried to help him by talking about his impending visit to her house. Though Shatz did not know it at the time, in fact this was not Ricky's meaning. He sought to clarify what he meant by dragging his toy house to the telephone, presumably in the hope that its proximity to the source of Shatz' voice would be sufficient for her to understand what he meant. What he was trying to communicate, it seems, was that he had been playing with his toy house. Although Ricky's attempt at clarification was inept in a cute kind of way, at least it revealed his insight into the fact that he and his grandmother did not share a mutual focus and that he had better take action to rectify things. Hence, we see a very primitive understanding of shared focus, both in gaze and in the earliest conversation. Indeed, as suggested previously, it is difficult to imagine how the child's language could develop if he or she lacked an understanding of mutual focus. In turn, this suggests that the infant has a rudimentary working understanding of mind.

Although in the example just described Ricky tried to achieve mutual focus in conversation by nonlinguistic action, nevertheless Ricky did have a basic grasp of achieving mutual focus through speech at the age of 17 months. For example, he handed an item to Shatz saying "urs". Shatz misinterpreted by asking "what hurts", whereupon Ricky repeated "urs!" more emphatically, causing Shatz to guess correctly that he meant "yours". Apparently, he was offering her a toy. Because Ricky was at the one-word stage, he was not equipped to elaborate in language, but he did grasp the urgency and necessity of achieving mutual focus on his intended meaning. He was very limited in his ability to achieve this goal, but in the example presented he succeeded just by the simple strategy of repetition and emphasis.

By the age of 24 months, Ricky was explicitly talking about his intentions and desires and his reason for these. For example, he was able to state that he wanted a drink, that he was going to get one, and that it was because he was thirsty. In doing so, he was behaving as though other people would be ignorant of these things unless he informed them. This is consistent with the possibility that Ricky, as a 2-year-old toddler, understood something about the difference between the contents of his and others' minds, and that verbal communication was a suitable tool for achieving a common understanding. Having said that, it would be entirely wrong to say there are grounds for claiming that Ricky was highly attuned to other minds. Often his communication was not well adapted to the informational needs of the person he was addressing, and it would have been better adapted if he had a more fully developed understanding of mind and communication.

Whatever Ricky knew about mind prior to his second birthday, that understanding was not expressed overtly in his mental-state language, which would have to involve such words as "think". He began using the word "think" between the age of 25 to 30 months, but not in a contrastive sense. By that, I mean that Ricky was not saying such things as "you think X but I think Y", or "I thought X but really Y". Instead, he apparently understood "think" as an expression of uncertainty. For example, in Ricky's presence, Shatz asked Ricky's mother if there were any toys in a bag. The mother replied, "Yes, some little people, I think." Ricky contributed by adding: "And a pig, maybe." In this case, the mother used "think" to express uncertainty, and Ricky seemingly understood this meaning by paraphrasing with "maybe". In other cases, Ricky also used the word "think" to express uncertainty, as his mother did in the example just given.

Between the ages of 31–36 months, Ricky was beginning to use "think" in the more mentalistic contrastive sense. Initially, this was used to explain such things as the actions of people who search wrongly because they hold a mistaken belief. For example, Ricky would be able to comment that the actor is searching in the wrong place because he thinks (wrongly) that the target object is there. There seemed to be a lag in Ricky anticipating that because a person thinks the wrong thing, so it will lead him at some unspecified future time to search in the wrong place. Shatz attributed this to a more general difficulty in using language to express something about a hypothetical situation. For example, only toward the end of the period under investigation (i.e. 36 months) did Ricky utter such things as, "If I had a ladder I would climb up it and change that light bulb."

Shatz (1994) was careful to stress that although one can partition development according to age, this does not necessarily mean that development consists of a sequence of discontinuous stages. On the contrary, Shatz argued that Ricky's development was smooth and seamless. However, one thing that is apparent from Shatz's description of Ricky is that it is possible to identify the different ways a child uses certain words at different ages. Her claim that Ricky initially used mental-state words, such as "think", not to refer to internal mental states echoes a claim that she had made a decade previously (Shatz, Wellman, & Silber, 1983). In the earlier work, Shatz et al. noted that prior to about 42 months of age, children tended to use mental-state words either to express certainty or in a purely conversational sense. An example of the latter would be the child's use of the word "know" in "Know what, I've got some Lego." As an expression of uncertainty, children of this age used the word "think" to mean "maybe", as in "I think I have some sweets left" to mean "Maybe I have some sweets left but I'll have to check before I can be sure." What the children lacked, apparently, was an ability to use the word "think" in a contrastive way, to express that a belief one holds contrasts with a different belief held by another person.

TALK ABOUT DESIRE AND BELIEF

One possible explanation for young children's failure to use the word "think" in a contrastive way is that they have some trouble with the underlying concept of belief as distinct from reality. This is a view taken by Wellman and Bartsch (1994). Other possibilities are that: (1) young children do not have a specific problem with the concept of belief as distinct from reality, but a more general difficulty with mental reference; (2) young children have little experience of mental reference in language because people do not usually speak to them in a way that contrasts mental states with reality. Wellman and Bartsch addressed themselves to this issue and specifically sought to eliminate the two alternative possibilities raised here.

Regarding possibility (1), it is Wellman's (1990) view that children aged 2 and 3 years do not have a general difficulty with the concept of mind but have specific difficulty with the concept of belief and especially that of false belief. He claims that actually the young child has an extensive understanding of mind, and that this understanding is a precursor of a more mature conception that incorporates an understanding of belief and false belief. Specifically, Wellman's claim is that the basis of a fully fledged understanding of mind is the conception of a tripartite relation between belief, desire, and action. In other words, action stems from a desire to achieve a certain preconceived outcome worked out in imagination, which amounts to the planning of behaviour that is about to be executed to that end. The preliminary action in imagination involves a mentalistic description of reality, which in fact could be a misdescription. So, for example, if the child wants chocolate, he or she will search for it. Precisely where the child searches depends upon where he or she thinks the chocolate is. If the child thinks the chocolate is in the cupboard, that is where the search will begin. If it turns out that the child is mistaken about the location of chocolate, then the desire will remain unfulfilled. This is merely a description of a simple relation between desire, belief, and action, but what we are concerned with is whether the young child understands anything about this three-way relation and each of its components. It is Wellman's view that the young child's understanding of desire and action precedes his or her understanding of belief. In that case, we ought to find the child's distinctive early understanding of mind reflected in spontaneous use of language. Specifically, we would expect the child to show mastery of the word (and underlying concept) "desire" prior to mastery of the word (and underlying concept) "think".

Wellman and Bartsch (1994) present a summary of their survey of archives of young children's spontaneous speech and claim that the findings are perfectly consistent with the suggestion that initially children are what they call "desire psychologists" and later graduate to being "belief-desire psychologists". They classified the use of mental-state words like "think", "know", "expect", "want", "wish", and "hope" as genuine references to mental states and distinguished this from mere conversational use of these words ("Know what, I've got a new toy."). The use of desire words (e.g. "want", "wish", "hope") as genuine references to mental states peaked at about 30 months, at which time such words accounted for more than 65% of all children's mental-state utterances. In contrast, use of belief words increased until about 48 months of age, at which time they accounted for about 25% of all mental-state words uttered. Between the age of 30 and 48 months, use of desire words diminished and use of belief words increased, such that the two categories of word converged by the end of this period.

Perhaps children have greater difficulty with the concept of belief, as reflected in their early language, because belief implies a contrast. For example, "I thought all the Lego bricks were used", implies that surprisingly some are still left, and hence thought contrasts with reality. Perhaps young children have difficulty with such contrasts and perhaps such contrasts are less evident in desire. For example, the child could say, "I want a drink of juice", which would be classified as genuine reference to desire that does not involve any contrast. To make a fairer match between belief and desire, Wellman and Bartsch (1994) focused specifically on contrastives in belief and desire. An example of a contrastive desire is "I don't want to leave it. Momma, why leave it?" (Adam, aged 31 months). In this case, a desire is stated by Adam in contrast to a reality. Even when confined to this contrastive definition of desire and belief, Wellman and Bartsch found that use of desire words emerged prior to use of belief words.

Another possible difference between belief and desire concerns subjectivity. Perhaps the concept of belief poses a special problem because it involves tacitly acknowledging that beliefs are person-specific, that I believe X while you believe Y. If the child finds it difficult to place him or herself in another person's shoes, then the concept of belief might pose a specific problem for this reason. Accordingly, Wellman and Bartsch (1994) classified children's belief and desire utterances in terms of individual contrastives. Here is an example of such a desire contrastive:

Sarah (2:11)	Eat ... you eat water?
Adult	No. I don't want any water.
Sarah	I want some.

In this example, Sarah, aged 35 months, seems able to contrast her own desire for water with that of the adult. Wellman and Bartsch found that when desire and belief were defined specifically in this individual contrastive sense (desires or belief contrasting between individuals), children were still using desire words at a younger age than belief words, the lag being about 8 months on average.

It seems safe to conclude that children aged 30 to 36 months do have some understanding of mind. This understanding is reflected in their ability to use desire words appropriately. In this respect, they show a good understanding of the difference between mind and reality and they also show a good understanding of the difference between individuals. Hence, they apparently understand that mind is substantive and not just a reflection of reality, and they understand that minds are subjective and differ between people. However well-developed their understanding of mind, it seems they specifically have some difficulty with the concept of belief and thoughts. Although we saw in a previous chapter that children understand that thoughts of things are different from real things, they seem to have specific difficulty using "think" in a contrastive sense, either to contrast a thought with reality or to contrast the thoughts of different people. We shall explore this issue in considerable depth in subsequent chapters.

Before proceeding, we should consider a superficial reason why young children might use desire words before they use belief words. It might be that parents or adults in general seldom use belief words when speaking to young children but frequently use desire words. If so, the relative lack of belief words in young children's speech would not be a sign that they have difficulty with the concept of belief but instead would just be a reflection of their linguistic input. However, Wellman and Bartsch (1994) found in their systematic study of adult utterances to young children that references to desire did not predominate over references to belief. The absolute frequency of word-usage by adults is probably not the only environmental factor that contributes to children's development of vocabulary. Presumably, the quality of the conversational context also counts. Nonetheless, it seems there might be something intrinsic to the child that is responsible for development in the use of words (and perhaps underlying concepts) of belief relative to desire.

THE ROLE OF COMMUNICATION IN THE DEVELOPMENT OF AN UNDERSTANDING OF MIND

At the beginning of this chapter I said that some kind of working understanding of mind would be necessary for the infant's first steps in acquiring language. At the very least, it is necessary for the infant to understand that meaning is the privilege of the speaker. As a consequence the infant, as listener, has to make an effort to decipher that meaning, which might involve checking precisely what it is that the speaker is looking at as an independent channel for gauging the speaker's reference. This benefit to early language development is repaid when subsequently the child's access to other minds via verbal communication promotes further understanding of mind. The work of Judy Dunn (summarised in Dunn, 1994) and colleagues has made considerable advances in our understanding of how early communication supports the development of an understanding of mind.

Dunn, Brown, Slomkowski, Tesla, and Youngblade (1991) conducted a longitudinal study in which they observed children from the age of about 33 months to about 40 months. Specifically, Dunn et al. focused on children's talk about causality with others, but especially with their mothers. Their talk of causality could be subdivided into children's causal talk about external physical events and actions and their causal talk about internal mental states. An example of the former is children explaining that "We're poo-poo coz we got mud on us." In this amusing example, provided by Dunn (1994), the child is explaining how a transformation in his appearance was brought about by an episode involving mud. An instance of causal mentalistic talk is "He doesn't know where it is coz he forgot." This is another example from Dunn (1994), in which the child was explaining the actions of a protagonist in a story book.

Dunn et al. (1991) studied the quantity and quality of causal talk between adult and child when the children were aged 33 months. They noted what proportion of conversation was occupied by causal talk, and also noted the nature of this causal talk. For example, when appropriate they encoded conversations as discussion of how specific action might have stemmed from a distinctive internal state of mind. This included such things as explaining why Daddy couldn't find his keys to the car—because he forgot where he left them. In this respect, considerable differences existed between families.

When the children were aged 40 months, Dunn et al. subjected them to a test devised by Bartsch and Wellman (1989) to assess their ability to explain wrong search behaviour by making reference to thought and belief. In this task, children watch an enacted scene in which a protagonist is searching for a bandaid to dress a friend's wound. It so happens that the bandaids have been moved from their usual box (unknown to the protagonist but known to the observing child participant) to a plain white box. The protagonist, due to his ignorance of the move, searches wrongly in the bandaid box and observing children are asked to explain why. A correct answer is to say that the protagonist thinks that the bandaids are in there or that he does not know they have been moved. In Bartsch and Wellman's study, some children aged around 40 months had difficulty offering such explanations, consistent with the children having little understanding of the link between belief and behaviour.

When Dunn et al. (1991) presented Bartsch and Wellman's (1989) test to their children aged 40 months, they also found individual differences, with some children readily offering explanations and some failing to do so. Intriguingly, there were significant correlations between children's performance in the bandaid task and the kind of conversations they had had with their mothers at the age of 33 months. Children whose mothers engaged them in lots of conversation about the causality of human action tended to be the very same children who were able to explain the wrong search of a protagonist by reference to his mistaken belief 6 to 7 months later. Hence we can see that not only are there individual differences between children in their grasp of mental states and also in the sociolinguistic environment of their home, but also that these two issues are interrelated.

It is highly tempting to suggest that the relation between the quality of conversation with the mother and ability to make judgements about mental states is more than just coincidence: Perhaps a mother who has the time and patience to explain the causality of human action actually promotes development of an understanding of mind in her child. Another explanation, however, is that a third variable, hitherto unidentified, accounts for the relation between conversations with mother and the child's understanding of mind. For example, it might be that both phenomena are accounted for by the general intelligence of the child. It might be that intellectually gifted children show a receptivity to their mother's conversation that has the effect of encouraging the mother to elaborate and pursue topics such as the causality of human action. Of course, it would not be surprising if the same children were also precocious in their understanding of mind.

It is very difficult to eliminate alternative explanations for correlations when the issue under investigation is a naturally occurring phenomenon such as the quality of conversation between mother and child. Fortunately, there is independent, if somewhat circumstantial, evidence to suggest that environmental experiences can actually promote an understanding of mind. This arises from a study by Perner, Ruffman, and Leekam (1994). They did not investigate the child's linguistic environment directly, but instead noted how many siblings the child had. Remarkably, the more siblings a child had, the more likely that child would be to acknowledge that people can hold mistaken beliefs. The latter was used as a diagnosis of progress in the child's development of an understanding of mind, so the conclusion drawn by the authors of this study was that the development of an understanding of mind is somehow promoted by having siblings.

The study by Perner et al. (1994) contrasts with Dunn et al. (1991) with respect to whether or not the correlation between understanding of mind and environmental experiences could be accounted for by the more general intellectual capacities of the child. In the study by Perner et al., it is most unlikely that the children with lots of siblings would score higher on a test of general intelligence than would children with few or no siblings. On the contrary, we might expect those with lots of siblings to be poorer in their measured intelligence. Zajonc (1983) found that measured intelligence correlated negatively with number of siblings, which he explained by suggesting that the intellectually beneficial input from parents was diluted for any given child as the number of siblings increased. Consistent with this, first-born children typically show higher measured intelligence than second- or third-born children.

In that case, how can we explain the positive correlation between number of siblings and ability to acknowledge false belief in Perner et al.'s (1994) study? We get a clue from another aspect of Dunn's (1994) work. Dunn notes that much of the mother's conversation is generally concerned with caring for the child, where some mothers go to considerable lengths to take into account the child's perspective while refraining from imposing her own emotions and beliefs. In contrast, we see quite a different kind of conversation with siblings. Siblings are notoriously irritable toward each other on occasions and go to enormous lengths to impose their own view on their brother or sister. Each child, therefore, is frequently subjected to his or her sibling's opposing desires, in some cases quite forcefully. Dunn illustrates this with the example of two girls sharing a costume, where one has claimed a queen's crown for herself. The other commented, "I should wear the crown because it matches my dress. It looks ugly on you." Being the recipient of such an insult surely forces the child to consider other people's perspectives. Hence, experiencing siblings with conflicting interests is very likely to stimulate the child into becoming wise to other minds.

Another feature of conversation between siblings that might be beneficial to the development of an understanding of mind is that which arises in the context of pretence. There is evidence, already mentioned in Chapter 2, to suggest that children who are skilled in role-playing in pretence also show a well-developed understanding of mind according to other criteria. Pretence offers an opportunity to enact situations from another person's perspective and thus is bound to help fine-tune the young child's understanding of mind. Presumably, the more siblings the child has, the more opportunities for this beneficial kind of experience.

It might even be possible to unite the findings reported by Perner et al. (1994) with those reported by Dunn et al. (1991). Although Zajonc (1993) could be generally correct to say that the stimulating input of the parent is necessarily diluted as it is distributed across ever more siblings, the quality of this diminishing input with respect to understanding of mind might increase. When a child is exposed to the conflicting interests of siblings in a typical domestic drama, the mother holds responsibility for being the peace-maker. In doing so, presumably the mother has to reason to explain to each sibling why the other's case has at least some reasonable basis. Hence, having a sibling allows an abundance of opportunities for the mother to explain the causality and especially the psychology behind another person's (sibling's) actions.

There is thus circumstantial evidence to suggest that children's early sociolinguistic experiences in the home promote the development of an understanding of mind. At the very least we can say that if the child lived in a vacuum, then there would be no need for any understanding of mind. By analogy, it would not be surprising if the vision of an individual reared in a severely impoverished visual environment (e.g. a room without light) had impaired vision. Presumably, a child reared in a socially impoverished environment would be impaired in understanding social cognition. It makes sense to suppose that features of the child's early conversation promote development of an understanding of mind, and evidence consistent with that has been presented.

UNDERSTANDING UNCERTAINTY AND BELIEF

As mentioned previously, Shatz et al. (1983) report that children's use of the word "think" to mean uncertainty precedes use of that word to refer to internal mental states. Perhaps using the word "think" to express uncertainty is actually a precursor of the use of that word for mental-state reference. We can see that in principle there is a link between the two uses of the word "think". The mentalistic use would be defined as a contrastive, in the sense of "I think X but you think Y" or "I think X but I used to think Y." Using "think" in this way is a tacit acknowledgement that what one thinks can be mistaken and as a consequence can contrast with reality or with what someone else thinks. However, using "think" to mean "uncertain" also carries connotations that the associated proposition could be mistaken. For example, if I say that I think it is going to rain today, I mean that it might rain, or in other words that I expect it to rain but I could be mistaken. Nonetheless the connotation of "mistaken belief" is much more obvious when "think" is used in a contrastive sense than when it is used merely to express uncertainty. It might be that using "think" weakly, to imply "mistaken belief", as in its use to express uncertainty, is a necessary preliminary step to be negotiated before the child is able to use "think" in the more explicit contrastive sense. This is something we can speculate from the knowledge that "think" as an expression of uncertainty developmentally precedes the use of "think" in a contrastive sense. From this speculation, we would predict at the very least that children's use of "think" to express uncertainty is related to their ability to contrast thoughts with reality. The work of Moore, Pure, and Furrow (1990) offers the relevant data.

Moore et al. (1990) assessed children's understanding of "think" as an expression of uncertainty by contrasting it with "know", which is an expression of certainty. They did so in a procedure in which the child's task was to find the location of a treat. Children knew that the treat was either in the red box or the blue one, but did not know which in particular. Two protagonists offered conflicting information to the children as clues to location. One of them said that he thought the treat was in the red box, while the other said that he knew it was in the blue one. Under a slightly different condition, the words "thought" and "knew" were exchanged for the words "might" and "must" respectively. These researchers found that children aged 3 years chose a location at random, and as such seemed insensitive to "knew" and "must" as expressions of certainty that contrast with "thought" and "might" as expressions of uncertainty. Meanwhile, children aged 5 years acted appropriately upon the expression of certainty in approximately 90% of occasions. In other words, older children tended to search in the location indicated by a protagonist using the expression "knew" or "must". Hence, considerable development in understanding expressions of certainty was occurring in the children aged 4 years.

In a further part of the procedure, Moore et al. (1990) assessed children's ability to acknowledge simple factual beliefs that contrast with reality. In this task, they had to anticipate where a protagonist holding a mistaken belief would search for the item he desires. They also had to recall an earlier belief they had held in error. Some of the children aged 4 years passed these tests while others failed. Interestingly, those who passed tended to be the same children who showed understanding of expressions of certainty and uncertainty. There was a strong relation between acknowledging that beliefs can be mistaken and systematically taking the advice of a protagonist who expresses certainty in preference to one who expresses uncertainty. It thus seems that children's continuing development of an understanding of mind might owe something to the associated understanding of words that express uncertainty. Having said that, we cannot be sure whether it is specifically grasping the meaning of words of uncertainty that is important, or the underlying concepts of uncertainty that those words denote. Even if the latter, it is likely that having convenient linguistic labels assists the child in processing and remembering the underlying concepts.

IS LACK OF LANGUAGE AND COMMUNICATION AN IMPEDIMENT TO UNDERSTANDING MIND?

We have looked at various ways in which early experiences in a linguistic context might promote the development of an understanding of mind. The evidence suggests that early conversation with the mother and with siblings might give an insight into the minds of others that the child would be denied if he or she did not have the benefit of a linguistic channel of communication. What people say gives a window on their mind, and any child who is exposed to this experience is bound to have greater insight into mind than a child who is unable to communicate with others. Additionally, it might be the case that words in themselves provide a medium for the child to process mentalistic information. It would follow that if the child were unfortunate enough to be deprived of this linguistic environment, then he or she might show evidence of having an impoverished understanding of mind.

Peterson and Siegal (1995) conducted an investigation with 26 children who had been deaf prior to acquiring language. These children were nonetheless able to communicate with sign language, which was taught to them in most cases by teachers in a special school the children attended for the profoundly deaf. The children were aged between 8 and 13 years. Although these children did have language, Peterson and Siegal suggested that their sociolinguistic environment would have been impoverished compared with children who had good hearing and communicated verbally. All but two of the children were from families in which all other members had good hearing and none could use sign language. Consequently, the children were deprived of the beneficial conversational experiences with their mother and siblings. Additionally, even when entering school, children would have had highly restricted linguistic experiences. Power, Wood, and Wood (1990) report that the school environment can be informationally impoverished for deaf children, primarily because much of the time is spent teaching nonproficient children to use sign language. A consequence is that the teacher will be likely to suppress initiative in the child's communication, which will be replaced by enforced repetition and persistent correction of grammar by the teacher. Because of the nature of the children's disability, there is little opportunity for them to benefit from informal conversation in the school environment, as well as in the home environment. Third, M. Harris (1992) suggests that communicating with signs restricts the participants to topics that are physical, tangible, and visible; it is more difficult when signing to discuss invisible internal mental states.

Peterson and Siegal (1995) assessed these children in their ability to make judgements about aspects of mind. Specifically, the children were asked to predict a protagonist's action who, they had been informed, held a mistaken belief. In this procedure, modelled on Baron-Cohen, Leslie, and Frith (1985), Sally put her marble in a box and then departed. In her absence, Ann moved it to a basket. Sally returned to get her marble, and observing children were asked to predict where Sally would look, the box or the basket. This story was supported with a succession of pictures of the scenes and the narrative was communicated in signs by a skilled adult.

By the time most children with good speech and hearing are 4 or 5 years of age, they judge correctly that Sally will look in the box, where she left the marble. Amazingly, only 9 of the 26 deaf children aged between 8 and 13 years judged correctly in the study conducted by Peterson and Siegal (1995). Perhaps the children gave incorrect judgements because they had general difficulty in comprehending the story. However, that seemed not to be the case, given the children's flawless performance in answering comprehension questions. Specifically, the children judged correctly that Sally had put the marble in the box initially and they also judged that currently the marble was in the basket. Apparently, they had no general difficulties with comprehension, but a specific difficulty in predicting Sally's erroneous search on the basis of her mistaken belief.

Perhaps the children tested by Peterson and Siegal (1995) were retarded in their general intelligence, and this accounted for their poor performance in predicting Sally's action under a mistaken belief. To find out, the researchers presented a test of nonverbal intelligence to the children and found that the group average IQ was 103. The population mean is 100, so there was no reason to suppose that the children were retarded.

Although Peterson and Siegal's (1995) finding is yet to be replicated, their results raise the startling possibility that if children are denied the wealth of early communicative experiences enjoyed by those who are able to communicate verbally, they risk substantial delays in their development of an understanding of mind. It seems that verbal children owe a great deal to their early communicative experiences in terms of their sophisticated understanding of the psychology of other people. However, not all the deaf children tested by Peterson and Siegal showed lack of insight into mistaken beliefs. It might be no coincidence that the two children in the sample who grew up in families that used sign language as a means of communication also succeeded in showing understanding about mistaken beliefs. It might be that although these children were not able to communicate verbally, their communication through signs was sufficient for the home environment to foster a good understanding of mind.

If deaf children have difficulty acknowledging belief, then we might expect to find that they are socially disadvantaged, not just because of their deafness and resulting communicative impediment, but also because they lack understanding of mind. One population said to have a severely delayed development in their understanding of mind is people with autism (see Chapters 9 and 10). Were these deaf children showing any autistic tendencies? Peterson and Siegal (1995) claimed that there was no reason to suppose that their participants were showing any signs of autism. However, it would be difficult to detect subtle evidence. The children already had difficulty with social interaction that is presumed to be due to their deafness, and it is difficult to determine if any of that is additionally due to lack of insight into mind.

In the next chapter, we shall look at further mutual developments in communication abilities and understanding of mind. The relation between mind and communication is a complex one that evolves over many years and perhaps even into adulthood. In particular, we shall look at the child's developing understanding of the literal meaning of a message as distinct from what is intended by the speaker of the message. We shall also examine how the child becomes skilled in adapting his or her speech to the specific informational requirements of the listener.

CHAPTER SIX

Further developments in language and communication

The advent of language in the history of our species allows us to learn much more about the world than ever would be possible if we only had first-hand experience to rely upon. A multiplicity of lifetime's experiences can be condensed and encapsulated in language. The accumulated wisdom of our ancestors is no longer lost with each generation but can be transmitted to our progeny and cultural heirs, initially just by word of mouth but now also by the more enduring written word. Flesh and blood is not immortal but the thoughts and experiences of those who lived centuries ago remain so. Largely via the medium of language, we thus inherit the cultural legacy of our predecessors. It would be difficult to overstate the role of language as a means of communication along with its role in the evolution of human culture, but on a more familiar level, that same language plays a vital part in children's formal and informal education. The young of our species would be very different if we were unable to communicate knowledge, moral values, and emotions with the aid of language.

However much we celebrate our faculty of language, it actually has an associated cost as a means of acquiring knowledge about the world. Although knowledge handed down from others saves us the toil and tedium of discovery by first-hand trial and error, there is always a risk that the information that filters through the mind of another person is going to be inaccurate. We cannot assume that what people tell us faithfully portrays reality. This is something recognised in law by the fact that hearsay does not qualify as testimony. As an example of the problem, it is common in the Western World for parents to communicate to their children about the existence of Santa Claus. There is nothing sinister about this nontruth—on the contrary—but it goes to show that children cannot take what they are told, even by their own parents, as being true of reality itself. Just as pretence should not be taken literally, so the same is true to an extent with verbal communication. There is a whole variety of reasons why what people say might not be an accurate reflection of reality. For one thing, they might be mistaken. Yet even if a person communicating to us has perfectly correct knowledge about reality, it would not necessarily follow that what they tell us is accurate. They may wish to conceal information and systematically tell a web of lies. Alternatively, they may have accurate information, wish to communicate truthfully, but articulate the wrong words just because they are not paying sufficient attention to monitoring what they are saying. In brief, there is a wealth of knowledge to be gleaned from what people tell us, but we have to treat that information with caution because it comes to us via another mind. Ideally, we should treat utterances as though they are "referentially opaque", meaning that we take utterances to refer to a model of reality that resides in the speaker's mind. That model might be faithful to reality but it might not, so we have to mark the information thus acquired as holding a special provisional status. Leslie (1987) and Harris and Kavanaugh (1993) suggested as much in another domain of children's symbolic activity, namely pretence. Leslie went so far as to claim that the young child's capacity for pretence implies a working grasp of referential opacity. The same process allows us to accord the special status to information presented to us by another mind via language. An understanding of referential opacity has a special significance given that both Leslie (1987) and Perner (1988) claim, independently of each other, that it is the concept that forms the core of a fully fledged understanding of mind. According to Quine (1961), who first defined "referential opacity", it is a concept that is fundamentally linguistic, so the child's earliest understanding of mind should be apparent within the linguistic domain.

UNDERSTANDING THE TENTATIVE INFORMATIONAL STATUS OF MESSAGES

A traditional vision of preschool children is that they are overliteral in their interpretation of speech. For example, they seem to accept the literal meaning of metaphors and sarcasm as the meaning intended by the speaker (e.g. Demorest, Meyer, Phelps, Gardner, & Winner, 1984;

Winner, Rosentiel, & Gardner, 1976). If children are overly literal, it is difficult to imagine how they could assume a tentative attitude toward utterances. Yet such a tentative attitude is at least a necessary precursor of an understanding of referential opacity in speech, if not sufficient to credit the child with a functioning grasp of opacity. There would be no scope for children to consider the mind behind the message if they took the message to apply directly and transparently to reality. However, sarcasm and metaphor qualify as linguistic conventions, and young children's overly literal interpretations in these domains could merely signal a lack of insight into these conventions rather than an irreducible compunction to interpret utterances—any utterances—literally and factually. Elizabeth Robinson, Rebecca Nye and myself (Robinson, Mitchell, & Nye, 1995) set about investigating whether preschoolers show any indication of assigning a tentative status to information presented in an utterance in a context that did not require insight into special linguistic conventions. We showed children aged around 3 years some boxes whose exterior purportedly proclaimed the contents: for example, a Smarties tube. Children had to guess what was inside from the exterior and all did so by saying "Smarties" or "sweets". Following this, under one condition the experimenter, but not the child, peeped inside and announced unexpectedly that the box contained only a pencil. Subsequently, an assistant appeared on the scene who enquired of the child what the box contained.

In this context, the child's initial belief was based on the flimsy evidence of the picture on the box's exterior and prior experience of finding that Smarties boxes contain Smarties. Surely the conflicting evidence in the form of the experimenter's utterance is much more trustworthy. Nonetheless, if children assign but a tentative status to verbal reports, even when delivered by an authoritative adult, they might be inclined to disregard what they were told and retain their initial belief in preference. In a first investigation we conducted, a surprising 42% of children aged 3 years retained their prior belief based on the appearance of the exterior of the box in preference to the conflicting message uttered by the experimenter. This was apparent from children informing the assistant that the box contained Smarties rather than a pencil. In a second investigation, the figure dropped to 21%. Nonetheless, in both investigations, children were significantly more likely to retain their initial belief about the box's content (Smarties) if they were told that it contained a pencil than if they directly saw that it contained a pencil. In the latter condition, with one or two rare exceptions, children reported to the assistant that the box contained a pencil.

Before considering the theoretical significance of this finding, we should pause to eliminate a trivial and superficial explanation for children's tendency to disregard what they were told when that conflicted with a belief they had already formed about the box's content based on its exterior. Perhaps the familiarity of the box, coupled with the highly salient and flamboyant picture on its exterior announcing its content, caused this source of information to eclipse the ephemeral and invisible conflicting information from the experimenter presented in a verbal message. Perhaps the child's initial source of information (Smarties) was so prominent that he or she was unable to assimilate and retain the conflicting information presented by the experimenter. If so, then children would not only continue judging that the box contained Smarties, even in the aftermath of the experimenter's conflicting message, but would also be unable to recall that the experimenter had said the box contained a pencil. At the end of the procedure, we asked children to recall what the experimenter said to check that possibility. A minority of children did wrongly judge the experimenter to have said that the box contained Smarties, but even so, many correctly recalled that she said "pencil". If we exclude children who failed to recall what the experimenter said, we still find that significantly more children retained their prior belief (Smarties) in the conflicting message condition compared with the condition where they looked in the box and saw directly that unexpectedly it contained a pencil.

A related finding is reported by Zaitchik (1991). Children observed "Big Bird" tell a lie to "Frog" about the location of a treat. Under one condition, the child participant knew that a lie was being told because the experimenter stated verbally that the treat was actually in a different location. Under another condition, child participants saw that the treat was in a different location. Finally, children were asked to judge where Frog thought the treat was. Those who saw the real location of the treat said that Frog thought it was there, whereas those who were told about its real location judged that Frog thought it was where Big Bird said it was. Hence, the information about the true location of the treat seemed to make more impact on the children when they had seen it than when they were told about it. Indeed, the impact was so great when they saw the true location that they seemed compelled (wrongly) to ascribe a true belief to Frog. On the other side of the coin, perhaps the verbally presented information was coded tentatively by the children such that they were liberated from making the realist errors that are typical when children are asked about belief (see Chapters 7 and 8).

If children aged 3 years are to develop an understanding of referential opacity, that speech is to be interpreted with respect to mind, then they must at least be willing to assign a tentative status to information communicated by messages. This could be manifest as a tendency to mistrust information from messages, especially when the information conflicts with information from another source. However, we do not yet know whether children assign a tentative status to information from utterances *because* they are sensitive to the fact that this information has issued from another mind. An equally plausible possibility is that they give priority to some sensory input above others, irrespective of whether minds are implicated. For example, they might be more willing to disregard prior knowledge based on touch than on seeing when faced with contradicting information. Indeed, pilot work supervised by Elizabeth Robinson suggests that they do precisely this. Nonetheless, children would have no scope for developing a working understanding of referential opacity if they were unwilling to encode utterances tentatively. Furthermore, if children were generally overly literal, beyond the domain of communication, it is difficult to image how they could effectively draw a distinction between fact and potential fiction. Leslie (1987) noted that such a distinction was necessary for the young child to engage in pretence, and Harris and Kavanaugh (1993) extended the argument to cover the child's comprehension of stories.

A working understanding that information presented in utterances should be accorded a tentative status is perhaps rather primitive. The findings reported by Robinson et al. (1995) do not tell us whether children have any reflective and explicit insight into the principle that people might assign a tentative status to the information presented to them in utterances. To explore the latter, we (Mitchell, Robinson, Nye, & Isaacs, in press) conducted a further study based on some earlier work by Perner and Davies (1991) that was motivated by a different question. Perner and Davies told children aged around 5 years a story about two protagonists and their football. John was in the garden, whereupon he noticed the football near the pond. Later, John was inside the house when Mike announced that the football was in the garage. Observing children were asked where John thinks the football is in the aftermath of his receiving conflicting information. Perner and Davies reasoned that John should accord more weight to what he has seen directly in preference to Mike's conflicting message, and thus should retain his prior belief that the ball is by the pond. Under another condition, John did not see the football, so his only source of information was Mike's message. The observing children judged that John retained his prior belief based on his seeing in the first story described here, but that he believed Mike's message in the second story. Crucially, children judged in this pattern irrespective of what they knew independently about the ball's location from their informationally privileged vantage point. Hence, they seemed to understand a principle that people treat utterances tentatively, such that they will disregard what they are told if it conflicts with what they see directly. They understand this as a principle, in the sense that they avoid confusing John's belief with their own knowledge of the ball's real location.

Perner and Davies' (1991) purpose in conducting their study was to show that children aged 5 years understand that minds interpret information—that, for example, how a given piece of information is received will depend upon extant information stored in the mind. Specifically, children understood that Mike's message that the ball was in the garage would be believed in one circumstance but disregarded in another. Previously, Chandler and colleagues (e.g. Chandler & Boyes, 1982; Chandler & Helm, 1984) had claimed that children do not understand that minds can interpret a given piece of information in different ways until they are about 7 years of age. Before proceeding, we should exercise some caution in using the word "interpretation" here. Perner and Davis evidently mean something different from Chandler and Helm. Perner and Davies mean that a protagonist will either believe or disbelieve a given message, depending on the protagonist's informational history. In contrast, Chandler and Helm appear to mean that one and the same piece of information can be interpreted as one thing by one person and as an entirely different thing by a another person. Perhaps it would be better to say that Perner and Davies were concerned with how children perceive that utterances are evaluated—either believed or disregarded—rather than with how they are interpreted.

An explicit understanding of the principle that information presented via utterances is assigned a provisional and tentative status might lead children as young as 3 years to judge according to the pattern identified by Perner and Davies (1991). However, there is an obstacle to finding such a pattern of judging in young children. Specifically, as will become clear in the next chapter, when we ask 3-year-olds to report simple factual beliefs held by themselves or by other people, they typically respond by reporting current reality. If we ask children aged 3 years to judge John's belief in the story devised by Perner and Davies, we could thus expect them to report what they themselves know of reality, irrespective of what John saw or what he was told. To avoid this problem, we (Mitchell et al., in press) presented modified stories such that observing children had no direct access to reality, thereby preventing them from committing a realist error. In this story, children witnessed Kevin look in a jug, and were told (but could not see inside the jug themselves) that Kevin saw orange juice in there. Kevin left the scene and later on he returned with his friend Rebecca. Without looking in the jug, Rebecca announced to Kevin that there is milk in there. The story was presented in two formats, either as a video, with real people playing the parts, or as a cartoon sequence of pictures.

The observing children, many as young as 3 years, were asked to judge what Kevin thinks is in the jug, what Rebecca thinks, and what they themselves think. On a group basis, children answered these questions in very different ways. They generally judged that Kevin thought there was orange in the jug (as he saw), that Rebecca thought there was milk in the jug (as she said), and were split as a group on what they themselves thought; some judged milk and some judged orange. This procedure achieved two things. First, it was successful in preventing young children from judging that everyone thinks the same thing, using known reality as the criterion of reference. Children did not know what was really in the jug, which seems to have allowed them to assign different beliefs to Kevin, Rebecca, and themselves. The second thing the procedure achieved was a demonstration that children aged 3 years seem to recognise that people assign only a tentative status to information entering their own mind from another mind via a verbal message. Children judged that Kevin would believe what he saw in preference to what he was told when the two were in conflict. They judged that he would believe what he saw (juice) more often than they judged that they themselves thought the jug contained juice.

There are several reductive and trivial explanations for children's judgements that Kevin would believe what he saw in preference to what he was told. One of these assumes that children aged 3 years have no understanding at all of the concept of belief, but managed to answer the questions on another basis. Perhaps they judged that Kevin thought the jug contained juice because only he was associated with juice in the story. That is, "juice" was introduced in the context of Kevin looking in the jug. Meanwhile, "milk" was associated uniquely with Rebecca. To eliminate this possibility, we associated Kevin with another drink. In one story, he pretended to give his teddy a drink of coke from the jug, but actually saw juice in there. Otherwise, the story was similar. Children still judged that Kevin thought there was juice in the jug, whilst judging that he likes to give his teddy coke. Hence, they used information about his pretence to infer his preference for teddy and used information about his seeing to infer his knowledge, knowledge that was given a higher weighting than the conflicting verbal information he received from Rebecca.

Another possibility, however unlikely, is that young children do not understand that utterances carry any information at all. To reject this possibility, we presented a story in which Kevin did not look in the jug but observing children were told that he likes to drink juice. Subsequently, Rebecca announced that the jug contained milk. Under this condition, children nearly always judged that Kevin thought there was milk in the jug, as he was told. In this case, they assumed that the utterance was sufficient to implant a simple factual belief in Kevin's mind, suggesting that they do understand that messages can inform, but are held tentatively and yield to directly obtained information based on seeing. The results further show that the children understood that Kevin's preference for juice lacked the epistemic content of his seeing juice. They understood that his preference for juice was not sufficient for him to believe the jug contained juice, at least to the extent that his preference should not take priority over what Rebecca told him in judging what he thinks. Hence, children understand that Kevin's belief is driven by information entering his mind from an external source (Rebecca's message) rather than from an internally generated desire.

It is now time to contemplate the implications of these findings. It is not too hard to see why children might *treat* messages as holding a tentative and provisional status. They live in a real physical and tangible reality and their first priority has to be to keep a track of this. In their quest for the truth, they have to apply caution such that they make a distinction between reliable sources and less reliable sources. If they did not do this, they would be less attuned to reality than is good for them. In assigning a lower factual priority to indirect sources of information (such as messages), than to direct sources (such as seeing), children have made at least the first step toward treating messages as though they were emanating from another mind. If children showed no sign of treating messages tentatively, it would make no sense even to begin to say that they are sensitive to the mind that resides behind the message.

It is an even more impressive feat when children display an explicit understanding of the principle that people attach more weight to what they see than what they are told. This is more than merely behaving in a way consistent with understanding that messages emanate from minds. It shows an insight into how minds prioritise different kinds of input. In other words, with respect to the tentative status of messages, young children seem to understand something about the implication for people's construction of a knowledge base. This does not actually tell us any more about children's understanding that messages come from minds, but it does show that they have a sophisticated understanding of the effect of messages on mind.

ADAPTING THE MESSAGE TO SUIT THE LISTENER'S NEEDS

If children have a fair amount of insight into the effect of messages on the content of mind, this conception could help them to show sensitivity to their listener's informational requirements. If children understood nothing about the role of oral communication in forming a bridge across two minds, they would not take care to communicate in a way that was understandable to a listener. Indeed, they might not be motivated to communicate at all. Of course, children are highly motivated to communicate, and frequently are extremely animated when doing so. A minimum criterion for showing that they have some insight into communication as a bridge between minds, then, would be any sign that they adapt the content of their utterance to match the listener's informational needs, such that they say not too little and not too much. To extend the bridge analogy, some structures are flimsy and narrow whereas others are wide and rigid. Whether the right kind and quantity of goods get across will depend on how suited the bridge is to the particular freight being transported. An engineer has responsibility for deciding what kind of bridge to construct in order to satisfy specific requirements. Likewise, the child has to engineer utterances to bridge a gap between minds that will satisfy the listener's informational needs without erring too heavily on the side of redundancy and inefficiency.

Early research conducted on children's sensitivity to their listener's informational requirements supported the old Piagetian notion that until about 7 or 8 years of age they are prone to "egocentric" communication. Krauss and Glucksberg (1969) reported that children of around 6 years of age communicate about the identity of abstract shapes by using idiosyncratic language, where they draw on knowledge peculiar to themselves and ignore the unique informational history of their listener. For example, one child described an abstract shape as "Daddy's shirt" and then used exactly the same phrase to describe the next shape in the sequence, which was clearly different in its form! This research seemed to suggest that until about 7 or 8 years of age, children know very little about their listener's informational requirements.

However, the findings reported by Krauss and Glucksberg (1969) do not square with one's ordinary experiences of interacting with small children. Evidently toddlers are not always good communicators (neither are some adults for that matter), but it seems far too harsh to say that they are insensitive to their listener's informational requirements. Perhaps the difficulty Krauss and Glucksberg report has something to do with the unusual task of describing abstract designs. Other more down-to-earth tasks might reveal a sensitivity to the listener's informational needs. A variety of studies have demonstrated precisely this.

Maratsos (1973) began by asking children aged 3 years to communicate to the experimenter which of a set of toys they had chosen. Under one condition, the experimenter had his eyes closed so could not see, whereas under another condition there was no obstacle to the experimenter's view. Children gave more explicit descriptions when the experimenter could not see (more gestures also, not that they could have been much use to an unsighted experimenter!). An even more impressive demonstration was reported by Menig-Peterson (1975), who tested children around the same age. In her study, an incident was staged in the children's nursery in which juice was spilled and the children assisted in a clean-up operation. A week later, an adult interviewed them about the incident and children were invited to report what happened. Crucially, under one condition, the adult had been witness to the incident the week previously, whereas under another condition the adult had been absent. Children gave more detail to the adult who had been absent than to the adult who had been present, thereby showing that they were sensitive to their listener's informational history and attempted to tailor their utterances accordingly.

Other studies point to young children's sensitivity to their listener's needs in different respects. Shatz and Gelman (1973) offered a novel toy to children aged 4 years and allowed them to play with it for a while. Subsequently, they were asked to explain how it worked, and to address their explanation either to a 2-year-old or to an adult. When addressing a younger child, the 4-year-olds used simple sentences and a restricted vocabulary. In contrast, when addressing an adult, they used longer sentences and a wider vocabulary. Related results were reported by Guralnik and Paul-Brown (1977). They observed children aged 4 years who attended a school with a mixed intake of normal achievers and children with learning difficulties. When the children addressed those with learning difficulties, they used simpler sentence structures and a limited vocabulary, compared with when they addressed normally achieving peers.

The most obvious interpretation of these studies is that young children have two distinct kinds of insight regarding mind and communication. The first is that the children seem sensitive to their listener's state of knowledge or ignorance, a sensitivity which apparently governs the level of detail included in their message. The second is that children seem to have some working insight, however primitive, into the power of oral communication as a means of imparting knowledge. In effect, young children meet others' minds when communicating orally, and it is highly tempting to go one step further in attributing their skill in this domain to an understanding that minds are shared through the medium of language. This is a view advocated most strongly by Golinkoff (1986), who asserts that toddlers' primary motivation in communication is to meet the minds of others, premised on the assumption that young children have a pre-existing awareness of their listener having a mind.

It is highly provocative to ascribe such competence to a very young child, and Shatz and O'Reilly (1990) responded by trying to show that early communication is motivated instrumentally, rather than by an inclination to share minds. Shatz and O'Reilly conducted an investigation of the circumstances under which 30-month-old children repair, or clarify, their failed communications. The researchers focused on two kinds of utterance, assertions and requests. They found that if an adult showed signs of failing to comprehend, then the children were significantly more likely to offer clarification if the utterance was a request (94% of the time) than if it was an assertion (84% of the time). Moreover, the offered clarification was more likely to be successful in the case of a request (77% of the time) than in the case of an assertion (60% of the time).

Shatz and O'Reilly (1990) suggest that their results offer a small clue that carries major implications regarding what drives early communication. They point out correctly that repair of requests could be motivated not by an orientation toward the mind of their partner in conversation, but as an entirely noninsightful quest to satisfy needs, where language serves as a purely instrumental means to those ends. If they are right, there is no more reason to suppose that the child understands the role of other minds in communication than there is to suppose that a rat understands that a mind lies behind the lever in a Skinner box contraption. Moreover, Shatz and O'Reilly suggest that if children were attuned to the role of other minds in communication, they should repair assertions more, not less, than requests. They say this because assertions made by children were about three times more common than requests, so children should have more experience of repairing these, and as a consequence have a higher expectation and preparedness to do so.

It is extremely difficult to infer what kind of evidence could inform us on what toddlers understand about mind in communication, and in that context, Shatz and O'Reilly are to be congratulated for their ingenuity in generating an operational definition of instrumental speech and speech that is purely informative. However, there are reasons for supposing they overinterpreted their data. First, the toddlers are surprisingly competent, it would seem, in clarifying their failed assertions. If we took the conditioning model on board fully, this would be very hard to explain. Behaviour that is not reinforced becomes extinguished, so there should not only be no sign of any repair to assertions, there should be no sign of assertions at all, if Shatz and O'Reilly are correct to say that making assertions does not lead to reward. Well, perhaps there is some reward in making an assertion and repairing it. That counter will not do, though, because then Shatz and O'Reilly could not make the very distinction that motivates their research—namely that they can identify some utterances that are instrumental and some that are not. Nonetheless, we still need to explain why toddlers are better at clarifying requests than assertions. There are two fairly obvious reasons. One is that because toddlers make many more assertions than they make requests, and because adults often give a blank nonreaction to assertions (more so than to requests: Shatz & O'Reilly, 1990), presumably their experience is telling them that at least some of the time it is futile to make assertions, and that not much response can be expected. If so, then presumably they learn that it is not always worthwhile to persist in trying to clarify assertions. Another reason why toddlers might repair requests more than assertions is that requests are probably inherently a good deal easier to clarify. If one's conversational partner shows noncomprehension to a request, clarification can often be achieved simply by pointing to the object that is being requested. In contrast, it is likely that to clarify an assertion, more elaborate dialogue, not less, is needed.

What we find so far, then, is that by toddlerhood, children have at least acquired an attitude toward messages that provides the necessary conditions for them to develop a richer understanding of the link between messages and mind. There is also evidence, albeit tentative, to suggest that they understand how communication can form a bridge between minds. It is now appropriate to begin assessing the emergence of children's more sophisticated and explicit understanding about communication and mind. The core concept underpinning such understanding has to be that of referential opacity.

A DIRECT TEST OF REFERENTIAL OPACITY

We (Robinson & Mitchell, 1992, 1994a) have devised a procedure that seems to be a direct test of understanding referential opacity. It is known as the message–desire discrepant task, and utilises the following scenario, or any other scenario that is structurally similar with respect to certain key features. Mum and Jane are in their living room tidying away two bags of material. They put one bag in the drawer and another in the cupboard. Mum leaves and, in her absence, Jane gets out the bags again to have a play. When she has finished playing she puts the bags away, but in doing so she gets them mixed up. The bag that used to be in the drawer is now in the cupboard, while the bag that used to be in the cupboard is now in the drawer; they are swapped the other way round. Later, Mum is sewing when she discovers that she needs some more material. She needs just one of the bags of material and it is very important she gets the right one, or the dress she is fixing is going to look silly. Mum calls to Jane, "I need one of the bags of material, it's the bag in the drawer." The observing child participant is then asked to give Mum the bag of material that she really wants. A crucial feature of the story is that we cannot actually see the dress Mum is fixing, so there is no direct or visual way of working out which of the bags of material she wants. All we have to go on is her request, stating that she wants the bag in the drawer.

Utterances are referentially opaque, in the sense that they refer to things residing in the speaker's mental model of reality. The utterance presented in the message–desire task is no exception and moreover, if the child interprets the utterance opaquely, he or she will reach not to the location mentioned in the words of the message (the drawer) but will reach to the nonspecified cupboard. This follows in that if we conjure up an image of Mum's mental model of the scene, we find that the bag residing in the drawer within that (i.e. Mum's mental model of the scene) is actually located in the cupboard in current reality. This is because Mum did not see the change that Jane effected on reality, so Mum's mental model is out of date. The findings were that a few children aged 3 years, several aged 4 years, and many aged 5 years correctly interpreted Mum's request opaquely by reaching for the bag in the cupboard.

A trivial and theoretically uninteresting explanation for children's reaching to the nonspecified location is that they somehow feel that a nonobvious response is required of them without actually understanding anything of referential opacity. This possibility can be eliminated by a control condition we devised, called the message–desire consistent task, and by another control task described by Leslie (1994). In the message–desire consistent task, the story is very nearly identical to that in the message–desire discrepant but with the sole exception that, after playing with the bags, Jane returns them to the places they were stored originally when Mum was present earlier. So Mum's belief remains a true one and when she requests the bag in the drawer we can be confident that the drawer is the correct location to search. It was very rare for any children to search in the nonspecified location of the cupboard in the message–desire consistent control. Children were significantly more likely to reach to the nonspecified location in the discrepant task than in the consistent control.

In Leslie's (1994) control, Jane proceeded to swap the bags, as in the discrepant task, but crucially, Mum remained on the scene, meaning that her mental model was updated in accordance with the change in reality. So when she requested the bag in the drawer, we can assume she really wanted that, despite Jane's swapping of the bags. Leslie found that many children aged 4 years correctly reached to the drawer in this condition, but reached to the nonspecified location of the cupboard in the condition in which Mum did not see the bags being swapped. It seems that we can say with considerable confidence that some children aged around 4 years are able to demonstrate their understanding of referential opacity in the context of interpreting utterances.

At this point, it would be useful to try to specify precisely what the demonstrated understanding of referential opacity amounts to, and to place the ability within a wider context of children's early communication skills. For one thing, we can say children understand that meaning is the prerogative of the speaker and not something that is restricted to the words in the utterance. That is not to say that children were overlooking the literal meaning of the message. On the contrary, children must be able to process the literal meaning efficiently in order to map that onto their construction of the speaker's outdated model of reality. However, they are clearly attuned to the meaning as something internal to the speaker's mind rather than external in the form of the spoken message. How can we describe children's strategy, then? Presumably, on hearing the message, they first check the speaker's knowledge, in this case by noting the speaker's visual input. They discover that the speaker cannot actually see the mentioned location, so they trace memory back to a point when the speaker could see the mentioned location. Children will then detect that the scene as witnessed by the speaker is different from how it is currently. The child's task is then to transpose the prior scene, with respect to the speaker's message, into the current scene, and hence the problem of reference is solved.

A substantial part of this description of what the child is doing can actually be mapped on to Baldwin's (e.g. 1993a) account of toddlers' reactions to their mothers' naming of things, described in the previous chapter. Toddlers also behave as though meaning is the prerogative of the speaker. When they hear the mother make an utterance, they do not remain fixated on whatever they had already been looking at, as though the mother were referring to that thing. Instead, they check the mother's line of sight, and realign their gaze to focus on the object at the end of that. It seems that infants are behaving as though the words uttered have to be interpreted in relation to the speaker's view of reality. In our message–desire discrepant task, the young children do the same only in a more elaborate way. They not only check what the mother is seeing right now, but also trace back through the recent past to note what the mother had previously seen of the array that she is now referring to. In Baldwin's scenario, the toddlers seem to grasp that the point in space that is the object of conversation is the prerogative of the speaker (and one has to find information about this that lies outside the message), whereas in our task young children seem to grasp that time as well as space is the prerogative of the speaker (and again, information outside the message has to be imported to infer what this time is). We feel entitled to say that success in our task qualifies as a demonstrable understanding of referential opacity. It might be going too far to say that toddlers are showing understanding of referential opacity in Baldwin's task, but evidently the child's competence, as described here, is not far off the mark.

OVERLITERAL INTERPRETATIONS IN THE MESSAGE–DESIRE DISCREPANT TASK

Although children's success in the message–desire discrepant task can be celebrated as a sign of a sophisticated understanding of mind and communication, what we should make of children's overly literal interpretations is yet another matter. Very many children aged 3 years interpreted Mum's request by reaching to the mentioned location of the drawer in both the discrepant and consistent version we presented (Robinson & Mitchell, 1992, 1994a). Can we assume a symmetry, in the sense that children who give a correct judgement (reaching to the nonspecified location) understand opacity, whereas those who give a wrong judgement (reaching to the mentioned location) do not understand opacity? In other words, can we use failure on the message–desire discrepant task as a diagnosis of a lack of understanding of opacity? Children's errors in the task do not provide a sufficient reason for arguing that they lack understanding of opacity. Their errors could arise for a different reason. For example, children might react impulsively to the location that is mentioned in the request, not because they lack understanding of opacity but because they are overly eager to offer an interpretation. In other words, children could make errors either because they lack understanding of opacity or because they impulsive.

Robinson and I (Mitchell & Robinson, in prep.) introduced a variation to the task to find the reason for children's errors. We manipulated the wording of the speaker's request in a way that was at once both subtle yet profound in its effect, which was to allow a correct judgement in the discrepant task without the child having to interpret the request opaquely. Specifically, Mum requested the bag she *put* in the drawer: "I need one of the bags of material. It's the bag I *put* in the drawer." In this case, the child need not treat Mum's request as referring to a model of reality that resides in her mind. All the child need do is identify which of the bags (as it happens, the one in the cupboard) Mum put in the drawer. At the very least, there is no need to consider Mum's visual access and infer the implications with respect to her knowledge. Lacking an understanding of referential opacity would pose no impediment to the child's correct judgement in this discrepant task that employs the *put* wording. We compared children's judgements in the two versions of the task, one that required the child to interpret opaquely and one that did not. We found that children aged 3 and 4 years pointed to the location Mum mentioned whether or not her request included the word *put*. Meanwhile, nearly all children aged 4 and 5 years correctly pointed to the nonmentioned location when Mum's request included the word *put*, but many persisted in wrongly pointing to the mentioned location when that word was absent. In other words, even if the younger children were able to make use of an understanding of opacity in interpreting Mum's request, they would be prevented from doing so owing to an impulsive tendency to reach to the location mentioned in the request—that affects transparent interpretations as much as it affects opaque interpretations. In contrast, slightly older children were not compelled to react impulsively to the request, and thus showed a specific difficulty in interpreting opaquely.

FURTHER DEVELOPMENT: EVALUATING MESSAGES AND THE SAY–MEAN DISTINCTION

A view widely held about a decade ago was that, below the age of around 7 years, children know very little about the difference between what people say and what they mean (Beal, 1988; Bonitatibus, 1988; Robinson, Goelman, & Olson, 1983; Robinson & Whittaker, 1987). In other words, the claim being made was that children below 7 years are not attuned to the mind behind the message. If that account were correct, then we would be forced to conclude that young children have difficulty putting to good use their understanding of referential opacity, and consequently, at least in some respects, have only a very fragile understanding of mind. Much of the evidence arose from 6-year-old children's difficulty in interpreting and evaluating ambiguous verbal messages. Robinson (1994) provides a detailed account of the implications of this difficulty for the child's developing conception of mind.

In a standard procedure, the child participant and the experimenter sit facing each other on either side of a small table. Both have an identical set of pictures, for example three pictures of men, two of them wearing hats. However, each "player" (child and adult) is unable to see the other's pictures on account of an opaque screen bisecting the table and obscuring each other's view. The aim of the game is for the players to take turns in selecting and then describing a picture, such that the other player is able to identify the same picture in his or her own set. Following this the screen is removed so that the two players can check whether or not they have selected the same card and finally there is a post mortem in which the child evaluates the message and apportions blame if the two players have not selected the same card. When the experimenter plays the role of speaker, his or her messages are specially contrived such that some of the time they are ambiguous. For example, "I have chosen a picture and it shows a man wearing a hat."—there are two pictures showing men wearing hats. The procedure is described in more detail in Robinson and Whittaker (1987).

Children aged about 7 years and below made various distinctive judgements in this task, which distinguished them from older children. Specifically, they did not acknowledge the difference between ambiguous and unambiguous messages according to a variety of criteria. First, they were eager to interpret an ambiguous message as though there was no impediment to making a correct selection. In contrast, older children were hesitant and often stated that they could not make an interpretation because they could not tell which of the men wearing hats the speaker meant. Second, if asked whether they were sure they had chosen correctly, children aged 7 years and below tended to say that they were, when hearing both ambiguous and unambiguous messages. Their overconfidence seemed all the more peculiar given that children had no difficulty in acknowledging that there were two men with hats when asked explicitly about this. Third, when asked if they had been told enough or if the experimenter had done a good job of telling them about the picture, the young children judged positively. Older children, in contrast, asserted that they had not been told enough and that the experimenter did a bad job. Finally, when it became apparent that the experimenter and child had selected different pictures, the young children blamed the listener for having chosen wrongly, whereas the older children blamed the speaker for not saying which of the men wearing hats they were to select. The children judged in the same way whether they were playing the role of listener, speaker, or whether they were a passive observer of two other people playing the game. In sum, children aged 7 years and below judged that ambiguous messages were good and they judged that it was the listener's fault for choosing the wrong picture. They seemed unable to grasp that messages could be ambiguous, resulting in the speaker's intended meaning remaining obscure. In this respect, children aged around 7 years and below seemed unable to distinguish between what is said and what is meant.

Moreover, children who seemed unable to detect ambiguity in utterances presented to them, also tended to be less effective in communicating clearly in their natural and spontaneous speech (see Robinson & Whittaker, 1987, for a review).

The claim that children below the age of 7 years lack an understanding of the say–mean distinction is patently wrong. If children can make a correct interpretation of the speaker's request in the message–desire discrepant task, then they understand the say–mean distinction. In making such a correct judgement, children are demonstrating an understanding that the words that form the message (bag in drawer) are not isomorphic with what the speaker means—defined in terms of what would satisfy her desire (bag in cupboard). Yet the child initially must process the literal meaning of the message (bag in drawer) in order to identify what would satisfy the speaker's desire (bag in cupboard). Hence, even some children as young as 3 years of age can demonstrate an understanding of two levels of meaning of a message. Evidently, they do not have a problem with the say–mean distinction in this case.

It remains to be explained why children aged 6 and 7 years have so much trouble with ambiguous messages. According to some researchers (e.g. Beal, 1988; Bonitatibus, 1988; Olson & Torrance, 1983), the answer is to be found in children's experience of living in a literate culture and of becoming literate themselves. Within a Vygotskyan tradition, these researchers suggest that the development of literacy (in culture and within the child) has the benefit of allowing the child to regard language itself as an item for cognitive scrutiny. This arises from the child being exposed to the written word, detached in time and space from a real-life context, that nonetheless makes reference to events that could or have occurred in reality. Being able to interpret squiggles on a page alerts the child to language itself as a vehicle for communicating ideas and events, but a vehicle that has its own distinct and substantive existence within the confines of a book.

Along these lines, Bonitatibus and Flavell (1985) predicted that 6-year-old children who have the opportunity to read an ambiguous message (as well as hearing it) will stand a better chance of recognising its inadequacy than children who merely hear the same message. To find out, they presented one message in legible writing (plus spoken), another in illegible writing (plus spoken), and another just orally. The children were asked to evaluate these different messages, some of which were ambiguous, and those most successful in judging the ambiguous message to be inadequate happened to be the ones who received a legible written message. Children receiving the other kinds of message tended wrongly to judge the ambiguous communication to be good.

It might well be, then, that children are limited in their ability to evaluate a message, which necessitates perceiving the message as an item for cognitive scrutiny, until they become more immersed in the literate aspect of culture. It might be that although 3- and 4-year-old children can draw the distinction between what is said and what is meant, which allows them to interpret a request opaquely, they lack the reflective awareness of language necessary for evaluating messages. Perhaps the latter only becomes possible when the child has sufficient experience of being literate. If so, we can make a striking prediction about children's evaluation of the speaker's request in the message–desire discrepant task. We can predict that although children aged 4 and 5 years will be effective in judging that Mum wants the bag in the cupboard (when she said "drawer"), nonetheless they will wrongly judge that she said the right thing (drawer) for the bag that she wants. If they judged that she said the wrong thing, then they would be explicitly acknowledging that Mum's message was inadequate in relation to her desire, which is supposed to be beyond the ability of younger children because they have insufficient literate experience (e.g. Beal, 1988; Bonitatibus, 1988; Olson & Torrance, 1983).

We put the prediction to the test (Mitchell & Robinson, 1994). We asked some children aged 4 and 5 years if Mum said the right thing and we asked others which of the bags Mum really wanted. Contrary to the prediction arising from proponents of the literacy theory (e.g. Beal, 1988; Bonitatibus, 1988; Olson & Torrance, 1983), children were just as effective in evaluating the discrepant message (judging that Mum said the wrong thing) as they were in interpreting her message (the bag in the cupboard). In a variant of the story, Mum's message was ambiguous because there were two drawers, and this time children wrongly judged that her message was good. We can conclude that children do not have a general difficulty in evaluating messages or regarding them as items for cognitive scrutiny that is only overcome at an older age, when they might be expected to become more attuned to the written word. Instead, it seems they have a specific problem with the concept of ambiguity.

WHY DO CHILDREN HAVE A PROBLEM WITH AMBIGUITY?

According to Ackerman (1981), children aged around 6 years and below suffer from a "performative bias", which means that the perlocutionary effect of the speaker's utterance is for them to make a selection from the materials in front of them. Having made a choice, it seems that children then come to assume that their choice is correct. Research conducted by Elizabeth Robinson and myself (Mitchell & Robinson, 1990, 1992; Robinson & Mitchell, 1990, 1994b) supports this view. We showed children aged around 5 and 6 years a set of unfamiliar cartoon characters and asked them to guess which was "Murkor" (an invented name). Children eagerly pointed to one of the pictures, though there was a complete lack of consensus over which of them was Murkor—which is not surprising given his unfamiliarity. We then asked the children if they knew that the picture they had chosen was Murkor or whether they didn't really know. There was a tendency, more prominent in the younger children, to claim that they really knew their chosen picture was Murkor.

These erroneous positive judgements could have reflected nothing more than a general tendency to be overconfident and to overestimate what they knew. However, we were able to offer a more specific interpretation of the phenomenon. Under another condition, we asked children if they knew who Murkor was in the absence of any picture cards, and they usually judged correctly that they did not. Hence their overconfidence seemed specific to choosing a card. Perhaps when children saw the pictures, they had a false sense of recognition. Again, we ruled this out by demonstrating that children judged that they knew their chosen card showed Murkor even when the cards were presented, and remained, face down! Perhaps having chosen, children felt compelled to justify their eagerness to select a card by claiming that they had knowledge of Murkor. This possibility could also be eliminated, because children judged that they would know which card was Murkor when merely anticipating being able to choose, and before seeing any pictures.

We concluded that children aged 5 and 6 years (and presumably younger ones as well) evaluate their own knowledge in a performative way in some cases. It seems that they were assuming that the act of choosing, or anticipating being able to choose, was sufficient justification for claiming that they had chosen correctly. If we apply this to the case of ambiguity, it might be that being able to make an interpretation is sufficient for children to assume that they have interpreted correctly. On making such an erroneous assumption, children may not pay enough attention to the details of the message that would allow them to identify the ambiguity along with the ensuing impediment to correct interpretation. Even so, it might be that the development of a literate perspective heightens the child's awareness of language as an entity in its own right to a point where the child can overcome an inclination to apply a performative criterion for judging that his or her interpretation is actually correct.

DEVELOPING AN ADVANCED UNDERSTANDING OF COMMUNICATION AND MIND

What do children understand about the role of the speaker's mental activity in the formation of his or her utterance? Specifically, what do they understand about the possibility of the speaker's memory failure causing him or her to generate a description that is imprecise? Following earlier work by Ackerman (1979), James Russell and I (Mitchell & Russell, 1989) set about finding an answer. We told children a story about John and Mary, who were going to do some reading. Mary asked John to fetch her book, which had the word "reading" on the cover and a picture of a dog. John went to the place Mary suggested and found only one book there, which had the word "reading" on the cover, but a picture of a cat. Under one condition, Mary was portrayed as having a very good memory for what her book looked like, whereas under another condition she was depicted as having a bad memory. Observing child participants were asked if this book that John found was the one that Mary wanted. Those aged 9 and 10 years tended to judge that it was if Mary was said to have a bad memory, but that it was not if she was said to have a very good memory. These children seemed to understand that Mary's memory failure might cause her to give incorrect details about the item she was requesting. On the other hand, they seemed to understand that if Mary had a good memory then it was likely that her description was accurate, with the consequence that the book John found was not the one Mary actually wanted.

In contrast to the older children, those aged 5 and 6 years did not discriminate between the conditions in which Mary was depicted as having either a good or bad memory. Generally, they frequently judged that the book John found was the one Mary wanted, irrespective of whether she was said to have a good or bad memory. Seemingly, these children accepted that Mary might have misdescribed the thing she wanted, but they seemed unable to grasp the implications of Mary's memory quality in relation to the accuracy of her description. There seemed to be a lack of integration of knowledge about her mental state of memory and the verbal output of her message. It might be that children aged around 5 and 6 years do not have much insight into the integration of various mental processes, such as speech and memory, though this suggestion is a speculative one.

Although misdescriptions are far less common than accurate descriptions in everyday life, the sheer volume of messages that we process means that nonetheless we have considerable experience of processing misdescriptions. When facing a suspected misdescription, all is not lost since it is still possible to make a judgement on whether or not an object that approximates to the description is in fact the item intended by the speaker. One source of input to this process of inference is any information we might have about the speaker's state of mind, such as whether the speaker has a good or bad memory. Another source of information is the extent to which the object that one might find is discrepant with the description uttered by the speaker. This is something we investigated in another study (Mitchell & Russell, 1991). We adapted the story about Mary and John, where under one condition the book John found differed according to one attribute (the picture on the cover) whereas under another it differed in two of its attributes (the picture and the word). In these stories, there was no information indicating the state of Mary's memory. Children aged 9 and 10 years tended to judge that the found book was the one Mary wanted when it differed from her description according to just one attribute, but not when it differed according to two attributes. In contrast, children aged 5 and 6 years judged in the same way under both conditions. The younger children seemed unable to use the magnitude of discrepancy as a clue to whether or not a given item was the one intended by the speaker.

These young children showed a related difficulty in another study (Mitchell, Munno, & Russell, 1991). Children had an opportunity to make an inference not about what the speaker intended but whether or not a discrepant message was good enough for the speaker's intended meaning to be transmitted to the listener. In this case, observing child participants were told explicitly that Mary's description was discrepant with what she intended. In one condition, her description was grossly discrepant whereas in another it was only mildly so. Observing child participants were given the task of judging whether or not the listener would be able to determine which item in an array the speaker intended. Children aged 8 to 10 years usually judged that the listener would know what the speaker meant when the description was only mildly discrepant, but judged that he would not know what the speaker meant when the message was grossly discrepant. In contrast, children aged 5 and 6 years were not influenced at all by how inaccurate the speaker's message was in their estimate of whether the listener would understand.

The results of this series of studies show that by middle childhood, children have a sophisticated understanding of verbal communication as an interface between minds. They understand something about how we can integrate clues with the message to assess precisely what it is that the speaker means. Similarly, they can make good judgements about the circumstances under which a listener will be able to make sense of an inadequate message. These subtle abilities are not so obvious in children aged around 5 and 6 years. Generally, then, although younger children seem to have a grasp of referential opacity, which is the core concept in an understanding of mind, it is bound to be the case that they build on this early understanding to achieve more subtle insights into communication and mind over the ensuing decade of development.

SUMMARY AND CONCLUSION

It would be easy to underestimate what is involved in the development of understanding the link between mind and communication. Some research suggests that, even during infancy, children are equipped with remarkable insights that allow them to grasp that reference is the privilege of the person uttering the message. As Baldwin (e.g. 1993a; see previous chapter) demonstrated, toddlers do not egocentrically assume that what is being referred to is the thing they are looking at, but the thing that is the focus of the speaker's direction of gaze. Accordingly, it would be tempting to claim that toddlers have a working understanding of referential opacity. That may be true on one level, but certainly not on another. Children aged 3 years might be able to utilise a speaker's immediate direction of gaze, but seemingly they do not make use of a speaker's prior direction of gaze, as in the message–desire discrepant task. In the latter, children would have to encode the significance of prior visual input with respect to the speaker's obsolete knowledge base, and interpret his/her request in relation to that (rather than in relation to the scene as it currently stands). By age 4 or 5 years, however, children show a surprisingly precocious insight in their ability to interpret nonliterally in the message–desire discrepant task. Moreover, they are able to reflect on such a message sufficiently to evaluate it, and judge that the speaker said the wrong thing.

Even so, significant further developments take place. These involve coming to understand how speech might not provide an adequate clue to what the speaker wishes to communicate. An obvious example is ambiguity, which children seem not to be attuned to until about 7 years of age. Even further developments concern the understanding of what constitutes a good verbal clue as opposed to a bad clue to what the speaker means. The child will also develop insights into the relation between the mental states of the speaker and the consequent quality of message. In sum, development unravels over a long period of childhood, and as it does so, the child is both better informed about mind and in a position to gather more information about mind. This follows in the sense that the more proficiency the individual develops as a communicator, the better the prospects of learning about mind. After all, speech opens a window on the minds of other people, and proficiency in communication stands to potentiate that experience.

CHAPTER SEVEN

Young children's difficulty with false belief: A conceptual shift in the development of thinking?

From the preceding chapters, we see that children aged between 3 and 4 years already understand a great deal about mind. This is apparent in early skills in language, communication, and imagination, which together form a precursor of the concept of referential opacity. As I have noted already, both Leslie (1987) and Perner (1988) regard the latter concept as the central component necessary for an understanding of mind. Nonetheless, several researchers, notably Perner (1988, 1991) and Gopnik (1993), are adamant in arguing that only when children pass a test of false belief, which they claim is not achieved until about 4 years of age, do we have good justification for crediting the child with an understanding that minds represent reality. Well, there is not much difference in chronological time between 3 years and 4 years, so why trouble ourselves about a contention that revolves around a meagre 12 months of development? The reason is because it is not so much the child's age that counts, but a whole range of theoretical implications that we need to consider in deciding what qualifies as an understanding of mind and how its development progresses.

Gopnik (1993) advocates something called the "theory theory". It is the theory that children themselves acquire an informal "theory" of what the mind is. Perner (1988) and Flavell (1988) ally themselves with the theory theory, whereas Wellman (1990) generally leans toward it yet sometimes seems ambivalent. These researchers' combined contribution has dominated this area of research such that the theory theory is widely accepted as mainstream among many of those working in the field. The piece of evidence that forms the cornerstone of the theory theory is young children's apparent difficulty with false belief. In summary, the view is that until children can pass a test of false belief, at approximately 4 years of age, there are no grounds for crediting them with a genuine representational understanding of mind. When a child is able to pass such a test, this is thanks to the child having undergone a radical conceptual shift, in which cognition has been restructured such that it is possible to formulate a mental representation of other people's mental representations of reality. Hence, the theory theory posits that to qualify as a theory of mind, the conception in question has to be *representational*. The theory theory further holds that the human understanding of mind is akin to a scientific theory, whereby the child formulates and applies rules to calculate what people do and do not think. Just as Einstein constructed a general theory of the universe with his formula $e=mc^2$, so we are being persuaded that children formulate a rule or set of rules that allows them to calculate the existence and content of minds. However, the child's ability to formulate these rules will supposedly be hampered by an immature failure to grasp that people can be mistaken in what they think. The researchers who subscribe to the theory theory each hold their own unique view of the details of the child's theory or lack of one. What I present here as the theory theory is more a composite of those views, and each individual researcher would no doubt take issue with some aspects of my portrayal, and perhaps wish to distance himself or herself from these.

THE SIGNIFICANCE OF FALSE BELIEF

Dennett (1978) set about stipulating the conditions under which we should say that an individual has demonstrated that he or she possesses a theory of mind. The demonstration should be that the individual acknowledges that people hold simple factual beliefs about reality, and that these beliefs govern their behaviour. This seems like a disarmingly simple requirement but in fact it is rather tricky. The main problem is that in checking whether an individual understands that people hold beliefs it would be futile to question the individual on what he or she knows about other people's *true* beliefs. Suppose we tell the child that we are going to show Sam, the child's best friend, a Smarties tube and that we are going to ask Sam what he thinks is inside. Suppose we ask the child to anticipate what Sam will say, and the child correctly replies with "Smarties", should we ascribe to the child an understanding of

Sam's beliefs and hence credit this child with a theory of mind? To do so would be premature, because we would be fooled into assuming that because the child gave a correct answer to a question asking what another person thinks, that it means the child necessarily understands about thoughts. The problem is that, irrespective of how we phrase the question, with or without the word "think", we can never be sure whether the child is genuinely reporting what Sam *thinks* of reality or just reporting current reality. What we require to solve the problem is a task that detaches belief from reality, such that if the child were to respond correctly, he or she would not just be reporting current reality. A test of *false* belief fits the bill nicely.

Wimmer and Perner (1983) are credited with conducting the seminal study setting out to test young children's ability to acknowledge false belief. In fact, what these researchers did had actually been achieved six years previously by Johnson and Maratsos (1977), which even pre-empted Dennett's (1978) pronouncements on what qualifies as evidence for a theory of mind. (Inexplicably, Johnson and Maratsos never received the full recognition they deserved.) In Wimmer and Perner's study, children listened to a story enacted with small dolls, which has become known as the *unexpected transfer* test. The story featured a young boy called Maxi, who had some chocolate that he deposited in a blue cupboard in his kitchen. He left the scene and in his absence his mother unexpectedly transferred Maxi's chocolate to a green cupboard that was also in the kitchen. Maxi was unaware of this event due to his absence from the scene. Subsequently, Maxi was about to return whereupon the experimenter turned to the observing child participant and asked him or her to predict where Maxi would look for his chocolate. Under another condition, children were asked where Maxi would say his chocolate was. If children judged that Maxi would look in the blue cupboard or would say his chocolate was in the blue cupboard, this would show that they were able to represent Maxi's belief and hold it in distinction to what they knew maintained in current reality. One of the great strengths of this procedure was that any difficulty children had in understanding the word "think" would not pose an impediment to correct judgements. All the observing children had to do was predict what Maxi would do or say.

The results were that only 42% of children aged 4 and 5 years judged that Maxi would look for his chocolate in the place that he left it. The rest judged that he would look for the chocolate where they knew it currently was. In contrast, 92% of children aged 6 and 7 years judged that Maxi would look in the place he left his chocolate, demonstrating that they could acknowledge another person's false belief. From this, the superficial conclusion seems to be that older children understand about mind, whereas younger children do not. However, there are problems in principle with this conclusion.

First, we shall consider the implication of young children's failure to acknowledge false belief. Actually, there is a whole variety of reasons why young children might fail to acknowledge false belief: One cannot argue anything with certainty on the basis of negative evidence. Logically, one cannot argue that absence of evidence of an understanding of false belief amounts to evidence of absence of an underlying understanding of mind. An absence of evidence indicates that the child may or may not have an understanding of false belief. That does not mean we have reached an impasse on what we can say about the young child's grasp of false belief. We can make progress by systematically eliminating reasons why they might have difficulty in answering the question correctly. That is, we can narrow down the range of possible reasons for children's difficulty. Second, older children's success could be explained without crediting them with any understanding of mind. In the unexpected transfer test, all the child participant has to do in order to be scored correct is to judge that Maxi will search in a place that he visited previously; there would be no reason to hold any representation of Maxi's representation to judge according to that simple principle. All one has to do to answer correctly is to judge that Maxi's previous behaviour forms a pattern that he will repeat in the future. Namely, he will go to the place he went to before. Fortunately, we know ultimately that people are aware of other minds because we have first-person evidence to this effect: We know that we ourselves are aware of other minds, so we can assume other people also have the same insight. In any case, as will be seen later, children are able to make a variety of related judgements that all contribute to the impression that they judge insightfully.

ELIMINATING EXPLANATIONS FOR YOUNG CHILDREN'S DIFFICULTY WITH FALSE BELIEF

If we were to assume that really young children do understand about false belief, then we might account for their difficulty in Wimmer and Perner's (1983) task by supposing that they misunderstand incidental aspects of the story presented to them. For example, it seems odd to test young children's understanding of mind by asking them to make judgements about inanimate objects that do not have minds, namely little plastic dolls. To get round this problem, Perner, Leekam, and Wimmer (1987) devised the *deceptive box* test of false belief. They showed children a Smarties tube and asked them to guess what was inside. Children dutifully replied with "Smarties" but the experimenter proceeded to disconfirm this expectation by showing that the box actually contained a pencil. The experimenter returned the pencil, closed the lid, and asked the observing child participant to anticipate what another person, who had never seen the tube before, would say or think it contained. Only 35% of children below the age of 40 months responded with "Smarties" as they themselves had done only moments earlier. The figure rose to 50% in the case of children between 42 and 48 months. In other words, very many of the children were reporting what the Smarties tube currently contained (a pencil) when asked to anticipate another person's false belief. Evidently, whatever the reason for young children's difficulty with false belief, it was not peculiar to their judgements about the thoughts of inanimate dolls.

Not only was the deceptive box procedure effective in ruling out reluctance to attribute mental states to dolls as the source of young children's difficulty, but it also broadened the phenomenon and indicated that it was robust. This impression was strengthened further by the results of a study conducted by Gopnik and Astington (1988). They also presented a deceptive box task, but rather than ask children what another person would think was inside, they instead asked the participating child to recall what he or she had thought was in the box on first seeing it. Children aged around 3 years tended to answer this question in the same way that they answered the question asking about another person's belief: They reported the current content of "pencil".

Two superficial explanations for children's failure to recall their own prior false belief are as follows. One is that perhaps young children have a profoundly weak memory and quite simply would fail to recall any trivial piece of information from a few moments previously. To find out, Gopnik and Astington (1988) presented children with a more general test of memory. They showed children a dolls' house and opened the roof to reveal an apple inside. They removed this and replaced it with a little man doll. The experimenter then asked children to report what was currently in the house and what was in it previously. Children aged 3 years had no difficulty answering with "man" and "apple", respectively, even though these very same children were unable to recall their own prior false belief. Evidently, children's difficulty with false belief could not be explained by general memory failure.

Another explanation is that children experienced ego involvement and would have felt some loss of face if they admitted that they had been wrong about what was in the box initially. Perhaps judging that they had thought the tube contained a pencil all along was their way of convincing themselves and the experimenter that they were smart. This explanation was eliminated by Wimmer and Hartl (1991; replicated by

Riggs & Robinson, 1995a), who tested children as they sat alongside Kasperl, who was known to them on TV as a silly puppet renowned for getting things wrong. The experimenter showed the child and Kasperl a Smarties tube and asked Kasperl to guess what was inside. He replied "Smarties". The experimenter revealed the unexpected pencil and then specifically asked the child what Kasperl had thought was in the tube initially. Children aged around 3 years tended to respond by reporting the tube's current content (pencil) just as much as when they were asked to report their own initial belief. They would have felt no loss of face in judging that Kasperl had thought the wrong thing. Indeed, there should have been an expectation that Kasperl would be wrong followed by public recognition of this fact—this was the usual script connected with Kasperl. Hence, there is no reason to think that children's difficulty in acknowledging their own false beliefs has anything to do with trying to avoid a loss of face.

THE BREADTH OF CHILDREN'S DIFFICULTY WITH FALSE BELIEF AND APPEARANCE–REALITY

Gopnik and Astington (1988) proceeded to present children with an unexpected transfer test, a deceptive box test of own prior false belief, and a test of appearance and reality. This last was based on a procedure devised by Flavell, Flavell, and Green (1983). They showed children an object that looked like a rock. However, when children handled it they discovered that in fact it was merely a sponge. The fake was good enough to fool children initially. Subsequently, the experimenter asked children what the object was and what it looked like. Children older than 4 years usually responded to the two questions correctly, by saying "sponge" and "rock" respectively. In contrast, many children aged about 3 years not only acknowledged that the object was a sponge but asserted that it looked like one. Gopnik and Astington went a step further to show that children who made an error on one of the tasks (whether acknowledging their own prior false belief, the difference between appearance and reality, or acknowledging another person's false belief), tended to make an error on the other two as well. In the light of this, they concluded that young children's difficulty on the three tasks is united by an underlying deficiency in understanding the difference between objects and representations (or beliefs) of objects.

Harris (1989) extended research into children's difficulty with false belief and the appearance–reality distinction into the domain of emotion. Harris and Gross (1988) report that although many children aged 3 years have difficulty in explicitly acknowledging that a camouflaged sponge looks like a rock, many also seemed to have a related difficulty with emotion. In particular, the children seemed to find it hard to acknowledge that somebody who is smiling could really be sad. Hadwin and Perner (1991) demonstrated another way in which they claim young children's lack of understanding of belief limits their understanding of emotion. In a variant of the deceptive box test, children were asked to judge how Sam would feel when he opened the Smarties tube. Young children judged that Sam would feel sad on not finding Smarties in there, but they judged that he would not be surprised (cf. Wellman & Woolley, 1990, summarised in Chapter 3). Hadwin and Perner point out that surprise is the emotion most associated with belief, in that if beliefs turn out to be true, then we are not surprised, but if unexpectedly they turn out to be false, then we will be surprised. Hadwin and Perner suggest that children's failure to anticipate a protagonist's surprise when shown that his belief is false, is further testament to their general difficult with the concept of belief.

Not only do young children make errors on various kinds of test of false belief, but the phenomenon is robust cross-culturally. Avis and Harris (1991) confirmed this when they paid a visit to the Baka tribe, which inhabits the rain forests of southeast Cameroon. The Baka are pygmies who live a traditional hunter-gatherer life and are nonliterate. They are largely uncontaminated by the values and philosophy of Western society. Children witnessed a staged scene in which an adolescent member of their tribe cooked mango. After he finished he stated that he was going to a meeting place for a chat and a smoke and would return later to eat his delicious mango. In his absence, an adult member of the tribe conspired with the observing child to trick the adolescent. Their scheme was to transfer the mango from the cooking bowl to a closed pot. Subsequently, the adult asked the child a sequence of questions about the adolescent's belief and emotion. The child was asked where the adolescent would look for his mango, and whether he would feel happy or sad before he opened the lid of his bowl and whether he would feel happy or sad after he had opened the lid. The results were that children aged 5 and 6 years of age usually judged that the duped adolescent would look for his mango in the empty bowl and that he would feel happy before opening the lid but sad afterwards. In contrast, younger children were more likely to make errors. Specifically, some of the younger children judged that the adolescent would search in the pot, where the mango currently was. When children answered in that way, the adult insisted that the adolescent would look in the bowl first of all, and proceeded to ask them how they thought the adolescent would feel. The younger children who failed the belief question tended to judge that the adolescent would feel sad *before* he opened the bowl.

Although according to logical dictate we are not entitled to claim on the basis of absence of evidence that young children lack an understanding of mind, they certainly seem to have considerable difficulty in acknowledging the difference between reality and representations of reality. This is evident in their difficulty with tests of false belief, extending into the realm of judgements of emotion and making the appearance–reality distinction. As I mentioned previously, we can only make progress by exploring various specific reasons why they might have difficulty with these tasks.

CHILDREN'S DIFFICULTY WITH THE QUESTION

A less exotic explanation for young children's difficulty with the various tasks is that perhaps they misunderstand the question the experimenter is asking. Recall that Wimmer and Perner (1983) were alert to this problem and were cautious about making a distinction between what children understand about belief as a concept and how they comprehend words that refer to beliefs (e.g. *think*). However, children might have a more general communicative problem. They might wrongly suppose that the experimenter is asking not where Maxi will look for his chocolate but where he will look in order to get his chocolate. In order to get his chocolate, he will look in the place where it is currently, namely the green cupboard. That is, he will only get his chocolate if he looks in the green cupboard and he will not get his chocolate if he looks in the blue cupboard, where he left it.

Siegal and Beattie (1991) identified this as a problem, which they investigated by presenting one version of the unexpected transfer test using Wimmer and Perner's (1983) wording and another version with a clearer question in which children were asked where Maxi would look for his chocolate *first of all*. The results showed that children aged 3 years were much more likely to answer correctly that Maxi would look in the place he left the chocolate when the question was suffixed with "first of all" compared with a version faithful to Wimmer and Perner's original procedure, in which this phrase was omitted. Siegal and Beattie took the view that what developed between 3 and 4 years of age was not so much an understanding of the concept of belief, but a more general ability to make appropriate interpretations of what they are being asked.

Lewis and Osborne (1990) made a very similar suggestion in relation to young children's difficulty with the deceptive box task. These authors noted that young children may misunderstand the experimenter to mean, "What will Sam think is in the tube once we have opened the lid and shown him the pencil?" They suffixed the question with "before we open the lid": "What will Sam think is inside before we open the lid?" They also report a statistically significant improvement in young children's correct attributions of false belief over a procedure employing the temporally vague wording formulated by Perner et al. (1987). Similarly, children were better able to acknowledge their own prior false belief when asked what they had thought was in the tube before the experimenter opened the lid.

At this juncture we should pause to reflect not just on the implications of children's improved performance when the question is better worded, but also ask how we could explain their preference to report current reality when questioned about belief. If children have no notion at all of belief, then why do they show a preference for current reality? On the face of things, perhaps we would expect children to show complete ignorance about belief, in which case they would not show any positive preference but random judgements. We would expect that in the deceptive box task, half the time they would respond with "Smarties" and the rest of the time they would respond with "pencil". In the unexpected transfer test, we would expect that half the time they would anticipate Maxi's search in the blue cupboard (where he left the chocolate) and the rest of the time anticipate his search in the green cupboard (where it currently is). How can we explain children's preference to report current reality when asked about belief?

These problems of conversation and preference for current reality seemed to be solved by one of the most powerful yet ingeniously simple experiments in the history of research on the child's understanding of mind, devised by Wimmer and Hartl (1991). This is known as the "state change" task. Wimmer and Hartl's assumption was that children aged around 3 years lack a conception of mind but even so make every effort to answer questions sensibly. When they hear the question, "What did you think was inside?", they are able to interpret most of what they are asked but not all of it. Because they have no conception of belief, they simply ignore any reference to that. Effectively, then, they reinterpret the question as, "What was inside?" Hence, in the deceptive box task, according to Wimmer and Hartl, children are not so much reporting what is in the box currently but what was in the box when they first saw it (which happens to be the same thing anyway: Pencils). However, the state change procedure allows for a demonstration that children are answering by reporting what was in the box when they first saw it, rather than what is in there currently.

In the state change procedure, the child is shown a Smarties tube and guesses that it contains Smarties. Unlike a deceptive box procedure, however, the tube actually does contain Smarties, and this is confirmed to the child when the experimenter opens the lid. As the child watches, the experimenter proceeds to tip out the Smarties and replaces them with a pencil. The experimenter closes the lid and then asks a standard question, "When you first saw the box, what did you think was inside?" In response to that question, Wimmer and Hartl (1991) report that a massive 85% of children aged 3 years answered correctly, whereas only about a third answered correctly in a standard deceptive box procedure. This is precisely the pattern of data that would emerge if children were interpreting "What did you think was inside?" as "What was inside?" Children thus only demonstrated problems if asked about false belief, where it was useless to treat a question about prior belief as one about prior reality. Hence, when asked to make a judgement about belief, children who have no grasp of this concept will not judge at random but will positively report reality, either past or present.

The state change true belief and deceptive box false belief conditions were so closely matched that Wimmer and Hartl's (1991) results help to show that children's difficulty with acknowledging false belief amounts to a lot more than difficulty in understanding the time reference of the question they are asked (*pace* Lewis & Osborne, 1990; Siegal & Beattie, 1991). If children misunderstand the question in a superficial way, to mean "What is in there now?", then they would report the current content in both the deceptive box test and the state change test. The finding that they generally give the correct response in state change shows that children have a more specific difficulty than can be accounted for by the conversation hypothesis.

THE FORMULA IN CHILDREN'S THEORY OF MIND

Wimmer, Hogrefe, and Perner (1988) outlined a simple rule that we apparently use in judging whether or not someone knows a fact. The rule comes from the old adage that seeing is believing, and it is that we should deny a person knowledge of a given fact if that person lacks the necessary informational access. We adults have this concept well formulated in that we understand the distinction between knowledge derived from ordinary perception and the hypothetical case of knowledge derived from extrasensory perception. Most people clearly understand the boundary between what we can and cannot derive through the senses. The corollary is that if one has acquired knowledge not through the channels of ordinary perception, then something paranormal has happened. Effectively, then, people can only gather information through the regular avenues of perception.

Perhaps young children lack a concept of the limitations of normal sensory perception; perhaps they feel perfectly comfortable with the idea of people obtaining information without needing perceptual access. On this basis, Wimmer et al. (1988) pointed out that, to understand that a person might hold a false belief, we need to recognise that limited or misleading perceptual access could leave one in a misinformed state. They went on to suggest that what children aged around 3 years do not understand about the unexpected transfer scenario is that Maxi's not seeing the chocolate being transferred to another location will mean that he does not know it has moved. In brief, they suggested that perhaps 3-year-olds do not understand that not seeing leads to not knowing, and neither do they grasp that seeing leads to knowing. To test this hypothesis they conducted the following study.

Children participants observed another person (who was an assistant of the experimenter) either look in a box or not look inside. The observing participant children were asked to report whether the other person looked in the box and whether she knew or did not know what was inside. Children were reliably correct in reporting whether or not the other person had looked in the box. However, they seemed to have surprising difficulty in judging whether or not the person knew what was inside. Those aged around 3 years by and large seemed to judge at random, sometimes saying the person knew what was inside when she had not looked, but sometimes denying that the person knew when she had looked. Children's judgements showed a similar pattern whether or not they themselves had seen what was inside the box. In contrast, older children showed a consistency in their judgements, in which they attributed knowledge if the person had looked, but denied knowledge if the person had not looked.

For various reasons, this seems a remarkable finding. For one thing, children apparently were not judging as though reality is transparent to people, since they were perfectly comfortable denying knowledge, except they denied it at inappropriate times. Also, they were not confusing their own knowledge with the other person's because occasionally they denied that the other person knew what was in the box when they themselves knew. Generally, then, the results were consistent with Wimmer et al.'s (1988) hypothesis that young children lack a theory of mind in the sense that they lack a rule that links seeing with knowing, and the converse.

Just as young children seem to have difficulty acknowledging their own beliefs, so Wimmer et al.'s (1988) suggestion can be extended to young children's lack of insight into how knowledge entered their own minds. If they do not possess the seeing–knowing rule, then presumably it would be inexplicable to them how the information stored in their mind got there. Consistent with this, Wimmer et al. report that 3-year-olds seemed to have difficulty in justifying how they knew a fact. Gopnik and Graf (1988) also investigated this issue. They either showed children what was inside a box, told them, or gave them a clue. For example, they showed children an egg carton and told them that what was in the plain box belonged in the egg carton. Children were then asked to state what was in the plain target box, followed by the critical test question. This asked them how they knew what was inside,, "...did you see it, did I tell you about it, or did you figure it out from a clue?" The results were that children aged 3 years were rather poor at reporting their source of information, in contrast to older children, and any who did report the source usually answered wrongly when questioned after a delay. In contrast, the older children continued to report their source correctly. The trouble with this study is that children who give a correct judgement by reporting their source of knowledge could do so without actually understanding how that experience led to knowledge.

More convincing results arise from the elegant study conducted by Povinelli and DeBlois (1992), which evolved from their research into apes' conception of mind. Children were offered conflicting information on the location of a treat. One communicator had seen the hiding of the coveted object whereas the other had not. Generally, children aged around 3 years did not discriminate between the two conflicting sources of input, whereas older children tended to search where the informed communicator indicated. This amounted to a demonstration that the older children (but not younger ones) understood that seeing leads a person to have a correct belief on where a prize is located, an experience that qualifies the person thereafter to communicate its whereabouts accurately. Other studies by O'Neill and Gopnik (1991), O'Neill, Astington, and Flavell (1992), and Perner and Ogden (1988) seemed to confirm that 3-year-old children continue to have difficulty in understanding the link between seeing and knowing even when the testing and task is presented in a simpler and more child-based way.

According to these theorists, then, children aged around 3 years do not have rules about how people (including themselves) get to know things, and hence it seems they lack a theory of mind. The particular rule in question concerns seeing and believing, but researchers (e.g. Wimmer et al., 1988) feel inclined to extrapolate to other kinds of perception and knowledge. On the other side of the coin, these researchers claim that children of 4 years and above do hold a seeing–believing rule, and moreover that this could be demonstrated by the presence of a tell-tale error showing that older children overuse such a rule. Identifying this error was the aim of a study conducted by Sodian and Wimmer (1987).

Sodian and Wimmer (1987) showed children the contents of a bag, a selection of balls all of the same colour (blue). The experimenter then transferred one of the balls to a box, and although the child was fully aware of this transfer, he or she did not see the actual ball involved. However, it would be possible to infer that the ball must be blue since the pool from which it was selected consisted entirely of blue balls. Children aged 4 years had no difficulty making this inference, and judged without hesitation that the ball transferred to the box was a blue one. Children were then introduced to Angelika, who was the experimenter's assistant. Angelika also looked in the bag and also knew that a ball was being transferred to the box but did not see the actual ball involved. Children were then asked if Angelika knew which ball was in the box. Children aged 4 years denied that Angelika knew, whereas those aged 6 years correctly judged that she did know.

It might have been that the 4-year-olds would deny that Angelika knew things in various domains, but the results of a control condition showed this not to be the case. Children were willing and happy to judge that Angelika knew the colour of the ball in the box when she saw the actual one involved. Sodian and Wimmer concluded that children aged about 4 years understand that seeing leads to knowing, and not seeing leads to not knowing, but they apply this rule too rigidly. This rigidity was apparent in that they would not accept that Angelika could know a fact by making an inference (that all the balls in the bag are blue, so therefore the transferred ball must be blue). Their denial was not based on any misconception about making an inference, since the children had no difficulty inferring for themselves that the transferred ball must be blue. Their difficulty seemed to amount to an overuse of the seeing–believing rule, coupled with a lack of understanding that people can know things by inferring them.

Wimmer and colleagues made a brave and clever attempt to pinpoint the cause of young children's difficulty with the concept of mind, and at the same time show that the child's conception of mind amounts to a rule-bound theory. The findings reported by Wimmer et al. (1988), coupled with those reported by Sodian and Wimmer (1987), combine to suggest that 3-year-olds lack an understanding about the relation between seeing and believing, and that older children who do grasp the rule tend to overapply it. The possibility that children overapply rules when they first grapple with them makes good intuitive sense, since parallels can be found in various domains of cognitive development. An example is children's initial use of the -ed rule to form the past tense of English verbs. Children aged around 5 years typically say "runned" instead of "ran", indicating an "over-regularisation" of the rule for formulating the past tense of verbs. Apparently, they have abstracted the past-tense rule, and proceeded to apply it too widely, without paying enough consideration to possible exceptions. A similar pattern, incidentally at the same age in development, seems to occur in children's grasp of the seeing–believing rule—at least that is what Wimmer et al. would have us believe.

PROBLEMS WITH THE
SEEING–BELIEVING FORMULA

There is a fundamental problem with the claim that children lack insight into what other people do or do not believe on the grounds that they do not understand the link between seeing and believing. The claim has a theoretical overtone, which is that young children understand the possibility of false belief, but do not understand the informational circumstances surrounding false belief. That leads to the supposition that young children should have no difficulty in acknowledging their own prior false beliefs, suggesting the Cartesian principle that we are innately rational and that, in particular, the mind is transparent to itself; in other words, for example, that we know that our own mind holds beliefs. This supposition is patently unsupported, though. Recall that Gopnik and Astington (1988) found that children aged around 3 years have at least as much difficulty acknowledging their own prior false belief as they do acknowledging false beliefs in other people. Gopnik and Astington argue that acknowledging one's own false belief merely requires access to a resident memory and there is no need to calculate whether oneself would be misled by the exterior of a Smarties tube. That issue is superfluous to the task of acknowledging one's own false belief, yet children still have serious difficulty.

Surely we cannot ignore the evidence that children in Wimmer et al.'s (1988) study seemed unable to make a link between seeing and believing. But as I have already stressed, absence of evidence of children's correct performance should not be taken as evidence of absence of their competence. We should proceed by enquiring whether there are any circumstances in which 3-year-olds are able to display insight into the link between seeing and believing. One study motivated along these lines was conducted by Pillow (1989, 1993). Instead of asking children to judge whether a protagonist did or did not know, Pillow asked them to judge which of a pair of protagonists knew the content of a box, the one who looked inside or the one who interacted with the box in an epistemically uninformative manner: He stood on top of it. Pillow found that children aged around 3 years had no difficulty in singling out the protagonist who had looked in this context. The results seem to be at odds with those reported by Povinelli and DeBlois (1992), mentioned earlier. In Pillow's study, perhaps the cues (ostentatiously looking in the box or standing on top of it) were more salient, giving the children a better chance to demonstrate their competence.

Pillow's (1989) results stimulated Pratt and Bryant (1990) to adopt a critical stance toward Wimmer et al.'s (1988) procedure. They noted that Wimmer et al. presented their participating children with a rather long and convoluted question, asking whether the protagonist knew what was in the box or whether he did not know that. Pratt and Bryant tried out the same questioning and found that children usually made their response after the experimenter had articulated about half of the question, and sometimes would change their response if the experimenter continued to the end of the question regardless. Pratt and Bryant pointed out the dilemma over which of the child's responses to accept and noted that Wimmer et al. not only failed to explain how to deal with the problem but did not even acknowledge that there was one. Pratt and Bryant simply repeated the procedure but presented a single-barrel question: "Does Lucy know what is in the box?" They found that between 75 and 95% of children aged 3 years answered correctly, according to whether or not Lucy looked in the box, across a pair of studies they conducted. In contrast, Wimmer et al. reported success in only 13% of 3-year-olds.

These results suggest that children aged 3 years have a good grasp of the seeing–believing rule. They also suggest that, whatever the reason for young children having difficulty with false belief, it is not that they lack a rule at the heart of their "theory" to the effect that seeing=believing; children who make that link, we can presume, still have difficulty acknowledging false belief. We already knew that their difficulty amounted to more than lack of the seeing–believing rule anyway, because they frequently fail to acknowledge their own prior false beliefs. We can say, then, that at least one feature of the theory theory has been dealt a severe blow. Nonetheless, the results reported by Sodian and Wimmer (1987) still stand as a tantalising clue to the effect that older children are not only using a seeing–believing rule but are overusing it. An alternative possibility is that children aged around 4 years have yet to grasp that people can know things by inference. Their overuse of the seeing–believing rule could have been a by-product of lack of understanding of the functions of inference rather than reflecting a positive preference for applying a newly acquired rule, akin to overuse of the -ed rule in language development. I shall say more about this specific point in the next chapter.

So what remains of the theory theory? The prevailing view to survive from this perspective is that advocated by Perner (1991) and generally endorsed by Gopnik (1993). Perner's view is that young children fail tests of false belief because they do not understand that people hold their beliefs in all seriousness as being about reality. Following Pylyshyn (1978), Perner asserts that young children do not understand the representational relation between beliefs and reality, or in other words, the attitude one holds about one's beliefs. The attitudes people hold about their beliefs is by definition what we can call a *factive* attitude. In other words, people routinely suppose that their beliefs are true and act upon them accordingly. Perner suggests that young children might grasp that people have thoughts and understand that people engage in pretence, but know virtually nothing about their attitudes toward their own mental representations. Hence, if a child assumes, for example, that a person with a false belief does not take his or her own belief seriously, then the child will not expect him or her to act on that belief as though it is held as a true model of reality. Consequently, the child would be unable to predict that a protagonist would search where a desired item is not located, and would be surprised and puzzled if the protagonist did so. How Perner supposes the child progresses from this state to acquiring a genuine understanding of false belief is unclear, though his recent research suggests that he is sympathetic to the idea that interactions with peers can generate a beneficial sociocognitive conflict that forces children to accept that people do take their own beliefs seriously (Perner et al., 1994). He is now also willing to accept that some form of understanding of mind exists at an implicit preverbal level before it blossoms into a verbally explicit theory. Clements and Perner (1994) found that young children showed understanding of false belief on an implicit level, as revealed by their direction of gaze. When the experimenter vaguely asked where the protagonist would look for the treat, children tended to look to the place where the protagonist had last seen it rather than where it was currently. But when they judged verbally, the children resorted to reporting current reality.

If we could show that children's difficulty in acknowledging false belief arises for a hitherto unconsidered reason, then Perner's claim that young children are ignorant of the attitude people hold toward their beliefs would become redundant. The only reason for accepting Perner's argument is that children have difficulty with false belief, and therefore his is a circular argument. Its inherent weakness would be highlighted by evidence pointing to other factors responsible for young children's difficulty. This is the province of the next chapter where, additionally, we shall explore the possibility that development is actually gradual and entirely unlike the scientific (conceptual) revolution occurring at the age of about 4 years as portrayed by advocates of the theory theory.

CHAPTER EIGHT

The reality masking hypothesis: The idea of a smooth developmental progression

There are three main pieces of evidence that advocates of the theory theory use to support their claim that the development of a conception of mind progresses through a radical conceptual shift around the time of the child's fourth birthday. One is the obvious, namely that children aged around 3 years tend to fail a test of false belief, while children aged about 4 years tend to pass. So on a group basis, children show a pattern that is consistent with their progressing to a higher developmental stage, akin to the transition from crawling to walking, from babbling to speaking, and from having milk teeth to having secondary teeth. Note that these latter three stages emerge reliably, within a relatively narrow age band, right across children in different cultures around the world. The same kind of supposition is made about children's emerging ability to acknowledge false belief, which at least superficially seems to conform to a stage-like transition.

Another line of evidence comes from the individual child. The child will progress from apparently being unable to acknowledge false belief to being able to pass such a test, so long as he or she is clinically normal. Putting it another way, we would not expect a child who passes a test of false belief to fail that same test when presented with it 3 months later. Although longitudinal data are rare, what we do have suggests that children do not subsequently regress once they begin to acknowledge false belief (Dunn et al., 1991). Hence, it seems that the 4-year-old has taken on board something that the 3-year-old lacked, in a permanent rather than transient sense. Whatever the child acquires at the age of 4 years is seemingly not fleeting or ephemeral.

The third line of evidence is that children who pass one test of false belief also pass other related tests. Gopnik and Astington (1988; also Sullivan & Winner, 1991) identified children who anticipate that Maxi will search for his chocolate not where it currently is but where he last saw it. These very same children also tended to be the ones who successfully recalled that when they first saw the Smarties tube they (wrongly) thought it contained Smarties (really it contained pencils). Moreover, they also tended to be the children who acknowledged that although an object presented to them was really a sponge, it looked like a rock, and thereby acknowledged the distinction between appearance and reality. In sharp contrast, children who failed one of the tasks tended to fail the other two as well. Gopnik and Astington concluded that children's success or failure on the set of tasks could be pinned down to an underlying aspect of cognition, namely, the presence or absence of an adequate theory of mind. A superficial alternative explanation, which these authors were able to reject, was that older children are simply more competent and perform better than younger ones, irrespective of the particular tasks presented. Gopnik and Astington showed that the correlation in performance between the three kinds of task they presented maintained independently of the children's chronological age. In other words, it was not the case simply that the older children got all the tasks right and the younger ones got them all wrong; age itself was not the best predictor of success across the tasks.

On the face of it, these three lines of evidence seem persuasive of a radical stage-like shift in development, which probably explains why the theory theory has been taken so seriously over the last decade. However, when we penetrate the surface in what follows, it is my contention that we will find that each of these lines of evidence in support of a stage shift crumbles and that, in the aftermath, the theory theory will appear somewhat implausible.

To begin, what can we make of the age trend, showing a very sharp improvement in acknowledging false belief between 3 and 4 years of age? We can start by questioning just how sharp this change with age actually is. As an example, Perner et al. (1987) present a table (Table 5 in their article) summarising a selection of studies (13 in total) in which children aged either 3–4 years or 4–5 years, or more typically both, were tested for their ability to acknowledge false belief. The mean success rate for the 3–4-year-olds over all the studies was 26%, whereas the mean success rate for the 4–5-year-olds was 67%. Undoubtedly, older children are more likely to pass a test of false belief than younger ones. Undoubtedly, also, some studies report a substantial difference in performance between 3 and 5 years (e.g. Wimmer & Perner, 1983, Experiment 2: 15% against 76%). However, the other side of the coin is that there is a considerable overlap, and some studies even find *no* significant difference between the performance of 3- and 4-year-olds. For example, in Perner et al.'s Table 5, the best performance in their 3–4-year-old column is 45%, whereas the worst performance in their 4–5-year-old column is 41%. It is not just that some tests of false belief identify a gradual increase in the children passing with age whereas others identify a sharper change. Rather, different studies that seem to have employed almost identical tests sometimes generate conflicting data on how sharp the age trend is.

The possibility that increases with age are not so impressive after all is corroborated by the results of research I have been personally involved in. For example, Robinson and Mitchell (1995) conducted a succession of six investigations modelled loosely around the unexpected transfer test. We shall take a look at the primary motivation for this research later, but incidentally, here we have an opportunity to look at trends in performance emerging between 3 and 4 years of age. The smallest investigation had a sample of 36 children and the largest had a sample of 66. The investigation with the widest age-range included children aged from 3:6 months to 5:4. In this, the older half of the sample were significantly more likely to give a correct judgement of false belief than those in the younger half. In one other study there was also a small but significant age trend. However, the most striking thing about the age trends was the lack of them. In four of the studies, no age trend even remotely approached significance. For example, 66 children were tested in the first investigation, aged between 3:6 and 4:11. Here we had a substantial sample with a fairly wide age range, yet the performance of the older children was not significantly better than that of the young children. This was not because all children were particularly good at passing the tests and neither was it because they were all particularly bad. There was plenty of scope within the distribution of scores for an age trend to emerge, but it did not.

Pretty much the same picture was apparent from another study, but this time employing a standard deceptive box task (Saltmarsh, Mitchell, & Robinson, 1995). Again, the primary motivation was to investigate something other than age trends, and I will discuss this later. There were four experiments in total, but only in the final experiment did the age-range justify an analysis of age trend. In Experiment 4, 70 children aged between 3:5 and 5:2 were divided into two groups according to age. The results were that the older children were no more likely to acknowledge false belief than were the younger ones. The younger children gave correct judgements about 28% of the time, which is typical, but surprisingly exactly the same percentage figure emerged from the older children.

More generally, both Saltmarsh (1995) and Steverson (1995) repeatedly found either no age trend between 3- and 4-year-olds, or at best very small trends. Moreover, Steverson found that even a minority of children as old as 6 years reliably failed to acknowledge false belief. Meanwhile, in virtually all of the published research, there are always some children, however young and however few in number, who seem able to give a correct judgement of false belief. In sum, the picture is that if we test a group of preschoolers on false belief, and compare them with a group of children aged around 6 years, there is no doubt that an age trend will be obvious. But to say that there is a sharp developmental trend between 3 and 4 years can often result in something akin to trying to knock a square peg into a round hole. Quite simply, it has become fashionable to claim that there is a sharp age trend, but in fact there is not.

Does this in itself mean that development is gradual? It does not, because even though a given child might be either developmentally delayed or precocious in acknowledging false belief, nonetheless that child's first success could mark the birth of a new underlying cognitive stage. In other words, perhaps we should not be fixated on the age at which the child passes a test of false belief, but realise that all or most children are uniform in that at an early age they have difficulty acknowledging false belief. So for any individual child, the first success in acknowledging false belief would signal the advent of a new stage of cognition that supplants an earlier and more primitive conceptualisation. What this boils down to is that we still have to explain why a child is likely to fail to acknowledge false beliefs when young, whereas when older, he or she is likely to pass. This is something we need to explain if we wish to advocate an account of developmental continuity in preference to discontinuity.

The main problem with a test of false belief is that the child can either be right or wrong and there is no scope for detecting shades of correctness that fall somewhere in between these two extremes. For this reason, a test of false belief is biased toward identifying shift-like changes in cognition, but is not well suited to identifying more gradual changes that occur as a matter of degree in the child's thinking. A logically invalid assumption made by advocates of the theory theory (see previous chapter) is that an absence of a correct judgement in the child's performance reflects an underlying absence in the child's cognition. Another possibility is that something changes gradually in the child, and when this gradual change reaches a certain threshold, the child will give a correct judgement. This begs the question of precisely what this something is that is changing gradually, and I will try to spell that out shortly. Meanwhile, consider this analogy. Suppose we were to define athletic maturity as the ability to sprint 100 metres in 20 seconds. Suppose that we had impoverished data, such as someone handing to us printouts showing age down one column and whether or not the individual satisfied the criterion (100 metres in 20 seconds) down the other. We might find that the average age for satisfying the criterion is about 16 years. Imagine how silly it would be, then, to suppose that at about 16 years of age people negotiate a radical athletic shift, marking a watershed before which the ability to run competently is absent, and after which it is fully developed, and so on. What is actually happening is that people gradually work up to this criterion and then, perhaps undetected, progress beyond it. In this light, it seems odd to posit a radical shift in children's thinking on the basis of their meeting an all-or-none criterion. If we become fixated on what it means to fail an-all-or nothing test, like a test of false belief, then we run the risk of being fooled into thinking that an absence of a correct judgement reflects an absence of the requisite underlying cognition.

There are two things outstanding that we need to discuss. One is that a process that undergoes gradual change has to be specified. Another is that the possibility that children are consistently right or consistently wrong across a wide variety of tasks demands explanation. The latter seems to add credibility to the theory theory argument that an underlying unifying concept develops in the child that allows him or her to pass not just one test but to pass all of them. How could we explain this without referring to a singular underlying shift in cognition? These two problems for the continuity hypothesis really amount to just one. Once we can say what it is that changes gradually, then we will see that this factor can also explain why children fail on a selection of tests intended to probe an understanding of mind. It is now time to unveil this mystery underlying factor, and it is the possibility that children fail to acknowledge false belief not because they have no theory of mind, but because *reality holds a magnetism and is therefore especially attention-grabbing* for younger children, but less so for older children. This is the *reality masking hypothesis*.

REALISM

On the face of things, to say that young children have a bias toward reality might seem like a mere description of the kind of error they make. Namely, when asked to report belief, they report current reality. However, I intend the term "realism" to be understood not just as a description of children's errors but as a comprehensive explanatory concept. First of all, there are plausible reasons for expecting young children's attention to be dominated by current reality when asked to report beliefs. Second, we are able to predict that certain manipulations should attenuate children's bias to current reality, and when they do so, children's underlying ability to acknowledge false belief should be unmasked. Third, we can predict that since development is assumed to be gradual, that some tests of false belief or related tests should be capable of detecting realist errors in older children and even adults.

I shall proceed by suggesting why reality should be especially salient to young children. To begin, Russell et al. (1991) are to be credited with the claim that for young children, when belief and current reality are in conflict, reality wins in capturing the child's attention, and hence they commit the usual realist error. However, they did not suggest any plausible reason as to why this should be the case, with the consequence that their argument seems like a circular one. That is, children are said to be attracted to current reality because they are demonstrably attracted to current reality when we present certain tests to them. Having said that, Russell, Jarrold, and Potel (1994) were able to formulate a prediction from their claim, which is that children should show a bias toward reality even in tests that clearly do not require judgements of belief.

Fodor (1992) also suggested that current reality captures young children's attention, but this was actually a corollary to the main point of his argument. Fodor's claim was that, since most beliefs are true anyway, there is not much point in attending heavily to the possibility that a person might be holding a false belief. If we are asked where Maxi will look for his chocolate, since Maxi is by default likely to be holding a true belief, a simple strategy is to report current reality: To report where the chocolate currently is. In other words, Fodor is claiming that young children do understand about belief, but they find it easier, due to certain performance factors, to report current reality than to report false belief. The trouble with Fodor's account is that it is formulated in such a way that he is only able to explain young children's difficulty in predicting a wrong search by an actor holding a false belief. He is unable to explain why young children would report current reality when asked either to judge another person's belief explicitly, or when asked about their own prior false belief. Fodor's view is that young children do understand about false belief, but are drawn to current reality when invited to indicate where someone will search for an item. I will give a more detailed critique of Fodor's suggestion later.

Another realism account has been formulated by Leslie and Thaiss (1992). They suggest that two distinct cognitive processes are involved in passing a test of false belief. They propose that a person must possess a "theory of mind mechanism" and they also suggest that one should possess a matured "selection processor", which is an attentional device. Leslie and Thaiss claim that young children do have an understanding of mind that amounts to a working understanding of referential opacity, but current reality dominates their selection processor, giving rise to the characteristic realist errors. However, Leslie and Thaiss do not present evidence to show that young children are able to acknowledge false belief under favourable circumstances and instead rely on indirect evidence in the form of early pretence to support their contention of an early understanding of mind. Also, there is no obvious reason why current reality should be attention-grabbing to young children, apart from the fact that they make realist errors. Hence, like Russell et al., they are in danger of presenting a circular argument.

The final realism account I shall report is the one developed by Elizabeth Robinson, Rebecca Saltmarsh, and myself (Mitchell, 1992, 1994; Mitchell & Lacohee, 1991; Mitchell, Robinson, Isaacs, & Nye, 1995; Mitchell & Saltmarsh, 1994; Robinson, 1994; Robinson & Mitchell, 1994a, 1995; Saltmarsh et al., 1995). I have already stated some of the predictions from our account (unmasking correct judgements of false belief in young children; gradual change and realist bias in older children and adults), and I shall report results pertinent to these later. In addition, I have attempted to spell out *how* current reality comes to be so engaging to young children (Mitchell, 1994). A summary of the argument is as follows. If we take a functional and evolutionary perspective on the utility of holding an understanding of mind, then it would be that it is something that is of value when we enter the social realm and have to live on our wits by making judgements about what others think and desire. This requirement becomes especially acute when the child begins to venture beyond the umbrella of care and protection provided by the primary care-giver and close members of the child's family. The child will not be sufficiently developed physically to venture beyond the safe haven of the family much before the age of 3 or 4 years. Until that time, the child is entirely dependent on the family for food, warmth and protection, and the family will oblige by offering these services for nothing in return (other than perpetuation of the family genes).

In sum, we can take it for granted that the young child will receive all sorts of benefits from the immediate family, and there is no need for the child to be a diplomat or psychologist to bring about that privileged state—it happens by default. In contrast, when children are propelled more into the social realm, then they will have to become wise to the minds of others if they are to win friends and influence people. The child cannot take it for granted that unrelated people and peers will act benevolently. Hence, attention to beliefs is likely to be at the forefront of the older child's mind but not of the young child's. What I am overlooking, here, is that sometimes the family environment is not always as harmonious as one might hope. In particular, siblings are capable of teasing each other and generally competing for attention and resources. Children with siblings have alternative views and wants forced upon them, which we might suppose would promote an early venture into the psychological world. In that context, it comes as no surprise that children with siblings tend to show greater insight into mind than those without (Perner et al., 1994).

Although the young child will often have no great need to be attuned to the psychological sphere, current reality (what is going on in the physical world around the child) is extremely likely to grab attention. Although young children need not worry much about what other people are thinking, they do need to be concerned about physical aspects of the environment. Humans are nomadic creatures by nature, and have a tendency to migrate to a wide variety of geographic and climatic regions. They also have a flair for introducing gadgets into their environment, so much so that the civilised milieu looks quite unlike that which provided the setting throughout the millennia of our evolutionary development. For these reasons, children are born into a physical environment that their genetic inheritance could not have prepared them for in any specific way. In this respect, we are completely different from many other creatures, who depend on a highly predicable habitat, and wither if they are denied that.

So how do young children get to grips with the unpredictable environment they are thrust into? It might be that they are equipped with a learning strategy that helps to get them rapidly accustomed to their world. Perhaps they have an attentional bias that makes current reality highly salient, especially anything that is novel or has recently changed in some way. The picture I am presenting, then, is that for young children current reality holds an attentional magnetism, because they are striving to get to grips with the world, and meanwhile beliefs are of low priority attentionally speaking. Additionally, since people's beliefs are usually true anyway, it is not surprising, according to this account, that young children fail to acknowledge false belief. On the other hand, it is entirely predictable that they report current reality when asked about belief. Nonetheless, there are lots of reasons for supposing that young children do have considerable insight into mind, including the special case of false belief, and many of these are presented in the previous chapters.

It seems that from a very early age, children are equipped with a symbolic faculty that allows them to acquire and understand language and it also allows them to express themselves in pretend play. Symbolic activities like language and pretence are once removed from reality, so this in itself shows that whatever the young child's reality bias, this is not so profound as to curb all processes that are detached from reality. However, having a symbolic capacity is not incompatible with having a realist bias at the very same time. I wish to stress that a realist bias exists in people as a matter of degree, and claim specifically that such a bias is sufficient in most 3-year-olds for them to commit realist errors in a standard test of false belief.

CHILDREN'S EARLY UNDERSTANDING OF FALSE BELIEF

If young children have an underlying competence that would allow them to acknowledge false belief in principle, then we ought to find improvements in their judgements if we could direct their attention away from current reality and on to belief. Emma Steverson and I (Steverson & Mitchell, 1995a; also, Mitchell & Isaacs, 1994, Experiment 2) attempted this with a disarmingly simple procedure in which children made judgements about their own prior false beliefs in a deceptive box task. Under a standard condition, we simply asked children what they had thought was in the box initially, but under a novel suggestion condition, we put it to children that when they first saw the box, they had thought there were Smarties inside. This follows the maxim that a useful way to check what children know and can do is simply to tell them the correct answer and see how they react to it! Not surprisingly, when it was suggested to 3-year-olds that they had thought the tube contained Smarties, nearly all agreed, even those who failed a standard test of false belief. They also continued to make correct judgements when another person's false belief was suggested to them.

The reason this result is not surprising is because we might expect young children to agree to any suggestion made to them by an adult, given that they are notoriously compliant (well, sometimes!). The onus fell upon us to show that when children accepted the suggestion of false belief, it was not just because they accept any kind of suggestion made to them. We achieved this with a control condition in which the experimenter suggested not that the child had thought the tube contained Smarties, but that he or she had thought it contained jelly babies. Only a very few children did accept this patently false suggestion, and the vast majority had no difficulty rejecting it. Importantly, the children who failed a standard test of false belief were significantly more likely to accept a true suggestion of their prior false belief (Smarties) than they were to accept an untrue control suggestion (jelly babies). Looking at the data another way, those children who rejected a false control suggestion were significantly more likely to acknowledge false belief following suggestion than they were in the standard procedure.

Hence the results do now begin to look surprising, at least in terms of the theory theory. It seems that children were able to acknowledge false belief if they were helped to focus away from current reality and onto their earlier belief with the aid of a suggestion. Their consequent correct judgements seem like genuine judgements in that the children were not open to any kind of suggestion—only true and appropriate ones. A further value of this research is that it makes a link with the Vygotskyan idea of the zone of proximal development. This is the idea that the child's competence would not necessarily be apparent in any task that the child performs without the aid of a more skilled person, but that the competence could be revealed with such assistance. Making a suggestion to the children perhaps served the purpose of supplying adult support and guidance on the correct judgement, which the child had no difficulty recognising when he or she encountered it.

SUPPLYING THE FALSE BELIEF WITH A COUNTERPART IN REALITY

Given the nature of the reality masking hypothesis, the obvious way to proceed would be to ossify a false belief in some sort of reality. This was the motivation behind the first study we conducted that is relevant to the hypothesis (Mitchell & Lacohee, 1991). Children participated in a deceptive box task in which they were asked about their own prior false beliefs. Under a novel "posting" condition, children were asked to select a picture of what they thought was in the box at the moment they first saw it and prior to discovering the true (unexpected) content. For example, in the case of a Smarties tube, children were presented with a set of seven picture cards, one of which showed Smarties. They selected and then posted this into a special postbox, where it remained out of sight until the end of the procedure. The purpose of this was to endorse the child's initial belief (Smarties) in the reality (albeit invisible) of the posted picture that rested inside the postbox. The experimenter proceeded to open the Smarties tube and reveal a pencil in there, closed the box and then asked a modified test question: "When you posted your picture in the postbox, what did you think was in here (gesturing to the Smarties box)?"

About three-quarters of the children we tested aged around 3 years gave a correct judgement in response to the test question under the posting condition. In contrast, those tested under a control condition involving a standard deceptive box procedure for own false belief tended to make a realist error by responding with "pencils". Although we had found a significant improvement in correct judgements in this study, we needed to pinpoint the factor responsible for the observed facilitation. Our hypothesis was that it was caused by the child's initial belief being supported by a reality counterpart, but an equally plausible candidate was that the "When you posted your picture" clause in the test question identified precisely which moment in time the experimenter was referring to. Lewis and Osborne (1990) suggested that young children might have trouble with false belief because they are unclear on exactly which previous moment in time the experimenter is asking about. Taking on board this point, it might be that the posting, followed by the question making reference to this event, clears up the ambiguity for the child.

However, we were able to eliminate this alternative interpretation with the aid of a control condition in which children posted a picture that was not relevant to their initial belief. In this, after saying initially that they thought a Smarties box contained Smarties, children posted a picture of their favourite cartoon character. Subsequently, they were asked the distinctive "posting" false belief question, and under this condition there was no significant improvement in children's correct judgements. It seems, therefore, that for whatever reason children were giving a correct judgement when they posted a picture of Smarties, it was not just because the procedure helped to disambiguate the time reference in the test question.

Another reductive explanation for children's correct judgements in the posting procedure is that they thought they were being asked not what was in the Smarties box, but what is currently in the post box. When they reply with "Smarties", they may have meant that there is a picture of Smarties currently in the postbox rather than that they used to believe the Smarties tube contained Smarties. If children did misunderstand the question to refer to the content of the postbox, then they would answer the test question by stating the name of their favourite cartoon character in the control condition, since a picture of this would have been resident in the postbox. However, not a single child responded in that way.

Since our original work, Freeman and colleagues (Freeman, 1994; Freeman & Lacohee, 1995; Freeman, Lacohee, & Coulton, 1995) have replicated our findings but challenged our interpretation. Our interpretation was that posting a picture promoted facilitation in children's correct judgements of their own prior false belief because it supplied that belief with a counterpart in reality. In contrast, Freeman argued that children were aided specifically because it was a picture that was posted. He suggests that the picture of Smarties (or a picture of anything for that matter) is representational and therefore already in the appropriate domain for the child to make a link with his or her initial belief (which is also representational). His prediction was that posting a sample of the object itself would not give rise to any facilitation. To find out, he presented a novel condition in which children posted a sample of real Smarties into a postbox at the time they held their initial belief.

Freeman's (1994) results showed some sign of facilitation, but the effect was not as strong as that generated by the picture posting condition, which he claimed was largely in support of his hypothesis. In other words, Freeman's claim is that supporting the child's initial belief with a reality counterpart is not the crucial ingredient that helps them to make correct judgements. However, it might be that Freeman's sample posting was not a fair test of the realism hypothesis. First, there was some sign of facilitation in the sample posting condition. Second, it might be that children did not construe the Smarties as a sample of their belief about the content of the Smarties tube. If, as intended, they assumed the tube was pristine, then the sample of Smarties they posted could not have been from the tube they were making a judgement about. Hence, the sample could not be the real-world counterpart of the child's belief.

The posting procedure has also been replicated by Charman and Lynggaard (1995), but Robinson and Goold (1992) found only a weak effect and Robinson, Riggs, and Samuel (1996) found no significant facilitation. In the light of these latter findings, it might be that the posting effect is not as strong or as reliable as we had thought initially. Nonetheless, some of the results remain encouraging.

Even if the results from the posting experiment were strong and stable, the evidence in support of the reality masking hypothesis would seem flimsy if it rested just on this. I shall proceed to review further evidence in support. One avenue of research relevant to the hypothesis is that pioneered by Bartsch and Wellman (1989), concerning children's ability to explain false belief in an unexpected transfer task. A crucial modification was that children witnessed the protagonist, who was acting under a misapprehension, search in the wrong location. The observing children were then invited to explain his erroneous search. Many children who failed a standard unexpected transfer test successfully explained the protagonist's wrong search by reference to his false belief. According to the reality masking hypothesis, the facilitation observed in this study was due to the protagonist's false belief having a counterpart in current reality in the form of the protagonist's erroneous search (Robinson & Mitchell, 1995), though Bartsch and Wellman offered a different interpretation.

These results aroused a substantial amount of controversy. As usual, Perner (1991) argued reductively, that children may have been judging not that the protagonist (wrongly) thought the item was where he was searching, but that he was thinking of it being there—akin to daydreaming. Intuitively, this seems a rather tenuous and unconvincing criticism, but the attack on Bartsch and Wellman (1989) was fuelled by results reported by Moses and Flavell (1990) that seemed to amount to a failed replication. Moses and Flavell showed children a video of a protagonist searching for crayons in the bag where she had left them, but in her absence they had been exchanged for rocks. As she approached the bag, children were asked what she thought was in there, and most 3-year-olds replied with "rocks", making the classic realist error. Children nonetheless performed better in this task than in a standard test of false belief, but only just.

From the perspective of the reality masking hypothesis, the trouble with Moses and Flavell's (1990) procedure is that the wrong search does not offer a counterpart to the protagonist's false belief. Searching in the bag does not of itself indicate that the protagonist thinks there are crayons in there or that she wants crayons (though the children were told that she did). Additionally, the attentional pull of the rocks residing in the bag may have prompted the children to blurt out "rocks" when asked what the protagonist thinks is in there. In contrast, in Bartsch and Wellman's procedure, the protagonist searched in a bandaid box (which was empty), which suggests that he wanted bandaids and thought they were in there. This, coupled with there being no alternative item in the box, could have allowed the child to give a correct judgement of false belief. Nonetheless, it would be better if we could offer supplementary evidence in support of the reality masking hypothesis with respect to false search.

Moses (1993) offers such evidence. He presented children with a scenario in which a protagonist searched for his aeroplane in his aeroplane box, only to find the box full of orange peel. Children were better at judging that the protagonist thought there was an aeroplane in there than they were at acknowledging false belief in a standard unexpected transfer task. Another study that offers consistent evidence was conducted by Elizabeth Robinson and myself (Robinson & Mitchell, 1995). Children observed a scene featuring twins of identical appearance. They jointly deposited a ball in location 1 and then one but not the other left. In his absence, the other moved the ball to location 2.

Subsequently, both twins were back together when Mother appeared and asked them to get the ball. Both reacted to the request, but one went to the place that the ball used to be, while the other went to the place where the ball currently was. The observing child participants could not directly tell which twin was which due to their identical appearance, but they were invited to work out which was the twin who went to the empty location—the one who went outside or the one who stayed inside? A substantial and significant majority of children aged 3 and 4 years judged correctly that he was the twin who went outside. In contrast, when children did not see the wrong search of this twin, but instead were asked to predict where the twin who went outside would search, the great majority made the classic realist error in judging that he would search in the place where the ball currently was. In accordance with the reality masking hypothesis, we concluded that the protagonist's wrong search provided a reality counterpart to his false belief, allowing children to acknowledge this. They did so by linking the wrong search with the protagonist's absence at a critical point earlier on. We argued that this finding was not susceptible to Perner's (1991) criticism that children assumed that the twin searching in the wrong place was daydreaming. There would be no reason for children to link the twin's erroneous search with his lack of informational history if they merely thought he was daydreaming.

The controversy does not end here. Riggs and Robinson (1995b) engineered a manipulation in which the experimenter conspired with the child to deceive the experimenter's assistant on the location of his coffee mug. The assistant left his mug in location 1, then departed, then the child and experimenter transferred the mug to location 2. The assistant returned and searched in location 1. Subsequently, children were asked to recall where the assistant searched and also where he thought his mug was. Children had no difficulty recalling that the assistant searched in the empty location, yet persisted in judging that he thought his mug was in location 2, where it really was. Moreover, witnessing and recalling the erroneous search offered children no help in acknowledging false belief over a standard task. So this was a case where the assistant's false belief had a reality counterpart in the form of his wrong search but without any discernible facilitation. Why?

Perhaps the reason why is illuminated by results reported independently by German (1995) and by Rebecca Saltmarsh and myself (Saltmarsh & Mitchell, 1996). In German's procedure, children were reminded, with the aid of video playback, of themselves searching in a location where they left their chocolate, only to find the location empty (the chocolate had been displaced surreptitiously). Under this condition, young children were usually correct in judging that they thought the chocolate was where they left it. In our procedure, children were videoed in a deceptive box procedure. After they were shown that a Smarties tube really contained pencils, they were asked to judge what they had thought it contained initially. Under one condition, children saw the video of themselves either saying that they thought it contained Smarties or the film was paused just before they articulated their initial false belief. Under both conditions involving video evidence, children were significantly more likely to acknowledge their own prior false belief compared with a standard deceptive box task. How do we reconcile the success in these studies with the lack of success in Riggs and Robinson (1995b)?

In Riggs and Robinson (1995b), the wrong search behaviour signifying the assistant's false belief was ephemeral and merely a historical episode at the time the child was asked the belief question. Although the child could recall the episode of wrong search, perhaps this was not sufficient in itself to promote correct judgements of false belief. Perhaps what the children needed to help them was some point of reference in current reality (like the protagonist standing by the wrong location right now) to help them resist judging that the protagonist thinks or thought the mug is where it currently is. This condition was satisfied in all the studies that report successful facilitation. In the Bartsch and Wellman (1989), Moses (1993), and Robinson and Mitchell (1995) studies the protagonist was standing by the empty location at the time children answered the belief question. In the German (1995) and Saltmarsh and Mitchell (1996) studies the condition was satisfied thanks to the replay of video evidence. In sum, it seems that so long as the false belief is seen to have a physical counterpart in current reality, then the child stands a good chance of giving a correct judgement.

DOES STATE CHANGE POSE AN EMBARRASSMENT FOR THE REALITY MASKING HYPOTHESIS?

If current reality is so salient, then why are children able to resist this in the state change procedure? This procedure, devised by Wimmer and Hartl (1991), arguably offers the most powerful support for the theory theory. I stated my admiration in the previous chapter, and briefly it is as follows. Children are shown a Smarties tube or any other appropriate box and asked to guess what is inside. After the child replies with "Smarties", the experimenter confirms this by revealing the expected contents, but then proceeds to replace them with a pencil as the child watches. The experimenter then asks the child what he or she thought was inside initially, and we are told that the vast majority of 3-year-olds respond correctly with "Smarties". This does not imply an understanding of belief, however, since according to Wimmer and Hartl, children get the correct answer by reinterpreting the question as "What was inside" on account of their having no understanding of what the word "think" means (as used in the test question). But if current reality dominates their attention, as the reality masking hypothesis suggests, then surely children should make an error by judging "pencils", since this is the current reality.

The status of the reality masking hypothesis depends upon being able to refute Wimmer and Hartl's (1991) interpretation of their state change results. Rebecca Saltmarsh, Elizabeth Robinson, and I set out to do just that (Saltmarsh, Mitchell, & Robinson, 1995). We presented a novel deceptive box task that had a succession of two unexpected contents over the course of the procedure. For example, the child was shown a Smarties tube and asked to guess what was inside. After the child replied with "Smarties", the experimenter revealed the true content as a pencil but then removed this as the child watched and replaced it with a straw. Finally, children were asked under one condition what they had thought was in the tube when they first saw it and under another condition were asked simply what was in the tube when they first saw it.

According to Wimmer and Hartl (1991), young children should treat those two questions as equivalent, and in both cases should reply with "pencil". When they first saw the tube there was a pencil inside, and if they interpret "What did you think was inside?" as "What was inside?", then they should reply with "pencil". However, the results were entirely different from what Wimmer and Hartl would have expected. When asked what they had thought was in the box initially, children usually made a typical realist error by reporting what was in there currently (a straw). This was not because they had forgotten about the initial content, since when asked explicitly what was inside initially, they usually responded correctly with "pencil". Hence, when asked about belief, young children tend to report *current* reality, and they are not interpreting the question "What did you think was inside?" as "What was inside?", contrary to Wimmer and Hartl's conjecture.

We still need to explain why children gave correct judgements in Wimmer and Hartl's (1991) state change task and why in particular they were able to resist reporting current reality. Actually, there is no big mystery at all. Correct judgements in the state change task could have been predicted from the results of our (Mitchell & Lacohee, 1991) posting experiment. To echo Freeman (1994), instead of a picture serving as a counterpart to the child's initial belief, a sample of that belief would suffice. The belief was that the tube contained Smarties and it turned out that it did. The Smarties in there existed as a physical embodiment of the child's initial belief, with the consequence that the child was able to recall that belief thereafter. This differs from Freeman's study in which children supposedly posted a sample of their initial belief. In his study, the item posted would not be construed as being the object of belief, but merely something similar to the belief. In contrast, in state change the sample residing inside the Smarties tube is the very item of the child's belief.

This seems to work as an explanation for facilitation in state change, but it would be much better if we could show that children were giving a correct judgement *as a judgement of belief* rather than reality. The trouble with correct judgements of true belief is that belief is not detached from reality; we require a state change test of *false* belief. We (Saltmarsh et al., 1995) contrived that in the following way. First, we modified the state change task such that the child made a judgement about another person as well as him or herself. The child sat beside Daffy and the experimenter asked both Daffy and the child what they thought was in a Smarties box. After both replied with Smarties, Daffy left for a snooze. In his absence, the experimenter proceeded to exchange the Smarties for a pencil. Daffy returned and the experimenter asked the child participant both what he or she had thought was in the tube first of all and what Daffy had thought was in there. Children were effective in judging "Smarties" both in connection with what they had thought and what Daffy had thought. They succeeded in giving such a correct judgement significantly more often than in a standard deceptive box procedure. This finding is uncontroversial, and is precisely what Wimmer and Hartl (1991) would have expected, involving just a small modification of their true belief state change procedure.

However, the introduction of Daffy allows us now to convert the true belief state change task into a test of false belief. In a subsequent experiment, when Daffy surfaced from his snooze, the experimenter turned to the observing child participant and asked him or her not what Daffy thought was in the box, but *what Daffy thinks is in there now*. Daffy was not privy to the exchange of content, so he holds a false belief. Would children acknowledge this? According to Wimmer and Hartl (1991) they would not, because, having no grasp of reference to belief, they would interpret the question "What does Daffy think is in there now?" as "What is in there now?" In contrast, according to the reality masking hypothesis, children would be able to acknowledge Daffy's false belief, because the belief response that the child needs to give in order to be credited with a correct answer (Smarties) has a physical counterpart in reality (the child saw Smarties in the tube to begin with) and therefore will not be eclipsed by current reality (a pencil in the tube).

The results were entirely consistent with the reality masking hypothesis but offered no support for Wimmer and Hartl (1991). Children tended to judge correctly that Daffy thought there were Smarties in the tube, more so than under a control condition in which the tube had contained a pencil all along. Moreover, their correct judgements about Daffy's current false belief were just as common as their correct judgements about Daffy's and their own prior true belief in a procedure more faithful to Wimmer and Hartl's state change. Apart from supporting the reality masking hypothesis, and at the same time refuting Wimmer and Hartl's account, these results show that young children find it no easier or harder to acknowledge true belief than to acknowledge false belief, *all other things being equal*. Of course, all other things generally are not equal because usually only true beliefs have a counterpart in reality. Incidentally, this is relevant to a suggestion made by Wellman (1990). He proposed that children might understand true beliefs as beliefs, but find the case of false belief especially difficult to grasp. According to our results, that has turned out not to be the case once we recognise that false beliefs typically lack a counterpart in reality. Seemingly, it is the reality anchor rather than the truth of the belief that counts.

Apart from being directly relevant to the reality masking hypothesis, our results also urge caution in interpreting the results of a couple of studies ostensibly on children's early understanding of false belief in the context of deception. The first was conducted by Sullivan and Winner (1993). They contrasted a deception condition with a standard deceptive box task. The deception involved a box that initially was seen to contain its stereotypical content, which was then exchanged for something atypical specifically in order to trick the experimenter's assistant, who had left the room temporarily. Children were better at acknowledging the assistant's false belief about the box's content in the trick condition than in the standard deceptive box procedure. The authors concluded that it was the deception that was responsible for this effect. However, our results (Saltmarsh et al., 1995) suggest that the facilitation could have been due to the belief option having a reality counterpart specifically in the deception condition. Unfortunately, deception and counterpart in reality were confounded in Sullivan and Winner's study.

The second study was conducted by Chandler and Hala (1994). Their design suffered from precisely the same problem. However, they report that children were even more successful in the deception condition if they were involved in instigating the deception. In other words, there seemed to be an effect associated with deception that extended beyond the effect of the belief option having a counterpart in reality.

The results from our investigations into state change in which children stood a fair chance of acknowledging belief seem to stand in contradiction with poor performance on the unexpected transfer test. We argued that supplying the belief with a counterpart in reality can be sufficient to help some children to acknowledge that belief. As defined, this counterpart could be in the form of the protagonist's behaviour. In that case, why do young children have so much difficulty in acknowledging Maxi's false belief, given that his false belief had a prior counterpart in reality in the sense that the chocolate physically existed in the place that children ought to acknowledge as his false belief? The first thing to note is that children's difficulty with the unexpected transfer test might stem neither from a realist bias nor from a difficulty with false belief, but from a lack of proficiency in comprehending a narrative. Lewis, Freeman, Hagestadt, and Douglas (1994) report that much or even most of the variance in children's failure on an unexpected transfer test is accounted for by their general ability in comprehension. Children who comprehend the story easily stand an excellent chance of acknowledging false belief. Moreover, if children are assisted to comprehend the narrative, by getting them to repeat the story aloud, then they are highly likely to acknowledge the protagonist's false belief.

But what in particular might the children find hard about the narrative? Note that the unexpected transfer test incorporates a belief test question asking *where* Maxi thinks or will look rather than *what* he thinks, as in a deceptive box task. The "what" of Maxi's belief is the chocolate. It might be that children's realism primarily surrounds the "what" of belief, such that when asked about belief, they are compelled to report what that belief is. It so happens that the belief is about the chocolate. So perhaps in pointing to the chocolate's current location, they are not making so much a statement about where in space is the focus of Maxi's belief, but about what his belief is: His belief is about the chocolate, which incidentally is in the red cupboard at the present time. Now it might well be that assisting children to comprehend the narrative helps them to grasp that it is the "where" that is at issue rather than the "what". And when that finally penetrates children, they are able to acknowledge Maxi's false belief about the "where" of the chocolate's previous location because in the past the child participant saw that the chocolate physically resided there.

The results reported here generally suggest that under certain conditions, young children might be able to acknowledge false belief. Yet if there is a simple message to take away from these findings, I hope it is not something to the effect that "really young children can pass false belief tests". Young children have considerable difficulty with false belief, a difficulty that is not entirely eradicated by protecting them from the salience of current reality. If reality is overly salient for young children, then they will continue to be in danger of reporting *current* reality even when the belief to be judged has a physical counterpart. We can only conclude that the mean age at which a group of children pass a test of false belief can be lowered in some cases. The message I prefer is that children sometimes focus excessively on current reality, which can hamper their ability to acknowledge false belief. In other words, it is the realism that is important rather than the early success. Consequently, there is no need to fixate exclusively on ages at which children pass tests and neither is there any sense in this.

I said that once we know what the factor is that underlies realist errors, then we would be in a position to explain why children consistently pass or consistently fail a variety of different tests. In fact, the tests in question are all tests of false belief in various guises, and as such all allow the children to commit a realist error—to report current reality when asked to judge belief. This is obviously the case with respect to children's judgements about own and others' belief in the deceptive box and unexpected transfer tests, but it is less obvious in a test of appearance and reality. Nonetheless, this is still a kind of false belief test. Children are asked how a thing might be construed (how it looks—beliefs about it) and what it is really. Surely we should not be surprised when they commit a realist error on this task. Children's realist errors across these tests no more show that they lack a theory of mind than they show that current reality is especially salient and attention-grabbing. The obvious retort is that sometimes children commit what Flavell, Flavell, and Green (1983) called "phenomenist errors". For example, they claim that an object beneath a magnifying lens not only looks large but really is large. Here, they confuse reality with appearance, rather than the opposite. However, this almost certainly should still be classified as a realist error. As far as the child is concerned, the object really has become enlarged, so it is the child's *assumption* about what reality is that contaminates judgements. These are phenomenist errors only from an adult perspective of privileged knowledge about reality that stands independently of the information entering our eyes.

REALIST JUDGEMENTS ABOVE THE AGE OF 4 YEARS

Why is it that people above 4 or 5 years of age are no longer susceptible to realism? If there is but a gradual reduction in the salience that current reality holds with increasing age, why is there not some scrap of evidence of this continuing realism? The simple answer is that evidence actually exists in abundance. To demonstrate, I shall begin by reporting realism in children aged 4–6 years and then proceed to discuss evidence pertaining to realism in older children and even adults that hitherto has not been identified as such.

Emma Steverson and I (Steverson & Mitchell, 1995b) turned our suggestion procedure on its head to bias children toward current reality. We screened children aged 4–6 years to ensure that they could acknowledge false belief in a standard deceptive box test. Subsequently, we submitted them to a modified deceptive box task, with a different box and content. To illustrate, after the child had said the box contained Smarties initially, we showed that really it contained a pencil, returned it, and then asked the question, "When you first saw this box you thought there was a pencil inside, didn't you?" The vast majority of children agreed with this suggestion, including many of those aged 6 years. By using false suggestion as a control, like in the earlier study, we confirmed that children would not just accept any suggestion, but only one that matched current reality.

This demonstration requires a further control, however. Effectively, the experimenter was suggesting that the child had known all along what was inside the box, and perhaps children were loathe to dispel the experimenter's apparently good impression of their ability to know things. This problem stems from children's ego involvement in a deceptive box test concerning their own false belief. To eliminate this problem, we conducted another study in which the experimenter made an analogous suggestion about Sweep, a silly puppet who is infamous for getting things wrong. Sweep's notoriety is well established in a TV show, and the procedure began with the experimenter showing an excerpt in which Sweep is making patently incorrect factual judgements about things. The experimenter then introduced her Sweep glove puppet and tested him in a deceptive box procedure. Finally, the experimenter suggested to observing child participants that when Sweep first saw the tube, he thought there was a pencil inside. Children (who passed a standard test of false belief) frequently agreed with this, just as when the suggestion was about themselves. When their judgements were about Sweep, these could not have been motivated by being presented with an opportunity to save face. It was of no concern to them if Sweep had thought the wrong thing. Indeed, they ought to have anticipated this, given Sweep's renowned blunders.

The simple interpretation of the results is that current reality retains a salience beyond the age of 4 years. This reality bias is not so gross that it prevents the child passing a standard test of false belief, but it is manifest when the experimenter reminds the child of current reality. This finding is difficult to explain from the point of view of theory theory. That view depicts realist errors just as a default consequence of the child lacking a theory of mind. Supposedly, the child possesses a theory of mind once he or she can pass a standard test of false belief, so it is inexplicable that children should show a realist bias thereafter. Surely this could only happen if current reality retains an attention-grabbing status for the child. Our findings can be contrasted with conserving children's resistance to nonconserving suggestions (see Russell, 1982), showing that the development of conservation ability has much better credentials than a phenomenon that stems from a radical shift in cognition.

Perhaps we should not get over-excited about a couple of years one way or the other. So 5-year-old children can be lured into failing false belief ... The realism hypothesis would become seriously convincing if we could show that realism remains a force in judgements about mind right into adolescence and even beyond. One clue suggesting enduring realism comes from a study reported by Rosenberg (1979). He asked people aged 10 and 18 years to describe themselves. The children tended to describe themselves largely in physical terms, for example referring to the colour of their hair, what kind of clothes they wear, and so on. In contrast, the older participants were more likely to describe their inner psychological characteristics. These results are consistent with the older people having greater psychological insight into themselves than the younger participants, but they are also consistent with the children finding it difficult to detach themselves from reality.

Perhaps more compelling, though, would be evidence suggesting that a reality bias prevails even in adults' judgements of belief. Extant data suggest precisely this, but hitherto, they have come under the heading of "hindsight bias". I will argue that these data play a significant part in the general realism hypothesis and all that it entails, especially with respect to developmental continuity.

Fischhoff (1975) is to be credited with systematically identifying the phenomenon of hindsight bias. He presented adult participants with accounts of historical events, such as a battle between British and Gurkha armies in India. The participants were told about a variety of factors that might advantage one or the other side. Some were also informed of the "outcome"—either a Gurkha or British victory, depending on which experimental condition the participant was assigned to. Finally, participants were asked to rate the probability of various outcomes as if they had not known what really happened. Despite these instructions, participants tended to give higher ratings to outcomes they were told had actually happened.

Fischhoff and Beyth (1975) replicated this finding in a more naturalistic context, in which participants rated the probability of various events occurring during Nixon's visit to the USSR in 1972. After the visit, when participants knew what had actually happened, they were asked to recall their earlier probability ratings. Again, the hindsight bias was evident: In their recall, participants overestimated their rating of events that actually happened and underestimated their rating of events that did not.

The term "hindsight bias" could actually be a mischaracterisation of this phenomenon, and it would be more accurate to say that adults have a realist bias in some circumstances. This is highlighted by the third investigation of the series reported by Fischhoff (1975). Instead of being required to judge what they would have expected as an outcome as if they had not been informed, participants were asked to rate the probabilities other people, who were ignorant of reality, would assign to the likelihood of various events. The same realist bias emerged. In other words, participants were judging that others would be inclined to expect an outcome that the participants believed to be true; seemingly, the participants' own knowledge of reality contaminated their judgements of what others would think is true.

There is at least a surface similarity between adults and children in the sense that knowledge of reality appears to contaminate judgements of belief, but do children have a broader problem than adults? It seems that children aged around 3 years also have difficulty acknowledging the difference between the way a thing looks and how it really is (Flavell et al., 1983), and this can be related statistically with their realist errors in a test of false belief. Surely adults do not confuse appearance with reality. It may come as a surprise to discover that in certain respects adults do also show confusion between appearance and reality. This was demonstrated a long time ago in classic research by Robert Thouless (1931), who reported the curious case of "phenomenal regression to the real object", as he called it. Participants viewed a disc from an oblique angle and then had to select an ellipse from a group of alternatives that they judged best matched the shape (of the disc) they could see. Participants tended to select a more circular ellipse than the image as generated by the disc from their oblique perspective. The participants knew that the thing they were looking at was actually a disc, and it seems that their knowledge of the true identity of this thing contaminated their judgements of how it appeared.

Laura Taylor and I (Taylor & Mitchell, in press) conducted a more carefully controlled study to isolate prior knowledge of reality as the source of contamination in adult's judgements of the appearance of a shape. Participants looked through a peephole into a darkened chamber and could see an ellipse in there that glowed on account of it having a coat of illuminous paint. This ellipse was actually a disc that was swivelled on its axis. Because the chamber was totally dark otherwise, there were no visual clues to suggest that the ellipse was anything other than it appeared. Participants were given the task of matching a shape presented on a computer to the elliptical shape they could see through the peephole. Pressing certain keys squashed the ellipse presented on the screen and others expanded it. Under one condition, participants knew the shape in the chamber was actually a disc, whereas under another participants had no additional information and were allowed to believe that the shape was an ellipse, as it appeared. The findings were that when participants knew the thing was really a disc, they exaggerated its circularity, whereas when they assumed it was an ellipse, their judgements of its appearance were accurate to a surprising degree. Hence, knowledge of reality contaminates judgements of appearance in adults as well as in children, with the proviso that the procedures for testing the two populations are quite different.

WEIGHING SCALES

According to Riggs, Peterson, Robinson, and Mitchell (1996), the phenomenon of difficulty with false belief can be better understood if we think in terms of people constructing, inferring, or formulating judgements of belief as and when a relevant query is presented. In the deceptive box test, where the child is asked what he or she thought was inside to begin with, Riggs et al. suggest that children (and people generally) do not search their memory for an outdated resident belief of what they used to think, but reconstruct by mentally simulating the prior episode and inferring what they would have thought in that kind of circumstance. Hence, their old prior belief does not swim around in consciousness or subconsciousness available for consultation. Once we dispense with the notion of resident albeit outdated beliefs, it then becomes appropriate to ask what kind of demands one might face in making an inference of false belief. We have to select between two apparently eligible premises in making the inference. One derives from the item that is currently in the box and the other derives from what is usually in the box, or what one saw or might have seen in there previously. In the unexpected transfer test, the two analogous premises are where the item is currently and where it used to be. It so happens that it is correct to judge that the protagonist thinks it is where it used to be because that is where the protagonist last saw it. Consequently, the child is faced with the task of selecting the correct premise in making an inference of false belief, in conjunction with limitations in the protagonist's informational access. Riggs et al. suggest that if one can subtract the premise associated with current reality, this would clear the way for a correct attribution of false belief. In other words, young children have difficulty with false belief because it is difficult for them to suppress current reality. Older children, in contrast, have become more adept at this process.

Emma Steverson and I (Steverson & Mitchell, 1995b) illustrate the kind of development that might be involved here with the aid of the weighing scales analogy. Suppose on one side of the fulcrum rests current reality and on the other rests what would be left if current reality were subtracted. To illustrate more concretely, suppose that on one side of the scales is the current reality of pencils and on the other side is the stereotypical content of the box—Smarties. If one had not seen the pencils, then by default one would think the box contained Smarties. But judging what anyone believes about the content of the box, in the present or in the past, will depend critically on the balance of the two premises. The scales may weigh more heavily toward "Smarties" if the participant enters into the equation any information indicating that the protagonist has not seen the atypical content of pencils.

So why do children have difficulty with false belief? One possibility is that they do not make sufficient use of information about the protagonist's impoverished informational access (Wimmer et al., 1988); another is that they simply do not grasp that beliefs can be false (Perner, 1991); and yet another, which I prefer, is that early in development, the scales are tipped toward current reality. Young children are able to acknowledge whether or not someone has knowledge based on informational access (e.g. Pratt & Bryant, 1990) and under some circumstances they are able to acknowledge false belief (e.g. Saltmarsh et al., 1995). What might develop with increasing age and experience is a gradual adjustment such that current reality is no longer weighted so heavily. Consequent implications are that there is no radical shift in conception, that development is gradual, and that vestiges of the realism that plague early childhood are detectable in older children and even in adulthood under certain conditions.

RESISTANCE TO REALISM AT 5 YEARS OF AGE

There is one important piece in the jigsaw that does not quite fit. Some of those who support the idea of a radical conceptual shift point to independent evidence to suggest that the 5-year-old has recently acquired a rule. This is marked by overuse of the rule in question: That seeing is equated with believing and not-seeing with not-believing. The study apposite to this was conducted by Sodian and Wimmer (1987), described in the previous chapter. In brief, they found that children aged around 5 years tended to deny that another person could know a fact even when that person had opportunity to infer the fact. The authors concluded that children based their denial on the protagonist not seeing directly. Hence, not-seeing apparently was equated with not-believing, even though in this case the belief in question could have been formed by the alternative route of inference. One way of looking at this finding is to say that perhaps 5-year-olds have just acquired a rule that is so appealing to them that they overuse it, with the implication that it is the novelty of the rule that is making it so attractive. This would be consistent with the radical shift view. Another way of looking at the finding would be to say that part of the processes of overcoming the excessive realism of early childhood involves the meticulous application of a simple rule like "seeing is equal to believing."

On the face of it, these alternatives might seem so similar that they amount to the same idea dressed in different language. However, there is a real and testable difference. If "inference neglect", as Sodian and Wimmer (1987) called it, marks the advent of a representational theory of mind, and realism is just a default consequence of lacking such a theory of mind, then there would be no such thing as realism as a substantive phenomenon beyond the age of about 5 years. Elizabeth Robinson and I, along with our colleagues, set out to investigate the existence of developmentally late realist judgement in the context of belief (Mitchell, Robinson, Isaacs, & Nye, 1996).

Borrowing a procedure devised by Perner and Wimmer (1985), developed for entirely different purposes, we told children aged 5 and 8 years and adults the following story. Susan was in the park and saw the ice cream van there. Subsequently she went home. Unknown to her, the van then moved to the church. Susan's friend John saw the van by the church and then rendezvoused with Susan at home. He reported to her that the ice cream van was by the church. At this point, Susan has two contradictory inputs, that she saw the van in the park, but that she is told that it is by the church. Observing participants were then given the task of judging what Susan would believe about the ice cream van's whereabouts. In this particular version of the story, it so happens that John's message was true whereas Susan's existing belief, based on what she saw, had become false. Under another condition the story was contrived so that her belief remained true and John's message was false. The children were strongly inclined to judge that Susan would believe the van was wherever she saw it, irrespective of whether that was known by the observing participant to be true or false. This finding replicated a result reported by Perner and Davies (1991). It is consistent with the children applying the simple rule that people believe what they see—and maybe overapply that rule, since in real life people might update their existing beliefs in the face of a contradicting message.

In contrast to the children, the adults we tested sometimes judged that Susan would believe what she was told. Their judgements in this respect were highly systematic. The adults often judged that Susan would believe John's message if they (the observing adults) knew it was true. Conversely, if they knew the message was false, they tended to judge that Susan would retain her prior belief based on what she saw and disregard John's contradicting message. In other words, the adult participants' privileged knowledge of reality contaminated their judgements of what Susan would believe. In this respect, our adult participants exhibited a tendency similar to that reported by Fischhoff (1975), which he called a hindsight bias. What is novel here is that the children tested showed no such bias, suggesting that their concentration on the seeing–believing rule suppressed the realist bias that is so prevalent in both younger children and in adults.

It would be very strange to think that people make a retrograde step as far as realism is concerned as they approach adulthood. More likely, people (children and adults) are seduced by what they know or assume of current reality, but perhaps during middle childhood children are better at resisting the seduction due to overapplication of a rule like seeing=believing. However, heavy reliance upon that rule evidently leads children into difficulties. For one thing, they deny that people know things when in fact they could have inferred them (Sodian & Wimmer, 1987). For another, they apparently underestimate people's willingness to be informed by messages. Hence, applying a seeing= believing rule does not mean the child has acquired a rule-based representational theory of mind. What it does mean, perhaps, is that the child has acquired a strategy that helps to overcome the excessive realism characteristic of early childhood.

WHAT THE REALITY MASKING HYPOTHESIS IS NOT

The reality masking hypothesis is not to be confused with Fodor's (1992) account of children's heuristics in solving the problem of false belief. Fodor posits two hypotheses that a person might use in making judgements of belief:

H1   Predict that the agent will act in a way that will satisfy his desires.
H2   Predict that the agent will act in a way that would satisfy his desires if his beliefs were true.

Fodor suggests that H1 would be used by default. Since beliefs are usually true anyway, applying H1 would result in a correct prediction of where a protagonist would search in nearly all circumstances. He further claims that H2 is available to young children, but because its implementation makes heavier demands on processing resources than H1, the triggering of H2 has a higher threshold in younger than in older children.

Fodor goes on to suggest conditions under which even a young child might apply H2. He suggests that if application of H1 did not afford a unique prediction, then the child would be stimulated into working out which of the potential predictions are correct. He points out that in an unexpected transfer test, if the bait is moved from the initial location (A) and distributed between two new locations (B and C), then H1 can no longer afford a unique prediction—searching in either B or C would satisfy the protagonist's desire, so to determine where the protagonist will look, the child must consult what he or she knows of the protagonist's belief (and hence apply H2). Consequently, the child is likely to judge correctly that the protagonist will search where he or she last saw it, which is location A. Similarly, Fodor predicts for the same reasons that if the bait were annihilated after the protagonist had seen it initially at A, the child participant will successfully predict search at A. In both these cases, a unique prediction of search cannot be made from knowledge of the protagonist's desire alone, which should promote application of H2 along with ensuing correct judgements of false belief.

There is a fundamental problem in principle with Fodor's (1992) account. He focuses exclusively on the unexpected transfer test, in which children's ability to acknowledge false belief is gauged by their prediction of the protagonist's search. However, as should be abundantly clear from this and the previous chapter, children also have a problem with false belief if asked directly where the protagonist thinks the bait is (rather than where he will look) in an unexpected transfer test and also in a deceptive box task. Realist errors are apparent in the latter whether children are asked about their own or another person's false belief. It is particularly difficult to imagine how Fodor's H1 and H2 could account for children's errors in acknowledging their own prior false belief in a deceptive box task. Children are not asked to predict action in this and their desire does not seem to be a relevant factor. At best, Fodor's account only describes a fraction of the data.

Even in relation to prediction versions of the unexpected transfer test, it seems Fodor's (1992) account does not hold water. As mentioned earlier, he predicted that so long as the child cannot make a unique prediction of a protagonist's search from H1, then correct judgements of false belief should follow. However, Wimmer and Weichbold (1994) conducted the test suggested by Fodor, in which the bait was distributed between locations B and C. Children were no better at judging that the protagonist would search at A under this condition compared with a standard unexpected transfer test involving only locations A and B. German (1995) replicated this procedure and obtained the same result. German reports that whereas in a standard procedure, young children tend to predict that the protagonist will search at B, under the split bait version their realist predictions were distributed evenly between locations B and C, with correct predictions of search at A remaining uncommon.

Although that finding runs counter to Fodor's (1992) expectation, it is perfectly consistent with the reality masking hypothesis. The hypothesis predicts that current reality will grab the child's attention and accordingly lead to realist errors. The fact that in Fodor's novel procedure there are two current realities (bait in B and C) makes no difference (or we might have expected even more realist errors). Fodor's novel procedure does nothing to reduce the salience of current reality. However, the reality masking hypothesis predicts that his other suggested procedure would yield facilitation. This is where the bait is annihilated after it moves from location A. In fact, such a procedure has been around for a long time and even formed part of the series comprising Wimmer and Perner's (1983) seminal investigation. In this, after Maxi left the kitchen, his chocolate was removed from the scene altogether. German (1995) did a replication in which the experimenter ate the chocolate to ensure that it no longer existed! In these studies, children were more likely to judge correctly that Maxi would search at A compared with a standard test.

One objection to the facilitation in children's correct judgements in the vanishing bait test is that perhaps children are hard-pushed to judge search at anywhere other than A since A is the only location associated with the bait. However, German (1995) neatly dealt with this problem by having the bait transfer to an intermediate location before vanishing altogether. Children still made correct judgements. These findings are precisely as predicted by the reality masking hypothesis because the annihilation of the bait effectively eliminates the attentional bias to current reality. The reality masking hypothesis offers a more comprehensive and plausible explanation of the results than does Fodor's H1–H2 account.

CONCLUSION

Perhaps a legacy of the Piagetian constructivist stage-model of development has been an over-readiness to accept the idea of stages of development of an understanding of mind. Researchers have employed tests that allow either a right or wrong answer with no degrees of correctness in between. The results of this, coupled with a prevailing conceptual set to the effect that development is stage-like, might have been sufficient to fool researchers into thinking that children experience a radical conceptual shift akin to a paradigm shift in the progression of natural science. In this chapter, I have introduced an alternative account of the data in the form of the reality masking hypothesis. The hypothesis posits that an understanding of the representational mind can exist in some form prior to the child's success in a standard test of false belief. It posits that development is gradual, and is in the form of a diminution of a realist bias that is prominent in early childhood, but one that never fades altogether. I suggest that extant data are largely consistent with this hypothesis, but do not always support the conceptual shift theory theory. Indeed, some data seem inconsistent with that.

What I have not yet done is to integrate the data from children's early communication and other symbolic activities. Neither have I said much about the factors that might play an important part in allowing the child to progress from having a limited understanding of mind to having a comprehensive one. The reality masking hypothesis is about a constraining factor in understanding mind, and it does not tell us positively what the child does know about mind with increasing age, and how this knowledge is acquired. This is the province of the final two chapters, which seek to shed light on such processes by looking at what happens when development goes wrong: The case of autism.

CHAPTER NINE

Psychopathology and the development of an understanding of mind

We have an understanding of mind and we take that for granted. For that reason it is very difficult to imagine what it would be like not to have such understanding. If we met someone who lacked an understanding of mind, how would we know—what would be the clues? At least on a surface level, we might expect abnormalities in socialisation, since it would be hard for the individual to make a "connection" with others. The individual might show indifference to others' interests, feelings, beliefs, hopes, and so on; if the individual was ignorant of these psychological states, then he or she would show little curiosity in them.

An individual who lacked understanding of mind would also be very poor at communication. This would follow for at least two reasons. First, as noted in previous chapters, distilling the speaker's intended meaning from his or her message requires a synthesis of the literal meaning of the utterance with the speaker's belief framework. In other words, we treat utterances as if they were referentially opaque, as referring not directly to reality but as referring to reality via the speaker's distinctive belief framework. Second, an individual who lacked a conception of knowledge or ignorance is unlikely to appreciate the informational benefits of listening to messages uttered by other people, and consequently would not show much interest in listening to what others have to say. At best, we might regard utterances as interesting input when they impinge upon us, but we would certainly not seek out communications in others with the aim of becoming better informed.

An individual who lacked an understanding of mind would probably (but not necessarily) display impoverished imaginative abilities. A manifestation of imagination in young children is their pretend play. In pretence, children substitute the identity of one object for another. Leslie (1987) gives the classic example of a child pretending that a banana is a telephone. According to Leslie, such object substitution, which we could regard as a defining feature of pretence, implies that the child has a working understanding of referential opacity, and hence the basis for understanding the representational character of mind. If an individual lacked this working understanding of mind, then there would be little sign of pretence or related symbolic and imaginative activities. Apart from this, a lack of aptitude for pretence could pose an obstacle to imagining (simulating via pretence) another person's mental states. If one lacked an understanding of mind, it would not be surprising if this could be traced back, at least partly, to deficiencies in the capacity to simulate through imagination.

In sum, I have suggested that anyone who lacked an understanding of mind would show impairments in socialisation, communication, and imagination. Those three capacities were not ones I plucked out of the air but actually form Wing's (Wing & Gould, 1979) *triad of impairments in autism*. In other words, if we wish to know what an individual would be like who lacked an understanding of mind, then perhaps we need look no further than those unfortunate individuals who have autism, individuals whom Wing identifies according to the triad of impairments listed here.

The triad of impairments suggested by Wing and Gould (1979) is reflected in the checklist that a clinical practitioner will consult when diagnosing autism. The current version of the standard checklist is known as DSM IV, published by the American Psychological Association. Items on this include such things as "Pervasive lack of responsiveness to other people". The list places special emphasis in impairments in language and communication with "Gross deficits in language development" and "If speech is present, peculiar speech patterns such as immediate and delayed echolalia and pronoun reversal" and "Abnormalities of speech, such as question-like melody or monotone robotic-like voice". Further items include "... inability to be consoled when upset ..." and "... lack of appropriate fear reactions ...". The clinician is guided to be on alert for an inability to form friendships with other children, absence of pretend play, and lack of imitation of adults. The checklist also mentions aspects of behaviour that are not obviously linked with a lack of understanding mind: "Bizarre responses to various aspects of the environment (e.g. resistance to change ...)". To differentiate between autism and other disorders like schizophrenia, the checklist insists that there should be an "Absence of delusions, hallucinations, loosening of associations and incoherence".

Wing and Gould's (1979) identification of the triad of impairments is entirely compatible with a "theory of mind hypothesis of autism", which was actually articulated explicitly by Baron-Cohen et al. (1985). They prepared a variant of the unexpected transfer test of false belief in which Sally put a marble in her basket and then left the scene. In her absence, Ann transferred the marble to a box. Sally returned to get her marble, and observing children were asked where she would look for it. A substantial majority of children with autism, diagnosed according to standard criteria, judged that Sally would look not in the place where she last saw it (her basket) but where it currently was (the box). In this respect, the pattern of judging in the children with autism was indistinguishable from that in the clinically normal children aged below 4 years. Does that mean autism amounts to a lack of a conception of false belief? Before considering such a possibility, we need to eliminate some theoretically uninteresting explanations for poor performance in autism.

Children with autism tend to have learning difficulties, often resulting in a verbal mental age well below their chronological age. How can we be sure that learning difficulties were not responsible for the poor performance of the children with autism, rather than lack of understanding of mind? If the children with autism had a verbal mental age below 4 years, their poor performance on a test of false belief is to be expected. Their limitation would then be attributed generally to their intellectual immaturity, rather than specifically to their autism. Baron-Cohen et al. (1985) eliminated this obstacle to interpretation by selecting high-functioning children with autism, specifically those who had a verbal mental age above 4 years. Many of these children were adolescents according to their chronological age. It was not possible to explain the poor performance on a test of false belief in these teenagers by appealing to their intellectual immaturity.

Even so, it could still be that children with autism perform badly on a test of false belief because of their general learning difficulties rather than because of their autism. To investigate this possibility, Baron-Cohen et al. (1985) included a control group of children with Down syndrome. The average mental and chronological age of these children was less than that of the sample with autism. These children generally had no difficulty with the test of false belief, and predicted correctly that Sally would search in her basket, where she had left her marble. This finding allowed Baron-Cohen et al. to conclude that children with autism have a difficulty with false belief that is not easily explained by reference to their immaturity or their learning difficulties. On the other hand, the findings were consistent with children with autism specifically lacking an understanding of mind, as diagnosed by their inability to acknowledge false belief.

Even so, there was still an obvious impediment to clear interpretation. If children with autism are impoverished in their imaginative abilities, then it makes no sense to diagnose their lack of an understanding of mind with a test that requires them to engage in make-believe. More fundamentally, why should anybody ascribe any kind of belief to a doll (Sally)? These were concerns raised by deGelder (1987). Essentially, the point is that failure on a test that requires imaginative abilities because it involves imaginary characters (Sally and Ann) does not tell us anything in addition to what we already know: Namely, children with autism are lacking in imaginative abilities.

To deal with this problem, Leslie and Frith (1988) captured the unexpected transfer procedure in a real-life interaction that the child was involved in directly. Frith deposited a penny under cup A and then left the scene. In her absence, the child assisted Leslie to move the coin to cup B. Frith returned, and the child was asked to predict where Frith would look for her penny. Children with autism still made a realist error by judging that she would search under cup B, where it currently was. Clinically normal children aged 3 years tended to make the same error but older normal children correctly judged that Frith would look under cup A, where Frith last saw it. Perner, Frith, Leslie, and Leekam (1989) simply presented a deceptive box test to children with autism and obtained much the same result. Perner et al. also found that children with autism have difficulty reporting their own prior false beliefs. It seems that children with autism do have a specific problem with false belief, one that is apparent in their real-life interactions as well as in their judgements about abstract make-believe situations.

ARE CHILDREN WITH AUTISM TRAPPED IN A PRE-CONCEPTION-OF-MIND STAGE?

If we assumed that children's understanding of mind progresses through stages of development, where a new stage supplants an old one following a conceptual shift, then superficially it would be tempting to suppose that children with autism are trapped in a pre-false-belief stage. It would be conceivable that children with autism are like normal 3-year-olds where their lack of understanding of mind is concerned, and that they remain that way. However, there is convincing evidence to suggest that the autistic understanding of mind (or lack of it) is not just a replica of the intellectual profile of the 3-year-old in this domain. Importantly, there is reason to believe that the limitations of many children with autism are more severe than those of 3-year-olds, even more so than would be predicted from their impoverished verbal abilities considered in isolation.

Clinically normal children begin to engage in pretence at about 18 months of age. According to Leslie (1987, 1994), this shows that they have an emerging capacity for referential opacity, without which pretence would be impossible. He goes on to say that referential opacity stands at the heart of an understanding of mind. Hence, according to Leslie, there is evidence that normal children have a rudimentary understanding of mind prior to their passing a standard test of false belief; acknowledging false belief cannot be a sign that the child has negotiated a radical conceptual shift in this domain.

Suppose we begin with the premise that children with autism lack an understanding of mind, however that is defined. If it turned out that children with autism did habitually engage in pretence, but fail a test of false belief, then this would go some way toward vindicating the test of false belief as a sign of possessing a theory of mind, one that is preferable to pretence. It so happens, however, that children with autism seldom or never engage in pretence spontaneously (Baron-Cohen, 1987), though in some cases they can be persuaded to pretend (Boucher, 1989; Jarrold, Boucher, & Smith, 1994; Jarrold, Smith, Boucher, & Harris, 1994b). A child with autism would not talk into a banana as though it were a telephone. Hence, according to Leslie, the lack of understanding of mind in autism is apparent in symbolic deficiencies signified by the paucity of pretence. These symbolic processes are more fundamental than processes required for success on a standard test of false belief because their advent developmentally predates success in acknowledging false belief. It follows that failing a standard test of false belief need not imply (though it might) that the individual has a deficient understanding of mind. In sum autism can serve as an assay for determining the criterion of what does and does not qualify as an understanding of mind.

Using a standard test of false belief is too stringent a criterion for assessing whether or not an individual is lacking an understanding of mind; arguably, an understanding of mind reduces to a process that is more fundamental than is required for acknowledging false belief (e.g. pretence). Acknowledging false belief may require additional competencies. By analogy, to use a standard test of false belief as a litmus test for understanding of mind is like using a test of membership for Mensa to assess whether someone has learning difficulties. Most people who fail the Mensa test are not intellectually impaired; perhaps many who fail a test of false belief (clinically normal children but not children with autism) have an understanding of mind, though one that is not as refined or effective as that of someone who passes a test of false belief. Perhaps, after all, pretence is a sign of a primitive capacity to handle referential opacity, and perhaps referential opacity both stands at the core of an understanding of mind and is an ability that is specifically impaired in autism. Accordingly, it makes no sense to say that as far as the intellect for an understanding of mind is concerned, children with autism are just like large 3-year-olds. Many children with autism at the very least have a more severe problem, and may even be unlike a normal child at any point in development.

The case would be strengthened if we could offer independent evidence in support of the claim that children with autism have a more severe problem than 3-year-olds. In any case, their limitation in pretence is something we have known about for a long time, ever since Wing included "impoverished imaginative abilities" in her triad of autistic impairments. Independent evidence was reported by Baron-Cohen (1989a). He used a procedure devised by Wellman and Estes (1986), described in Chapter 3, to assess whether children understand the distinction between things and thoughts. In particular, Wellman and Estes asked if young children understood that thoughts are intangible and unavailable to be touched or physically manipulated. They report that some children aged 2 years and many aged 3 years have no difficulty in understanding that thoughts of things, unlike real things, lack any physical existence. Baron-Cohen set out to check the same in children with autism. He showed them a picture of Sam and a picture of Kate. He told them that both were hungry. For this reason, Sam's mother gave him a biscuit, while for the same reason Kate was thinking about a biscuit. Baron-Cohen asked the children who could touch the biscuit, who could eat it, and who could give it to a another person. Children with autism were entirely unsystematic in their judgements, and were just as likely to say that Kate could eat the biscuit as they were to say that Sam could eat it. Basically, they responded as though they had no idea of what the experimenter meant when he talked of Kate thinking about a biscuit. In contrast, children with Down syndrome, who formed a control group, judged that only Sam could eat the biscuit, touch it, or give it to someone else. They performed much better than the children with autism, even though they were younger chronologically, and less intellectually advanced according to tests of verbal maturity. Looking at these findings in comparison with those of Wellman and Estes, we can say that normal 2- and 3-year-olds know something about thoughts that children with autism apparently do not know. Many children with autism have such a severe deficiency in their understanding of mind that they compare unfavourably with 2–3-year-olds.

One function of the brain as an organ is to provide its owner with a mind. Is the lack of understanding mind in autism so severe that afflicted children are ignorant of all the brain's activities? This was something else Baron-Cohen (1989a) investigated, this time borrowing a procedure devised by Johnson and Wellman (1982). Johnson and Wellman report that children aged around 5 years acknowledge that the brain is involved in things like thinking, but many deny that the brain plays any part in such activities as walking, seeing, or talking. For example, if asked about the brain's role in speech, children tend to claim that it is the mouth that does the talking and not the brain. They make similar claims about the eyes in relation to seeing and the legs in relation to walking. What about children with autism? Would they deny that the brain is involved in anything? Indeed, would they even deny the very existence of the brain as a bodily organ?

The results Baron-Cohen (1989a) reports are intriguing. He asked normal 5-year-olds, children with Down syndrome, and children with autism about the locations and functions of the heart and the brain. Most members of all three populations correctly identified the locations of these organs and all three were also usually correct in stating that the heart pumps blood round the body, or words to that effect. Only in relation to the functions of the brain were population differences apparent. As reported by Johnson and Wellman, 5-year-olds seldom acknowledged the brain's role in talking and walking. The same was true of children with Down syndrome. In sharp contrast, more than 70% of children with autism judged that the brain makes you walk and makes you talk, which might be because they were older and therefore better informed than the other children. On the other hand, over 80% of 5-year-olds and nearly 70% of children with Down syndrome judged that the brain makes you think. Meanwhile, fewer than a quarter of the children with autism judged that the brain makes you think. In sum, the children with autism exhibited a curious mixture of knowledge and ignorance about the functions of the brain. They knew its location and they recognised its role in behaviour, even more so than the other two groups interviewed. In contrast, and as expected, they seemed to have little idea of the brain's role in thinking, which is not surprising if they lack understanding of what thinking is. It is tempting to suggest (as Baron-Cohen did) that children with autism are behaviourists. They acknowledge the role of the brain in behaviour, but deny the existence of thoughts and do not acknowledge their role in governing actions. The pattern of their judgements across various questions gives rise to a profile of their understanding of the brain that seems unlike anything we see in normal development. Children with autism are not just trapped in an early stage of development. Advances in their understanding can occur but apparently only with respect to particular activities of the brain. It is tempting to say that they come to understand something about the brain but virtually nothing about the mind.

The evidence presented so far in this section is consistent with the claims made in the previous two chapters, that failing a test of false belief does not necessarily imply that the individual lacks understanding of mind. Accordingly, we would only want to deny that the individual lacked understanding of mind if he or she exhibited a more severe deficit. The other side of the coin, argued in the previous chapter, is that being able to pass a standard test of false belief does not necessarily imply that the individual has a fully developed understanding of mind. Children we tested aged 5 and 9 years were inclined to judge beliefs according to a simple rule to the effect that people believe what they see, and give this source of information priority over other sources such as hearing a message. Adults, in contrast, were more flexible, but showed a realist bias in some cases (Mitchell et al., 1966). What about autism? Can anyone with autism pass a test of false belief? If so, do they have (or have they acquired) an understanding of mind akin to that of a clinically normal person? Effectively, would their autism be cured?

Baron-Cohen (1989b) identified a subgroup of teenagers with autism who passed a standard test of false belief. Such children tend to have higher scores on tests of intelligence compared with those who fail tests of false belief (Eisenmajer & Prior, 1991). Happe (1995) also points out that there appears to be a relation between chronological age and passing a test of false belief in autism. Hence, younger people with autism who fail a test of false belief are not necessarily destined to fail such a test always. Does that mean that children with autism can acquire an understanding of mind, even if somewhat belatedly? A more stringent criterion relating to the development of understanding mind is the test of understanding second-order belief. Perner and Wimmer (1985) define this as an ability to represent a person's thought about another person's thought. They report that this is something normal children begin to grasp at about the age of 7 years. Baron-Cohen found that although his teenagers with autism were capable of passing a standard test of false belief, they failed a test of second-order belief attribution, suggesting a vestigial impairment that prevented understanding of higher-order representations. However, Bowler (1992) tested a group of high functioning young adults with autism on a second-order test of belief attribution and reports that the majority gave a correct judgement. Indeed, they were no different from a group of people with chronic schizophrenia matched according to IQ, and neither were they significantly different from normal controls.

Baron-Cohen (1989b) argued that autism engenders developmental delay in the acquisition of an understanding of mind, rather than a blanket impediment. He suggests that such a delay might interfere with normal developmental processes, resulting in the social impairments that are typical of autism. Nonetheless, Bowler (1992) correctly points out that the ability to acknowledge beliefs and even the ability to acknowledge higher-order beliefs does not protect the individual from social impairment. If it did, then when people with autism succeeded on such tasks, there would be an accompanying radical improvement in their social competence; but no such relation is apparent. At least the people with autism that Bowler studied continued to show social impairments, even if not as severe as those more heavily afflicted with autism. Sadly, the autism any individual suffers might never be defeated—though development and adaptation can occur. In sum, being able to pass a test of false belief, even involving higher-order belief, is not sufficient to make social impairments vanish in autism.

Data from autism do not instil much confidence in the standard test of false belief as a measure of a working understanding of mind. Children with autism who fail tests of false belief also tend to fail tests that we might regard as probing understanding of mind on a more primitive level. On the other hand, those who pass continue to show signs (in terms of impaired social interaction) of an impoverished understanding of mind. Perhaps being able to pass a test of false belief is neither necessary nor sufficient for possessing an understanding of mind. Using autism as an assay, these comparative data offer no support for the conceptual shift account of normal development that places monumental emphasis on being able to acknowledge false belief.

IS AUTISM MORE THAN A DEFICIENCY IN UNDERSTANDING MIND?

Frith (1989) suggests that the cognitive underpinnings of autism amount to a severe inability to mentally assemble phenomena into a coherent (theoretical?) whole. Normal people seem unable to refrain from imposing coherent meaning on events. An example is the gamblers' fallacy. If I had an unbiased coin, then heads would be on top on about half the occasions I flipped it. The probability of heads being on top on any one flip is 0.5. It remains 0.5 whatever the sequence of results that occurred previously (providing the coin is unbiased). Contrary to this simple statistical fact, the gamblers' fallacy is that if, for example, a sequence of five tails has just occurred, then there is increased probability that the next flip will give heads. Actually, that is not so, and the probability of heads remains 0.5. This fallacy is not confined to gamblers but is something that people commonly assume to be the case. Presumably, people conceptualise in the following way. They assume that if we flip the coin 10 times, then the most likely outcome (though one that is by no means inevitable) is 5 heads and 5 tails. Therefore, if the first five flips yield only tails, then Nature had better get to work in redressing the balance so that there is ultimately a symmetry between heads and tails. Consequently, the next five flips are likely to yield lots of heads. Yet however much sense we try to impose on the pattern of heads and tails, in fact the probability of heads on any given trial is 0.5, so long as the coin is unbiased.

The example of the gamblers' fallacy suggests that we are disposed to perceive connections between events that are actually independent. It seems that we are biased to find order even in the default random state that is likely to give rise to as many heads as tails. Ancient people went a step further and perceived not only order but also purpose in natural events, such as the vagaries of the weather, by supposing that they were the product of the will of a mysterious higher form of spiritual being. For example, they thought that thunder was God expressing his wrath at some misdemeanour that these hapless people were guilty of, and derived the implication that they should spend time in spiritual meditation to contemplate what this moral weakness might be. Normal people seem destined to link events and perceive causes when in fact this would be unwarranted. Apart from these examples, one need only consider the whole spectrum of psychological theories that are published, many founded on flimsy data, to appreciate that this is so! People with autism, it seems, are not predisposed to perceive coherent patterns in the world and fail to hypothesise about general and unifying underlying causes, and therefore do not assign a role to another entity's will, intention, and beliefs. This cognitive deficiency would give rise to an inability, or at least a difficulty, in making judgements about others' minds.

We are thus venturing into the territory of autistic intellectual difficulties that extend beyond the domain of understanding mind. Indeed, Kanner (1943) noted that children with autism show stereotypical behaviour and resistance to change in routine. It is not obvious how these characteristics relate to a failure to understand mind. Having a rigidity of thought raises the possibility that children with autism are suffering an "executive dysfunction". Ozonoff, Pennington, and Rogers (1991, p.1083) define executive function as:

> The ability to maintain an appropriate problem-solving set for the attainment of a future goal; it includes behaviours such as planning, impulse control, inhibition of prepotent but irrelevant responses, set maintenance, organised search, and flexibility of thought and action.

They note that, apart from the triad of impairments, people with autism are perseverative in focusing on one narrow interest to the exclusion of others and repetitively engage in stereotyped behaviours. Apparently, they are not future orientated and seem to fail to anticipate the long-term consequences of their actions. They seem impulsive, stimulus driven, and generally unable to inhibit inappropriate responses. These peculiarities could come under the heading of "executive function deficits".

Ozonoff et al. (1991) proceeded to test children and adolescents with autism on a couple of executive function tasks. Their participants were high functioning people, with verbal and spatial intelligence falling within the normal range. The two tests were the Tower of Hanoi problem and the Wisconsin Card Sort Test (WCST). In the Tower of Hanoi problem, the participant has to shift a tower of three loops of differing diameter from one peg to another. The largest loop is at the bottom and the smallest is at the top. The participant has to shift the loops one-by-one and is able to make use of a third peg in the process. A critical rule constraining the method of transfer is that a large loop must never be placed on top of a small one. In tackling this problem, participants have to inhibit a prepotent response, which is simply to move the loops one by one directly to the target peg (in which case the smallest would be at the bottom). To avoid this tendency, it seems the participant has to work out in imagination a sequence of steps to obtain the objective whilst avoiding violating the rules.

In the WCST, the participant is issued with a pile of cards that differ according to colour and shape and perhaps other dimensions. In a simple version of the test, there would be two target piles, each identified by an example card: For instance, a green square in one and a blue circle in the other. Participants aim to distribute their cards into the two target piles according to an unspoken principle held by the experimenter. To illustrate, let us suppose the principle is squareness, so all the squares go in the square pile, irrespective of colour, and all other shapes go in the non-square pile (headed by a circle). The participants can only discover the experimenter's selecting principle from his or her corrective feedback, stating whether each card is placed in the correct or incorrect pile. This phase of the task is quite easy for participants, including those with autism. However, it might pose a difficulty for people with autism if halfway through the task the experimenter shifts the selecting principle to colour (e.g. greenness) instead of shape. Clinically normal people are able to inhibit a prepotent response to select according to a principle that was previously successful and have the mental flexibility to identify the new principle. Perhaps people with autism would persevere with the old principle even in the face of negative feedback from the experimenter. This is what would happen if they had deficient executive control.

Ozonoff et al. (1991) found that the children and adolescents with autism they tested tended to have serious difficulty with both executive function tasks. Specifically, they tended to execute and persevere with prepotent responses. Members of a closely matched control group, composed of people with similar intellectual abilities but without autism, had no such difficulty with these executive function tasks. As expected, the people with autism also had difficulty with tests of false belief and appearance–reality. Importantly, there was a substantial and significant correlation between performance on the two kinds of test. Those who performed especially badly on the executive function tests also tended to perform badly on the tests intended to probe understanding of mind. Those who tended to perform well on one task also tended to perform well on the other. Does this finding entitle us to conclude that having a poor understanding of mind is an inevitable by-product of having a deficient executive function?

THE RELATION BETWEEN LACK OF UNDERSTANDING MIND AND EXECUTIVE DYSFUNCTION

Frith (1989) did not say in so many words that people with autism have impaired executive functions, but she did suggest that they lack the ability to link items of information into a coherent whole—which could amount to virtually the same thing. She also suggested that an inability to perceive coherence and lacking an understanding of mind were theoretically inseparable. Russell et al. (1991) stated the link between executive function deficits and impaired understanding of mind more strongly. According to these authors, failure to acknowledge false belief in children with autism is not due primarily to lack of an understanding of mind, but is a corollary of having impaired executive functions. They made this claim in relation to the results of their "windows task". This is described in Chapter 4, but here is a reminder. The participant is confronted with two boxes with windows. One contains a reward and the other does not. To get the reward, the participant has to point to the empty box, not the baited one.

Russell et al. (1991) found that most of the children with autism they tested persevered in pointing to the baited box over a succession of 20 trials, despite repeated frustration at not getting the reward. They argued that to gesture imperatively to the baited box is a prepotent response the children with autism were unable to inhibit. Russell et al. concluded that no amount of feedback or experience would allow the children to override this error because their primary problem is an inability to inhibit a prepotent response rather than to discover the principle of the task. In sum, they argued that children with autism were unable to disengage from the object of their attention, which incidentally would inevitably lead to errors in a test of false belief. The object of attention in an unexpected transfer test is the chocolate (or whatever the target happens to be), and in the deceptive box task it is the current content of the box. Acknowledging false belief requires the participant to disengage from this, something that children with autism apparently find very difficult. Accordingly, Russell et al. argue that we are not entitled to claim much or anything about children's deficient understanding of mind on the basis of their failure on a test of false belief, but only that they have a primary deficit in their executive function.

However, more recent evidence casts doubt on the existence of such a strong relation between executive dysfunction and impairments in understanding mind. The most damaging evidence comes from the results of Zaitchik's (1990) "false photo test". Zaitchik had an insightful hunch that young children's difficulty on the unexpected transfer test was not primarily due to a deficient understanding of mind. She set about devising a test that placed similar cognitive demands on the participant, but without asking them to ascribe beliefs. She did so by putting a model in location 1 and then took a photo of the scene. The undeveloped film issued from the front of her instant camera, but in the few remaining seconds before the image emerged from the murky chemicals, she moved the model to location 2. She asked observing children to predict where the model would be in the developing photo, and children aged around 3 years typically judged that it would be where it currently was rather than where it was at the time the film was exposed. It seems children were unable to divert attention away from current reality, preventing their reporting the first location of the model. This result, incidentally, is consistent with the reality masking hypothesis, which is also loosely consistent with Russell et al.'s (1991) account of difficulty on the windows task experienced by 3-year-olds and children with autism.

Zaitchik did not test children with autism, but subsequent researchers did, either using her original procedure or adaptations of it (Charman & Baron-Cohen, 1992; Leekam & Perner, 1991; Leslie & Thaiss, 1992). The results of these studies were both entirely consistent with each other and intriguing. Children with autism had little difficulty giving a correct judgement on the false photo test, by indicating the model's previous location, yet failed a test of false belief as usual. In contrast, 3-year-olds tended to fail both tests. If the false photo results allow us to conclude that normal children have a more general difficulty than deficient understanding of mind, which could be characterised as a reality bias or executive dysfunction, then we would have to concede that children with autism apparently do not have such a severe executive function deficit: They passed the false photo test, which presumably required them to inhibit a prepotent response to report or gesture to current reality (Happe, 1994). The children with autism were able to inhibit a prepotent response in one context but not another, suggesting that the mentalistic aspect of the test of false belief was the source of their difficulty.

A finding that makes a similar point was reported by Sodian and Frith (1992). They found that children with autism had considerable difficulty telling a lie to a competitor, the lie being that a baited box was locked (when in fact it was unlocked). However, under another condition they had no difficulty in actually locking the box to deprive the competitor of the reward. These two conditions placed the same demands in terms of the child's attention to a specific location and the box's coveted content. The only difference was that to succeed on one of the tasks, the participant required an understanding that misinformation has the power to implant a false belief in the recipient. In sum, the pattern of performance across tasks can be explained by invoking deficiency in understanding mind but not by invoking executive dysfunction.

Apart from these findings, Ozonoff et al. (1991) point out that deficits in executive function can be caused in adulthood by lesions to certain areas of the brain's frontal lobes without giving rise to autism. It is true that sometimes such lesions can produce deficiencies in social cognition and associated social incompetence. In particular, afflicted people can find it difficult to relate to others and show a lack of sensitivity to social conventions with accompanying impairments in pragmatic skills. However, these people quite patently have not become autistic and certainly would not meet the criteria for diagnosis of autism. Hence, autism is not an inevitable consequence of deficient executive function.

It might be that aberrations in the frontal lobes give rise to an abnormal course of development that is manifest as autism. That is, the difficulties on executive function tasks experienced by brain-damaged adults and the difficulties on these tasks encountered by people with autism may arise from the same underlying organic abnormality. However, the developmental consequences of such an abnormality might additionally give rise to the more general symptoms of autism. It might be that executive dysfunction at a crucial period in childhood could stand as an impediment to the acquisition of an understanding of mind or at least could produce deviations in this respect. Unfortunately, this appealing suggestion is actually implausible. Welsh, Pennington, Ozonoff, Rouse, and McCabe (1990) tested children with phenylketonuria (PKU), who had a strict diet free of phenylalanine from an early age. These children had normal IQ, which was testament to the parents' rigorous observation of dietary requirements. Nonetheless, the children showed considerable difficulty on the kinds of executive function tests Ozonoff et al. (1991) gave to children with autism. Sadly, it seems that the clinical condition of these children had led to subtle impairments in intellectual abilities. However, these children were not autistic according to the standard criteria of diagnosis. Hence, even within this developmental context, the intellectual profile that gives rise to executive function deficits, along with the accompanying neuropsychological classification, need not give rise to autism. In other words, the abnormality in the frontal lobes that gives rise to executive dysfunction does not necessarily cause autism either in adults or in children. Having said that, children with PKU are at risk of having autism. About a fifth of children with PKU not placed on a diet free of phenylalanine are diagnosed as being autistic (Reiss, Feinstein, & Rosenbaum, 1986).

Together, the findings suggest that there are at least two distinct cognitive impairments underlying autism. One is an impaired understanding of mind and the other is impaired executive function. These two deficiencies do not boil down to the same thing, but they might stem from a single dysfunction. If a person with autism lacked imaginative abilities and as a consequence tended to be locked into the present with the accompanying conceptual inflexibility, then as a consequence we would expect that person to have a deficient understanding of mind and to have a deficient executive function. Both could contribute to impairments in social interaction and interpersonal relatedness. These are different processes, but their existence might rely on a single underlying cognitive competence, namely a capacity for generating and manipulating hypothetical scenarios or configurations, which essentially relies upon a capacity for imagination. An incapacity in this respect might give rise both to a lack of understanding mind and executive dysfunction, but alternatively it might just be expressed as deficiency in executive function only. This view is entirely consistent with Wing's (1988) original formulation of autism and it is also consistent with Leslie's (1987) insight that a lack of pretence (as a manifestation of imagination) in autism is a sign that the child has a fundamental impediment to the possession of an understanding of mind.

IS AUTISM PRIMARILY A DISORDER IN THE COGNITIVE DOMAIN?

The account presented so far depicts autism as a cognitive dysfunction. However, Hobson (1993) argues vehemently that autism actually amounts to an inability to make an affective connection with others, concerning the sharing of experiences. He suggests that people with autism lack a sense of intersubjectivity, which can be defined as an awareness of multiple perspectives especially in the emotional domain. A consequence of this is an inability to perceive affective attitudes, which leads to difficulty in conceiving of others' minds (Hobson, 1990, 1993, 1994). Evidence consistent with autistic failure to perceive affective attitudes is to be found in the distinctive pattern of their judgements about faces. According to Hobson, we do not see another person's face as an unrelated set of elements, but as an integrated and possibly irreducible Gestalt of the person's psyche.

Hobson predicted that if people with autism are aberrant in perceiving emotional expressions, then this should be apparent in their reading of emotion from faces. Hobson, Ouston, and Lee (1988) provide support for this hypothesis. The task was to sort piles of different faces according to the emotions expressed in them. When shown a full face, people with autism actually performed better than participants without autism matched for verbal abilities. In contrast, when some of the features were occluded, although matching deteriorated in both populations of participants, it did so much more markedly for the people with autism. Hobson (1993) argues that clinically normal people are highly attuned to expressions of emotion, allowing them to continue making accurate classifications with impoverished data. The autistic sample, in contrast, seemed to be operating on more superficial visual similarities that could be picked up easily from full faces but not from part faces. In a follow-up study, people with autism showed specific impairment relative to controls in naming rather than matching the emotion in a face (Hobson, Ouston, & Lee, 1989). In that study, their deficiency also extended to naming the emotion expressed in tone of voice. Again, the level of their difficulty seemed to be at the general underlying domain of understanding emotion itself.

A further finding persuaded Hobson et al. (1988) that the capacity for face recognition in people with autism differs categorically from that of people without autism. When faces were presented upside-down, the participants with autism were relatively effective in two respects in making judgements about these stimuli. A target face was presented upside-down and participants had the task of matching faces to this that were also in an upside-down orientation. The task was either to group together faces of different people according to a given emotion, or to sort together the faces of the same person showing different emotional contortions. The participants with autism performed significantly better on both sorting tasks relative to the matched controls. Hobson et al. concluded that children with autism do not see the face as a Gestalt whole associated with a characteristic orientation, but as a set of elements in a certain spatial relation to each other that can be identified in various stages of rotation—they were claimed to be seeing the face as a meaningless pattern. The distinctive profile of performance yielded by the people with autism, including their success with upside-down faces, led Hobson et al. to suppose that this was a sign that they were deficient in attaching emotional meaning to faces. More generally, the interpretation is consistent with Frith's (1989) claim that people with autism have difficulty in integrating elements into a coherent whole. Hobson and Frith differ in that Hobson attaches special significance to the failure of integration of input, specifically in the domain of emotion.

Hobson et al.'s (1988, 1989) findings, along with claims made by others, stimulated Baron-Cohen (1991) to investigate further the nature of the difficulty children with autism have in understanding emotion. Specifically, he wanted to know whether deficiency in understanding emotion was primary (as Hobson, 1990, supposes), or secondary to a deficiency in understanding belief (as Leslie & Frith, 1990, suppose). Borrowing a procedure from Harris, Johnson, Hutton, Andrews, and Cooke (1989), Baron-Cohen told children about a character called Jane, whom he explained had cut herself. He asked children with autism how they thought she felt. They had little difficulty judging correctly that she felt sad. He also told of Jane having a birthday party, and in this case, children with autism judged that she felt happy. These findings show that children with autism have a good understanding of how various situations and events are related to emotion labels, which he supposes undermines the claims made by advocates of the emotion hypothesis.

Subsequently, Baron-Cohen (1991) also found that children with autism understood something of the relation between desire and emotion. They judged that if Jane wanted rice crispies and was given them, then she would be happy, but if instead she was given cornflakes, then she would be sad. However, they had considerable difficulty understanding the relation between desire and emotion if "belief" was added to the equation. In Jane's absence, participants saw cornflakes being placed in the rice crispies box, after the usual content had been removed. They were then asked how Jane would feel on being presented with the box, and children with autism tended to judge that she would be sad—as though they assumed reality were transparent to her. In another context, children with autism judged that Jane would be happy on being presented with a cornflakes box that actually contained rice crispies (even though it was obvious that Jane had no way of knowing about the exchange of contents). Hence, children with autism do have some difficulty understanding emotion, but according to Baron-Cohen, this is specific to occasions when understanding the particular emotion in question would require an understanding of false belief. Baron-Cohen took his findings as evidence that failure to understand belief is a primary deficit in autism, and difficulty in understanding emotion is secondary to that.

Let us reflect on what these findings do and do not tell us. Partly, they tell us something we already know, namely that many children with autism have difficulty understanding false belief. One consequence arising from this difficulty is that if they are asked to anticipate the emotion of a person who is holding a false belief, then they will show the same kind of difficulty as if they had been asked to anticipate the person's action or report the person's thoughts. That does not necessarily mean that a failure to understand belief is responsible for the general difficulty in understanding emotion that is apparent in children with autism. Perhaps what is more novel is that the findings tell us that children with autism do succeed in understanding how certain contexts evoke certain emotions. Similarly, children with autism understand something about the match between desire and outcome, and how that evokes positive or negative emotions. Baron-Cohen (1991) argues that the children's successful judgements in these cases arise because the children are being asked to judge about emotion in a manner that does not depend on an understanding of belief. However, the findings do not actually tell us this. There are many reasons why the children with autism may have judged emotions correctly in these cases. The most obvious is that, in a fairly mechanical way, they have learned about the convention surrounding an association between negative emotions and thwarted desires. Indeed, it is probably difficult for children with autism to avoid experiencing their peers or siblings throwing tantrums when not getting what they want. Presumably, something similar happens with respect to observing links between contexts and emotions. In other words, because the children are able to judge "happy" or "sad" appropriately, this in itself does not imply that they have any deep understanding of emotion. They may simply know how to use words that are substantially meaningless to them (happy, sad) in appropriate contexts.

We need to formulate the research question slightly differently: Are there any circumstances in which children with autism show impairments in affective contact with others? Importantly, can it be shown that any such impairments are independent of their lack of understanding of belief? This way of putting it differs from Baron-Cohen (1991), who seems to have asked if there are any circumstances in which children with autism can make correct judgements of emotion that do not depend on an understanding of belief. His data suggest that there are, but in his study the participants may have performed successfully in a trivial and noninsightful sense. Only when the research question is posed differently, as here, do we have the potential to reveal impaired understanding of emotion and affective contact that is independent of deficiency in understanding belief.

A study by Klin, Volkmar, and Sparrow (1992) provides the required data. These researchers investigated the basic social behaviours of children with autism aged around 4 years. Unlike normal children and matched controls with mental retardation and learning difficulties, the children with autism tended not to show anticipation of being picked up by a caregiver and they tended not to show affection for others or any interest in them. The authors were careful to demonstrate that this behaviour (or lack of it) was independent of any general impairments in motor functions in their participants. In other words, the children with autism were specifically impaired in the ability to make a basic affective connection with others. In normal development, these affective processes emerge in the first year of life, supposedly well before the child has developed a representational understanding of mind. Hence, in order to show a basic affective contact with others, one need not have the ability to acknowledge false belief. Indeed, domestic pets show an affective contact with their owners, but these animals presumably do not have much insight into mind (though it is often tempting to anthropomorphise).

Deficiency in socialisation was identified by Wing and Gould (1979) as one of the triad of impairments in autism. At the beginning of this chapter, I said that if an individual lacked an understanding of mind, then he or she would show impairments in socialisation, and I think that argument remains valid. However, there is an asymmetry here. If the individual shows impairments in socialisation, then those impairments do not necessarily stem from a deficiency in understanding mind. Baron-Cohen (1991) seems to have supposed there was such a symmetry, but Klin et al.'s findings suggest otherwise, in a way that is more consistent with Hobson's (1993) position. Hobson argues that being unable to make a basic affective connection with others deprives children with autism of the rich source of social experiences that otherwise would nurture a budding development of understanding the representational character of mind.

SUMMARY AND CONCLUSIONS

Many children with autism who fail a test of false belief are unlike normal children aged 3 years because they often show more severe deficits in their understanding of mind. Perhaps they lack an understanding of referential opacity, which would be evident not only in their failure on a test of false belief, but also in their lack of pretence and general ignorance of mental phenomena. However, some people with autism are able to acknowledge false belief and even higher-order belief. This may mean that they understand something of referential opacity, but even if it does, the autistic symptoms afflicting these people remain. There appear to be additional cognitive deficiencies that contribute to the autistic profile (executive dysfunction), plus impairments in understanding affect. An alternative possibility is that people with autism are able to pass a test of belief via some route that does not require understanding of opacity. An independent clue suggesting lack of ability to handle opacity is the paucity of pretence and impoverished imagination in autism.

People with autism have a constellation of symptoms that extend beyond those directly relevant to understanding mind. They also show signs of having impairments in their executive functions, and in particular display difficulty in inhibiting prepotent responses. But this does not account for their deficient understanding of mind, and neither does their deficient understanding of mind account for their impaired executive function. Both difficulties might, however, stem from an underlying deficiency in the capacity to work through problem solutions in imagination—a process of mental simulation. Children with autism also show a basic lack of affective contact with others, a deficiency that seems even more primitive than their lack of ability to represent others' beliefs and maybe even more primitive than a capacity for pretence or referential opacity.

One thing neglected in this chapter, which is something that tends to be neglected in the general literature, is consideration of the significance of deficient communication abilities in autism. The nearest we came to it in the present chapter was when we looked at very primitive impairments in emotional communication or connectedness. This is an issue I explore in detail in the final chapter, because it might offer a vital clue to the role of early communication experiences in the normal development of an understanding of mind. In turn, it might provide an insight into one aspect of aberrant development in autism that could pose a threat to the acquisition of appropriate social behaviour; it might be that impairments in communication stand as an impediment to the quintessentially human means of access to the minds of other people.

CHAPTER TEN

Communication and thinking: Autistic and normal development

According to Frith (1989), young children diagnosed as having autism are in very many cases referred for clinical assessment because of a language or communicative impairment. Indeed, a typical characteristic of autism is delayed language and communicative development, in some cases so severe that afflicted children do not speak much or at all before the age of 3 years. Frith suggests that where young children are concerned, linguistic and communicative impairments are much more likely to portend a subsequent diagnosis of autism than are early social-emotional abnormalities amounting to what Frith calls "failure to relate to people as persons". These latter children usually develop affectionately based contacts with people later on, but are mentally retarded. However, we can be thankful that only a tiny minority of young children who have linguistic and communicative impairments eventually receive a diagnosis of autism.

There are several rather ambitious aims in this chapter. First, we should explore in what ways children with autism are deficient in communication and how this relates to the claim made by some researchers (e.g. Hobson, 1993; Klin et al., 1992; Mundy, Sigman, & Kasari, 1993) that autism does entail a basic deficiency in affective contact with other people. We shall then explore which linguistic abilities do and do not develop in autism and how this relates to their lack of understanding mind. We shall look at the implications of this for the quality of autistic thought in general, and how that relates to autistic deficiencies in executive function tasks. In what follows I hope to generate novel ways of seeing the problem that might suggest avenues for research that could afford new insights into the development of an understanding of mind. My overarching aim is to make a link between the developments of communication and understanding mind in a way that unifies the phenomena of weak understanding of mind in autism on one hand, with the powerful understanding of mind in normal development on the other.

PRIMITIVE COMMUNICATION: ANOTHER LOOK AT ABNORMAL AFFECTIVE CONTACT IN AUTISM

According to Hobson (e.g. 1993, 1994), children with autism suffer a primary deficiency in forming an affective contact with other people in the sense that they have difficulty conceiving of intersubjectivity on an emotional as well as cognitive level. However, Baron-Cohen (1991) presented evidence (reviewed in the previous chapter) suggesting that children with autism have a fair amount of insight into emotion, so long as the emotion in question is not linked with belief. Yet Klin et al. (1992) demonstrated that children with autism apparently do exhibit impairments in primitive social behaviours. What Klin et al. were perhaps observing in their young participants with autism was a primary lack of capacity for sharing experiences. They used the Vineland Adaptive Behaviour Scales, constructed by Sparrow, Balla, and Cicchetti (1984) for gauging socialisation in children with autism. Many of the 20 items in this part of the scale are relevant to the sharing of experiences and information. For example, several items concern the child's interest in other people and treating familiar people differently from unfamiliar people. If the child was not disposed to share information or experiences with others, then this would be manifest as a lack of interest in others and as a failure to shift the manner of their interaction between familiar and unfamiliar people. One way in which we habitually make this discrimination in an observable way is by sharing information and experiences with familiar people but not with unfamiliar ones. Even a failure to anticipate being picked up by a caregiver could be interpreted as a disinclination to share. Anticipating being picked up could be a sign of eagerness to interact with the caregiver, an interaction that, by its nature, would involve sharing experiences and information. In short, it might be that children with autism show a primary deficiency in affective contact in the sense that they are disinclined to share experiences and information with others.

This brings us to the theory of autism articulated by Mundy et al. (1993). They suggest that autism reduces to a deficit in the capacity for joint attention. Primitive joint attention behaviours are defined by Bruner (1983) as gestures produced to share attention in relation to an object or event with another person. This would most typically take the form of pointing to an object in order to draw another person's attention to it. However, we have to be careful to make a distinction between gestures that are declarative and gestures that are imperative. The former mean "Take a look at that (just for the sake of interest)!" and the latter mean "I want that." Mundy et al. report that the use and understanding of declarative gestures is impaired in autism but that the use and understanding of imperative gestures is not. This is corroborated by Baron-Cohen (1989c). He made both imperative and declarative pointing gestures to children with autism and observed how they responded. An imperative gesture was defined as the experimenter pointing to an object in the room that the child could see, and should be interpreted as a request to fetch the object in the context in which the gesture was made. Children with autism showed no specific impairment in responding in the appropriate performative manner. A declarative request involved the experimenter wandering over to the window and pointing outside at something not within the child's immediate field of view. This gesture supposedly declared the existence of something interesting outside that should arouse the child's attention sufficiently to stimulate him or her to come over and take a look. That was precisely how the children with Down syndrome and the normal controls reacted, but in sharp contrast the children with autism remained still and assumed a blank expression. In the previous chapter, I suggested that if children lacked a concept of ignorance, then they are unlikely to appreciate the informational benefits of messages from other people, and would show little interest in attending to information that others have to offer for this reason. The distinctive way in which children with autism react to declarative gestures is consistent with the view that they do not perceive the potential of communication to supplant a state of ignorance with a state of knowledge.

Mundy, Kasari, and Sigman (1992) report that declarative gestures are typically accompanied by positive affect, suggesting that sharing experiences with others is usually pleasurable. They filmed infants aged around 20 months and asked independent judges to rate aspects of the infants' facial expression when engaged in various social activities. A robust pattern emerged from these ratings. Namely, when the infants were engaged in declarative joint attention, they tended to wear happy expressions, but when making imperative request gestures they were more likely to be wearing neutral expressions. In contrast, Kasari, Sigman, Mundy, and Yirmiya (1990) report that on the rare occasions when children with autism engaged in joint attention activities, they did not show any concomitant positive affect. In this respect, they differed not only from clinically normal controls but also from a sample of children with mental retardation.

Mundy et al. (1993) outline both similarities and differences between their account and the traditional "theory of mind hypothesis of autism" (e.g. Leslie & Frith, 1990). Considering the similarity first, they raise the possibility that joint attention might depend on the same underlying process that makes pretence possible. Both capacities appear at about 18 months, which is probably no coincidence. Something resembling joint attention does exist prior to this, which is actually likely to be the result of imitation and specific behavioural learning in the infant (Butterworth, 1994; Moore & Corkum, 1994). The special significance of pretence where conception of mind is concerned is that according to Leslie (1987) it requires the capacity to decouple a primary representation from a secondary one. This supposedly amounts to an ability to embed the primary representation within a secondary one, akin to the structure of embedding required for handling referential opacity. According to Mundy et al. (1993), declarative joint attention skills may themselves involve the kind of propositional embedding common to pretence and referential opacity. They suggest that being proactive in sharing an experience requires an understanding of the experience as an experience. Actively taking steps to share an experience is tantamount to having a meta-experience, or, propositionally speaking, embedding an experience within an experience. This view gains empirical support from an observation reported by Mundy et al. In a longitudinal study, they noted joint activity behaviours and play in children with autism and children with mental retardation. In both populations, the authors found that joint attention activities correlated with the level of pretend play. Obviously, both activities were suppressed in autism, but what there was followed the same pattern observed in the children with mental retardation. The authors also report that early joint attention activity correlated with communicative abilities.

After all, then, it seems appropriate to consider the possibility that joint attention and pretence are unified by the underlying capacity for handling referential opacity. The main difference remaining between Leslie's (1987) account and Mundy et al.'s (1993) is that the latter authors emphasise that joint attention activities are typically accompanied by positive affect. This was not something Leslie emphasised in his classic metarepresentational account of pretence, but he could easily have done so. It would be very surprising indeed if children wore miserable facial expressions when engaged in pretend activities. A defining characteristic of play, including pretend play, is that it is fun. One need only lend an ear to the jolly hubbub emanating from a children's nursery to appreciate that this is so. Why is pretence such good fun, and for that matter, why are joint attention activities so pleasurable? Perhaps we are prepared for handling referential opacity but are also disposed to derive satisfaction from using this capacity in its various guises, whether in the declarative communication of joint attention or in pretend play.

An auxiliary component of a capacity for handling referential opacity, then, might be a motivational energy that serves to ensure that the process is well-practised. This point echoes a suggestion made by Piaget, that "functional assimilation" exists as a motivational force intrinsic to the exercising of schemes. Schemes, especially newly acquired ones, give satisfaction purely by being exercised, irrespective of extrinsic reward. It is not inevitable that the practice of a given capacity or skill would arouse positive feelings. For example, disaffected sports people may have impressive specialised skill, yet to practise that might even arouse negative affect in some cases. Perhaps our capacity for handling opacity is such that in normal circumstances, practising this skill assures good feelings. If that is correct, we cannot be entirely sure whether the social impairments in autism reduce ultimately to a cognitive or to an emotional–motivational deficiency just on the basis of data reported by Mundy et al.

We can thus make a case for saying that early joint attention declarative gestures are a sign of a very primitive process that forms the heart of an understanding of mind. But what about imperative request gestures? Why should these be intact in autism, and is there any reason to suppose in principle that their existence might imply the rudiments of an understanding of mind? Perhaps imperative gestures are treated entirely instrumentally by children with autism. Indeed, perhaps there is no reason for the children even to think of others as sentient organisms as opposed to versatile machines that are capable of satisfying one's desires. Because imperative gestures are transparently and directly instrumental in nature, they could emerge in the absence of any social capacities.

THE DEVELOPMENT OF VERBAL COMMUNICATION AND LINGUISTIC SKILLS

Precursors of verbal linguistic abilities are the mainly gestural protocommunicative acts that are typical of infancy. Without these precursors, it is difficult to conceive of how linguistic development could occur normally (Bruner, 1983). They can serve to secure a mutual focus of attention between adult and child, but shared attention can be achieved more efficiently and powerfully when one is linguistically competent. That very linguistic competence in return could allow further understanding of mind by opening a more lucid channel of access to the minds of others, where what they say tells us what they think; yet many children with autism do acquire at least some linguistic competence, even if it typically lags behind the development of their nonverbal intelligence. Does this imply that we are entirely wrong, and that after all children with autism who acquire linguistic abilities are thus also learning about minds? Indeed, perhaps mastering the grammatical structure of language is sufficient to create an understanding of referential opacity in an accomplished language-user. This would be the case if referential opacity were actually encapsulated in certain linguistic formulations, as Quine (1961) seemed to suppose. Another possibility, however, is that grammatical competence is not sufficient for handling referential opacity. If so, then although linguistic competence and referential opacity might be highly related, they do not actually reduce to the same thing.

Quine (1961) seemed to regard referential opacity purely as a linguistic issue. He talked of propositions behaving strangely when placed within the context of verbs of propositional attitude (e.g. *think*). Specifically, coreferential terms cannot replace elements in the proposition without risking damage to the meaning when that proposition follows a verb of propositional attitude. Putting it plainly, saying that "Jane believes the Prime Minister lives at Number 10" does not necessarily mean the same as "Jane believes Major lives at Number 10". However, referential opacity is actually something that exists in the mind, not in language. If it existed only in language, then the verb of propositional attitude would be a necessary prefix as a linguistic device for creating the referential opacity of the ensuing proposition. In fact, the presence of this verb is not necessary. Rather, communication in general is referentially opaque and should be treated as such. Hence, if Jane says to us, "The Prime Minister lives at Number 10", we recognise that the proposition cannot be paraphrased with coreferential terms without risking loss of meaning; and we recognise this in the absence of Jane prefixing her assertion with a verb of propositional attitude.

Similarly, if Jane says "Clinton lives at Number 10", we do not take this as <Clinton lives at Number 10>, but as <Jane seems to believe (or she is being silly) that Clinton lives at number 10 but really Major lives there>. In other words, we read beliefs from utterances, implying that we perceive an affinity between the language of speech and the language of thought; and in reading beliefs from utterances, we encode them for what they are—referentially opaque. Utterances ostensibly report reality but do so via the cognition of the person articulating the message.

Hence, referential opacity is a state of mind, not of language. Sometimes we can experience the illusion that language is irreducibly referentially opaque (as Quine, 1961, seemed to suppose) but actually it is so only because it is a vehicle of communication used by minds. Ultimately, it is the minds themselves that are opaque.

Nonetheless, it might be that certain linguistic conventions of embedding support a budding ability to handle referential opacity. To illustrate, when we hear Jane say "Clinton lives at Number 10", to make sense of that untrue assertion we embed the proposition under the heading "Jane is saying ..." For example, consider the embedding in

The man the dog chased is eating a sausage.

Who is eating the sausage, the man or the dog? This is but a simple problem, for we embed the clause <the dog chased> within the proposition of the man eating a sausage:

The man [the dog chased] is eating a sausage.

It might be that the embedding that is a typical feature of ordinary language provides a structure for handling referential opacity. If so, perhaps the linguistic impairment in autism takes the form of a lack of ability to process linguistic embedding, with the knock-on effect of denying the child a vital framework that most of us utilise for the purpose of reading the content of mind from the meaning of the utterance.

However, Tager-Flusberg (1981) reports that the acquisition of grammar is not specifically impaired in autism, and that children with autism do not show a particular difficulty either in comprehending or producing embedded sentences. Tager-Flusberg goes even further to suggest that some children with autism understand the linguistic structure of sentences containing embedding connected with verbs of propositional attitude. She claims (Tager-Flusberg, 1993, p.142) that "... any difficulties [children with autism] might have understanding mental states cannot be due simply to syntactic limitations, or limitations in the linguistic expression of propositional attitudes." On the other hand, Tager-Flusberg and Sullivan (1994) present circumstantial evidence showing that children with autism who can handle the kind of grammatical embedding that would be entailed in referential opacity seem to stand more chance of acknowledging false belief than do children who lack such grammatical sophistication.

Is it possible to show a dissociation between linguistic competence and ability to handle referential opacity? Syntax might be sufficiently developed for dealing with referential opacity, but impairments in processing referential opacity might remain in a task that does not demand the kind of linguistic competence that Quine (1961) would have supposed was essential. We already know that children with autism have difficulty with referential opacity insofar as they fail to acknowledge false belief. However, that might stem from a realist bias rather than a lack of the concept of opacity (Russell et al., 1991). What we require is a test of opacity that cannot allow a realist bias to operate and that does not involve the processing of grammatically complex sentences. The message–desire discrepant task (see Chapter 6) seems to fit this requirement, and this is something we presented to children with autism (Mitchell & Isaacs, 1994).

One value of the message–desire discrepant task is that it does not allow for the possibility of a realist error. This is because we cannot tell what the real object being referred to is without interpreting the speaker's utterance in relation to her unique informational history and consequent belief framework. Hence, to select the object of reference is to solve the problem of referential opacity. Another value of this procedure is that the child's task is to interpret a linguistically simple sentence. It is the context that invites an opaque interpretation rather than any features of syntax or verbs of propositional attitude. If children with autism had a primary problem with referential opacity, then it would be reflected in their errors on this task.

We (Mitchell & Isaacs, 1994) found that children with autism who were generally linguistically competent (on account of their good performance on the British Picture Vocabulary Scale) nonetheless had serious difficulty in interpreting requests opaquely. Instead, they interpreted them literally. If the speaker requested the bag in the red drawer, then this is where children with autism tended to gesture. They did so whether or not the item in that drawer had been swapped for another without the speaker's knowledge. Moreover, there was a lack of correlation between acknowledging that the speaker was ignorant of the exchange and judging that the speaker wanted the item in the nonspecified location. In contrast, if clinically normal children acknowledged that the speaker was ignorant of the exchange, they stood a good chance of judging correctly that the speaker wanted the item in the nonspecified location. Seemingly, these children, but not the children with autism, understood that it is appropriate to take into account the speaker's state of knowledge or ignorance when interpreting her utterance.

However, there is a remaining impediment to the strong conclusion that children with autism have a problem with referential opacity. Although we can say that their difficulty does not stem from a realist bias or from difficulty with the syntax of referential opacity, it might be that a deficiency in executive function was responsible for their overly literal interpretations. Russell et al. (1991) seemed to equate a realist bias, which they defined as an inability to disengage from the real object, with a deficiency in executive function, which is an inability to inhibit a prepotent response. In the Mitchell and Isaacs (1994) study, disengaging from the real object was not an issue because focusing on the object of reference would solve the problem of referential opacity. Yet there remained the requirement to inhibit a prepotent response. It would have been a prepotent response if the child simply acted upon the location mentioned in the speaker's request—for example to gesture to the red drawer when the speaker requests the bag in the red drawer. Did children make an overly literal interpretation just because they acted upon a mentioned location (a prepotent response), or was it more specifically because they did not take into account the speaker's belief when interpreting her message (a difficulty with referential opacity)? Further experimentation was required.

We (Mitchell, Saltmarsh, & Russell, in press) conducted a follow-up study to investigate this. The study incorporated a control question asking children to identify the item that the speaker had put in location 1. In a sense this was a simple memory question, but one that required a nonobvious answer. Although location 1 is mentioned in the question, a correct judgement is to gesture to location 2, because that is where the item is now that the speaker originally put in location 1. Hence, children were required to inhibit a prepotent response of gesturing to the location mentioned in the question. The findings were that children with autism were much better at judging that the item the speaker had put in location 1 was now in location 2 than at interpreting the speaker's request for the item in location 1 by gesturing to location 2. Children answered the memory question correctly 80% of the time but answered the interpretation correctly only 55% of the time. Hence, it seems that children with autism found it difficult to interpret a request opaquely, and that this was more than just a difficulty in inhibiting a prepotent response. Incidentally, it seems that children's difficulty with the interpretation task cannot be explained merely as a memory weakness (forgetting that the items had moved). It seems likely, then, that children with autism have a specific problem with referential opacity, though it seems that this is likely to be compounded by an executive dysfunction that gives rise to difficulty in inhibiting a prepotent response.

In a small but possibly important way, the performance of the children with autism differed between the studies reported by Mitchell and Isaacs (1994) and Mitchell et al. (in press). In the former, children did not discriminate between a message–desire consistent and discrepant story. They were just as likely to interpret the speaker's request literally in both. In Mitchell et al. (in press), however, children with autism offered a nonliteral interpretation more frequently in the second, though not in the first, of the two message–desire discrepant stories than in the consistent stories. Even so, in a second experiment Mitchell and Isaacs (1994) did find that children with autism could acknowledge that they had verbally misrepresented a situation if this was suggested to them. After the children had discovered that a Smarties tube contained a pencil, the experimenter suggested that the child had said it contained Smarties when he first saw it. Children accepted this true suggestion, but rejected a false control suggestion, indicating that their reason for acceptance was due to recognition of the truth of the suggestion rather than simple compliance. Accepting that one had misdescribed the prior situation could also require an understanding of referential opacity; that the utterance was regarded as true when in fact it was false. The two studies are consistent, then, in raising the possibility that at least some of the children with autism had at least some understanding of referential opacity. This touches on the point identified by Bowler (1992), which was mentioned in the previous chapter. If the underlying deficit responsible for the manifestly autistic social impairments is a core deficiency in understanding referential opacity, then how can it be that individuals remain autistic even when they demonstrate some understanding of opacity?

Perhaps this problem no longer seems quite so paradoxical when considered within the context of the message–desire discrepant task. If clinically normal people routinely treat utterances as though they were referentially opaque, then by definition they are treating those utterances as though they are informative not just about reality, but also about the content of the speaker's mind. Speech provides a kind of window on the mind, with the potential to inform most directly and lucidly what one assumes, hopes, and fears. To a considerable extent, we discover the particulars of the psychology of those around us from what they say; but this would only be possible if we routinely regarded speech as being referentially opaque in the first place. If we did not, then we would be denying ourselves access to this rich channel of information about minds. Effectively, we would fall victim to a double jeopardy because difficulty with the core concept of referential opacity would be a disadvantage that was compounded by not being attuned to speech informing us about mind. In sum, even if children with autism had some understanding of opacity, this might be insufficient for them to use the concept as a vehicle for interpreting speech as a window on mind. Accordingly, it would not be surprising that people with autism who had some grasp of opacity remained socially inept.

As far as normal children are concerned, an incipient ability to handle referential opacity is seen in their early linguistic skills. At about 18 months of age, infants check the direction of their mother's gaze, apparently as an adjunct to their interpretation of reference when they hear their mother name an object (e.g. Baldwin & Moses, 1994, see also Chapter 5 for a review). Seemingly, infants do not assume that the object being named is the one they are looking at, but is the one that is the target of the *mother's* gaze. These infants seem to have the rudimentary but implicit insight that meaning is the prerogative of the speaker. Perhaps this becomes supported by other capacities such that from about 4 years of age they come to succeed in handling referential opacity in the message–desire discrepant task. Their good performance means that they are not condemned to literal interpretations, but rather are able to treat utterances as a product of mind—as a window on mind. It might be that an early ability to handle referential opacity bootstraps an almost limitless access thereafter to other minds via oral communication. Although people with autism engage in communication, this would not be greatly to their benefit in understanding beliefs if they did not treat incoming utterances as a window on the mind of the speaker. They might fail for two reasons: (1) the core ability to handle opacity may not exist; (2) even if it does, it might not function to bootstrap further understanding of mind. Nonetheless, it could be the case that more linguistically able people with autism show better insight into mind than those less able. We can therefore predict an association between development in linguistic-communicative skills and the development of understanding mind in autism.

Relevant to this, Sparrevohn and Howie (1995) gave children with autism a battery of tests designed to assess their understanding of beliefs. The children formed two groups, matched according to chronological age and nonverbal abilities, but differing in verbal abilities. The findings were that children with higher verbal ability were more likely to show good performance on the belief tests compared with those of lower verbal ability. This finding led the authors to conclude that (1) there is progression in the development of understanding mind in autism, albeit belatedly, and (2) that progression is linked with developing verbal abilities.

Happe (1995) reports the same result from a survey of several published studies involving participants with autism. Pooling the samples yielded an unusually large sample of 70. She found that the mean verbal age (assessed by the British Picture Vocabulary Scale) of those who passed was 9:7 years, whereas the mean of those who failed was 5:5 years. Happe raises the possibility that the direction of causality in the relation between acknowledging false belief and verbal mental age may be counter to the obvious (but see my interpretation of Peterson & Siegal, 1995, presented later). Contrary to Sparrevohn and Howie (1995), children may not make any progress in the development of understanding mind in autism if their good verbal ability is inadvertently a measure of understanding mind. Consistent with my earlier suggestion, she proposes that a rudimentary understanding of mind may play an important role in linguistic development. If so, then measures of linguistic development would be indirect measures of understanding mind. If that view is correct, then longitudinal studies of autistic development should reveal that younger children with autism who pass belief tests, but have not yet acquired good linguistic skills on account of their young age, would nonetheless be destined to make considerable progress in developing linguistic abilities; lack of good verbal ability would not in itself be an obstacle to success on belief tasks. In contrast, those who fail belief tests would stand less chance of becoming linguistically advanced. This is something awaiting investigation.

However, like Sparrevohn and Howie (1995), Happe (1995) also raises the more likely possibility that being linguistically able is causally responsible for good performance on tests of belief. Her suggestion is that children with autism might utilise their proficiency in language as a tool to "hack out" or calculate a correct judgement of belief. An assumption implicit in her account is that clinically normal children achieve correct judgements via another route, though she is silent on what this might be. My view is that Happe is right about autistic success in this respect, but that clinically normal children go through the same route also.

Evidence of a more direct nature concerning the link between linguistic proficiency and understanding of belief is presented in an earlier study by Happe (1993). She found that children with autism who were able to interpret metaphors nonliterally also tended to succeed in acknowledging false belief, whereas those who interpreted metaphors literally tended to fail false belief. Happe argues that a well-developed understanding of referential opacity is necessary in order to interpret metaphors nonliterally. A related finding is reported by Leekam and Prior (1994). They investigated the ability to distinguish between a lie and a joke, and how that related with verbal mental age, pragmatic ability, and performance on tests of both first- and second-order belief. The children with autism listened to a pair of stories, each featuring a protagonist who uttered an untruth. In one, the protagonist immediately admitted to the untruth whereas in the other he did not. In the former we might infer that the protagonist was joking, whereas in the latter we might infer that he was seriously intending to deceive.

Several children with autism correctly identified who was lying and who was joking, and those who did tended to have a higher pragmatic score, higher verbal age, and to pass a test of second-order false belief. As in the study reported by Happe (1993), it might be that children who acquire a finer understanding of communication, including metaphor, lies, jokes, and refined pragmatic skills, accordingly make more use of speech from others as a channel of access to other minds. Consequently, it is not surprising that they perform well on tests of belief. Nonetheless, Leekam and Prior report that the parents of children who performed well on the tests stated that their children seemed lacking in social sensitivity. It might be that despite a fair amount of competence, this was still insufficient for the children routinely to penetrate the minds of those around them in contrast with clinically normal children. Similarly, Frith, Happe, and Siddons (1994) report that children with autism who passed tests of false belief were still socially impaired, though they showed more social insight than those who failed false belief. On the other hand, clinically normal children's social skill presumably develops as they gain more and more insight into mind thanks to refinements in their concept of referential opacity over the first decade of life—and beyond. Most normal children aged 5 years are socially skilled in comparison with their peers but not by adult standards. Presumably, their further development in this domain owes something to a finer understanding of mind, which is gained substantially through growing competence and experience in communication.

Although the correlation between understanding mind and communicative abilities is consistent with impairments in specific aspects of communication restricting the development of understanding mind, it could be that the causality lies in the opposite direction (Baron-Cohen, 1988). However, data reported by Peterson and Siegal (1995) mean that we do not have to rely solely on correlational studies exclusive to populations with autism. They tested a group of children aged 8–13 years who had innate deafness but normal nonverbal intelligence (mean IQ=103). Despite the good intelligence of these children and their advanced age, 65% of them failed a simple test of false belief. Although these children were not autistic according to standard criteria, it might be that restrictions in breadth and possibly depth of their communicative experiences from an early age denied them the easy access to the contents of other minds that verbally able children (and adults of course) take for granted. This may have resulted in their not being habitually attuned to other minds, with the consequence that they were tripped up by a simple test of false belief. The findings lend support to the view articulated by Sparrevohn and Howie (1995), that restricted communicative abilities could be responsible for the slow development of an understanding of mind in autism.

A finding apparently inconsistent with this account is that congenitally blind children also seem to have specific difficulty in acknowledging false belief. Hobson and Minter (1995) tested 19 blind children by asking them to judge the contents of a warm teapot. After they responded with "tea", the experimenter revealed the unexpected content of warm sand. On discovering this, 42% of the children failed to acknowledge their own prior false belief by judging that they had thought it contained sand (or sugar) all along. Fifty-three percent also judged that another person would think the pot contained sand (or sugar). This group of children had a mean age of 6:10, and their verbal mental age was consistent with this. According to Hobson, this finding is consistent with his argument that understanding mind develops from an experience of intersubjectivity, an experience that will be impoverished if the child is unable to perceive the focus of other people's attention. In that case, do these data fall beyond the scope of the communicative hypothesis of a development of understanding mind? On the contrary, I shall argue that the data actually stand in support.

Blindness, it seems, has serious ramifications with respect to communication. First, blind children who are integrated into a school for sighted children exist not only in an environment that they cannot see but also effectively are treated by sighted peers as though they are themselves invisible. Sighted children tend not to interact with blind members of their class (Preisler, 1995), meaning that the school experience offers little in the way of a forum for a meeting of minds through communication. Second, when blind children do experience communication, they are likely to be confined to interpreting utterances literally rather than opaquely. A sighted person can usually tell at a glance whether what is being said matches what is out there in reality. This is not so for a blind child, who probably has to treat indirect sources of information (e.g. verbal messages) as though they were direct sources (e.g. seeing). Third, it seems that blind children are more locked into reality than sighted children, certainly at the age of 3 or 4 years. In the nursery, they devote much effort to exploring the physical environment, an activity that consumes virtually all of their time (Preisler, 1995). Presumably, children are compelled to tackle the physical side of their environment before they can indulge themselves in the province of the psychological (Mitchell, 1994). A sighted child can take in the physical environment at a glance, but it would take a blind child an inordinately long period to achieve the same through touch. While they are doing so, they are not attuned to the psychological aspects of their environment and their behaviour is not inviting psychologically informative communication from others (see Fraiberg & Adelson, 1977, for an account of impairments in intersubjectivity in the blind).

Blindness, then, might be an obstacle to the development of an understanding of mind because of the impact it has on communicative abilities and experiences. Just as autism might restrict the psychologically informative value of communication, so blindness might do the same. If so, then in both populations, compensation in the form of a peculiarly high verbal mental age might be necessary for the individual to treat utterances as the product of mind. Happe (1995) claims that the average verbal mental age for a person with autism who does show insight into mind is 9 years and 7 months. The same might be true of blind children. Hobson and Minter (1995) did not present a profile of the verbal abilities of their blind sample, but it might turn out that the more verbally able children succeeded in acknowledging belief.

THE CHARACTER OF AUTISTIC THOUGHT

Returning to normal development, perhaps coming to apply the concept of opacity to interpreting speech is but a small step along life's journey toward acquiring a deep understanding of the psychology of other people. In this respect, certain aspects of verbal communication (especially joint attention and the associated symbolic competence as expressed in pretend play) would be both a sign of an incipient grasp of referential opacity plus an instrument offering the opportunity to achieve a more intimate understanding of mind. Difficulty with the concept of referential opacity can therefore be seen as a serious epistemic obstacle to becoming intimate with minds.

In autistic development, why should the concept of referential opacity prove to be so elusive? It is not purely due to difficulty with embedding and it is not purely due to deficiencies in executive function. Neither is it due to an inability to conceive of alternative situations, since children with autism seem well capable of this when giving the correct judgement about the developing image in an outdated photo, which they implicitly contrast with the current situation (e.g. Leekam & Perner, 1991; Leslie & Thaiss, 1992). In the previous chapter, success on this task was presented as evidence that children with autism do not always show a realist bias, contrary to the executive dysfunction hypothesis. On the other side of the coin, their success shows a capacity to compare and contrast alternative situations.

Being able to handle referential opacity demands imagination and symbolic activity. We might say that the earliest sign of an incipient capacity for opacity is at 18 months, when the normal child begins to engage in pretence, which, coincidentally, is also the age when the infant first shows proficiency in joint attention activities (Butterworth, 1994). Prior to this age, pseudo joint attention skills are probably the result of specific learning experiences (Moore & Corkum, 1994). Handling referential opacity requires one to imagine a description of a hypothetical model of which the usual truth conditions are suspended. How could this require anything other than an act of imagination and manipulation of internal symbols (the hypothetical model is a symbolic model)? It might be that in contrast with clinically normal children, children with autism have something more akin to what Bruner (1964) called an iconic mode of thought. This is the idea that children rely on what Leslie (1987) refers to as the primary representation, which is a cognitive redescription of the thing of attention as it is. It would be possible to imagine this thing in its perceptual absence, but presumably direct perceptual input will hold attentional priority over daydreams to avoid the child losing touch with reality. Hence, the stored image will be faithful to the real object of attention, meaning that thinking in this mode is concrete and dominated by immediate input and surface appearances. The images generated in this mode of thought would be classified by Vygotsky (1978) as falling within "natural memory".

Having iconic thought might lead to realist errors in a test of belief and appearance–reality, but the reality masking hypothesis introduced in Chapter 8 does not reduce to a hypothesis concerning the early existence of iconic thought. If one has an iconic mode of thought, then of course one is going to be locked into the here and now, but that is not the same as saying that current reality holds a magnetism, which is what we suppose in the case of clinically normal children. Operating on the level of first-order reality in autism would be a default consequence of a concrete, image-driven iconic mode of thought. It amounts to the claim that children with autism do not habitually use language as a tool of thought—because they are lacking in symbolism and imagination. That is, they lack what Vygotsky (1978) called "mediated memory". Clinically normal young children, in contrast, might still prefer reality as a criterion for making judgements about such things as beliefs even if they have a capacity for imagination and symbolism—because reality holds a magnetism for them.

The symbolism that is necessary for linguistic communication might also play a part in the symbolism required for understanding referential opacity. Symbolism might be a necessary aid to imagination that allows the individual to act upon ideas as ideas that are once removed from reality. This would be possible if symbols and language in particular served as a tool of thought, in which case Bruner (1964) would say that the individual had a symbolic mode of thinking. If, on the other hand, the individual only had an iconic mode of thinking at her disposal, then there might be insufficient scope for the detachment from reality necessary to conceive of other minds; current reality has to dominate an iconic mode of thought if the child is to keep in touch with reality.

Evidence directly supporting this possibility was reported by Boysen (1993) in connection with the symbolic capacities of chimps. Briefly, she trained two chimps to play an adversarial game, where one communicated about the location of food to the other. This was very similar to Russell et al.'s (1991) windows task, since there were two baited locations, one with a large reward and one with only a small reward. To get the large reward, the communicating chimp had to gesture to the smaller of the rewards, but in fact they found this almost impossible in practice. Dramatic improvement occurred, however, when numbers symbolising the quantities were substituted for the real objects.

Perhaps the chimps routinely relied upon an iconic mode of thought, which compelled them to gesture imperatively to the food they wanted. Because they were operating on the raw image of the desired object, perhaps they were unable to go beyond this in imagination to think through the ramifications—that they would deny themselves the big reward. If, on the other hand, the image of the desired food were unavailable and represented instead symbolically, then a benefit might be that the chimp is being forced to process symbolically and can then profit from all the accompanying advantages such processing affords. This could serve as an allegory for autism. It might be that if children with autism were constrained to think symbolically, then they too would show improvements in conceiving of the mind. At the very least, we might find that if the windows task as devised by Russell et al. (1991) were to be modified to incorporate symbols in place of real objects, then a substantial improvement in correct judgements would ensue. This obvious and important manipulation is still awaiting investigation at the time of writing.

In the windows task with symbols substituted for real objects, a symbolic representation is imposed on the participant. In Boysen's (1993) version of the task, the individual would see the number 2 in one place and the number 4 in the other, these numbers representing the respective quantities of food. The chimp playing the role of communicator has no difficulty gesturing to the number 2. At the risk of anthropomorphism, the chimp might reason that the small number is standing in for the large quantity in this peculiar context. After all, symbols do have an arbitrary relation to the things they denote. This need not imply that henceforth the chimp has redefined the symbol "2" to mean four items, but just that it is treated in that way temporarily in the context of the gesturing game. Or, at least, the chimp has redefined "small number" to mean "large quantity". In contrast, the perceptual image of a large quantity of food has a nonarbitrary relation with the thing out there in reality—a large quantity of food. Note that this argument does not depend so much on the character of the particular symbols in question; the symbols could be coloured shapes or anything else, so long as they were not linked canonically with the object that they represented. Indeed, the arbitrariness in the relation is the essence of the point I am trying to make.

Viewed in this way, the externally imposed symbolism in Boysen's (1993) task shares something in common with the internally originating and entirely spontaneous symbolism of the young child pretending that a toy building brick is a gun. The perceptual image of a brick has a nonarbitrary relation with the thing that it is (a mundane geometrical piece of timber), but miraculously the child is able to assign a symbolic identity to the image such that it now serves as a pretend gun. Suppose Boysen's task had a different purpose. Suppose participants had to pretend that a wooden brick was a gun. This is something we can consider in principle but it would almost be impossible in practice if those participants were chimps. It would be terribly difficult for us to communicate what they were supposed to be doing and it would be hard to conceive of a way to make the task naturally motivating (in contrast to the windows task, where reward is contingent on correct perform-ance). Nevertheless, just imagine that it were possible. In one version of the task the item to act upon would be an ordinary wooden brick, whereas in another it would be a wooden block specially carved to form a word—the word *brick*. Let us suppose that the chimps were familiar with this word and recognised it as denoting an item that is a basic element of construction (i.e. a brick). It might be that the chimps would find it much easier to treat this wooden carving of a word as though it were a gun than they would its plain rectangular counterpart. The word, of course, has an arbitrary relation with the thing it denotes (in this case a brick), and for that reason perhaps it could temporarily be placed in a new arbitrary relation, this time with a gun. Temporarily, the word *brick* would aid in assigning another identity to the object, allowing it to be represented as a lethal weapon of war (i.e. a gun). In other words, "brick" would temporarily be taken to mean not <brick> but <gun>.

This is pretty much what Leslie (1987) had in mind when he spoke of pretending children engaging in object substitution at a level once removed from the first order encoding of the object at the primary level of the perceptual (iconic) image. It is also similar to Harris and Kavanaugh's (1993) suggestion that, in both pretence and narratives, children temporarily redefine the reference of mental symbols with the aid of a system of mental flags. I am saying that it might be possible to make a link with pretence and an emerging ability to handle the arbitrary relation between things and words. This suggestion could encounter scepticism from someone who has experienced the phenomenon of what Piaget called "nominal realism". For example, Markman (1976) reports that children of around 6 years and below judge not only that rain is wet but also the word *rain* is wet. Also, they judge that if all giraffes were to become extinct, then the word *giraffe* would vanish also! These intriguing findings suggest at the very least that until children are surprisingly old, they have not mastered the arbitrary relation between things and words on a level sufficiently elaborated and explicit to allow them to reflect on it verbally; apparently, as far as the child is concerned on this level of thinking, the relation is nonarbitrary. Although that may be so, the children nonetheless have a working ability to handle the arbitrary relation because they easily make links between words and things that by their nature are entirely arbitrary. To illustrate, it is certainly unnecessary for a word to have onomatopoeic qualities for the child to commit it to his or her lexicon.

If one thinks at least to some extent in terms of words rather than in terms of the images of the things themselves, and if one encodes these names as having an arbitrary quality, no matter how implicit the level, then it is but a simple step to assign a different value or meaning to those names. Hence, *wooden brick* can mean *gun* and *2* can mean *4*, or "small number" can mean "large quantity".

What about false belief? If we reason on this level of symbolism sharing an arbitrary relation with reality, then the same process can be brought into play for handling false belief. John thinks "here are Smarties in the tube" can be taken to mean "here are pencils in the tube". Alternatively, "here are pencils in the tube" means to John that "here are Smarties in the tube". John does not actually know there are pencils in the tube and, if he did, then he is not thinking of those pencils as Smarties. However, a way of mentally notating the situation that will prevent the child from slipping into ascribing a true belief to John is to think in terms of "What is pencils for me is Smarties for John". Obviously the child has to understand that John misrepresents the situation, meaning that they have to understand something about referential opacity in order to be credited with a basic understanding of mind. Yet this capacity alone may not always be sufficient for the child to engage in mentalistic reasoning. Such reasoning may benefit considerably from symbolically notating the relations in the problem. The child must reason something to the effect that John falsely believes there are Smarties in the tube when really there are pencils. Even if the child understands the structure of the problem, she might still struggle to keep track of the content. To repeat, perhaps the latter can be aided by thinking in terms of "What is pencils for me is Smarties for John".

This does not necessarily imply that a child who gives a correct judgement of false belief first has to formulate the problem into linguistically based propositions. By analogy, a child who pretends that a wooden block is a gun need not name the block linguistically as a prerequisite for engaging in this activity. Even so, because names stand in an arbitrary relation to the things they denote, an emerging competence in language would surely facilitate a more general developing capacity of symbolism, by helping to establish the necessary structure in cognition; and if private speech could be brought into play in conceptualising belief, then perhaps so much the better.

In sum, perhaps an emerging symbolic and especially linguistic capacity confers special advantages on children when it comes to reasoning at a level once removed from reality. That kind of reasoning is manifest in pretence and is eminently valuable when reasoning about other minds. According to Luria (1960; Wozniak, 1972), language becomes a tool for regulating what previously has been an immature and impulsive orientation toward the world. According to him this happens at roughly the age of 4 years, which corresponds with children's spontaneous success in acknowledging false belief in a way so striking that it seems certain to amount to more than just coincidence. Because children's thought is more heavily iconic prior to this age, it is not surprising that they show a realist bias. However, as I have argued, a realist bias in itself does not mean that the child is incapable of acknowledging belief (or understanding referential opacity). Rather, an emerging symbolic capacity, which first makes its appearance in normal development from 18 months, perhaps allows the child to realise her potential to grapple with the concept of mind. On the other hand, it seems that if children with autism share that potential, then it will be difficult for them to realise it given the possibility that they perhaps struggle to shed a mode of thought that is largely iconic. The clear implication is that if somehow children with autism could be encouraged to think symbolically, then that could have extensive ramifications in terms of promoting their mental and mentalistic development.

INDEPENDENT EVIDENCE FOR ICONICALLY DOMINATED THOUGHT IN AUTISM

In the appearance–reality task, clinically normal 3-year-old children typically make a realist error when questioned about the identity of the object (e.g. Flavell et al., 1983). For example, when shown a sponge painted to look like a rock, the children judge that not only is it really a sponge but that it looks like one. Yet the illusion is convincing, since prior to feeling it, the children were fooled into thinking that it was a rock.

If we knew that children lacked the ability to make a distinction between appearance and reality, this alone would not be sufficient to help us predict what kind of error they would make. It might have been that they maintained that it really was a rock, as it appeared, even after having felt it. It so happens, however, that in this case young children are willing to attach more importance to touch than seeing, even though they are currently seeing the illusory appearance and no longer feeling the object.

If children with autism have a mode of thought that is iconically dominated, then we would expect a different kind of error. We might expect them to be influenced more heavily by the current visual appearance of the object than by how it felt when touched a moment earlier. We would thus predict that they would say that it looks like a rock and that it really is a rock. We would expect them to maintain this assertion despite having just handled the object. Even in the absence of this strong prediction, results of this kind presumably would be seen as striking and in need of explanation. It is surprising, then, that this result has been recorded not once but twice, and on neither occasion did the authors consider it necessary to discuss what was happening. The two studies were conducted by Baron-Cohen (1989a) and by Ozonoff et al. (1991), and in both cases the children with autism judged that not only did the object appear to be X but that it really was X (despite tactile cues to the contrary). Unlike the normal 3-year-olds tested by Flavell et al. (1983), who made realist errors, these children with autism made phenomenist errors. The authors on both occasions simply concluded that children with autism have difficulty with the distinction between appearance and reality, but did not comment on the unique kind of error the children made.

Another sign of iconic thought in autism arises from the good performance in making judgements about faces presented upside-down. As reported in the previous chapter, Hobson et al. (1988) found that people with autism are actually better than controls without autism in matching faces by identity and by emotion when all stimuli are presented upside-down. Hobson et al. concluded that people with autism are perhaps perceiving the face as a pattern rather than as a Gestalt face. There might be a basic predisposition in people without autism to interpret faces in relation to a prototype face template (Valentine & Bruce, 1986), which actually gives rise to confusion when a stimulus face is presented upside down. This would not pose a problem for people with autism if they were processing the face at the iconic level of a pattern, instead of perceiving faces as having an integrated meaning beyond that.

There are advantages to possessing an iconically dominated mode of thought in a few other contexts (Bruner, Olver, & Greenfield, 1966). Some children with autism are renowned for having remarkable abilities in recalling calendar dates, memorising bus timetables, and performing obscure numerical feats. Perhaps most prominent of all, though, a few are famous for their drawing abilities (notably Stephen Wiltshire and Nadia; see Selfe, 1983). All the diverse islets of special abilities cannot necessarily be explained by a capacity for iconic thought (though it might be possible), and it certainly is not the case that all or even most children with autism are good at realistic drawings (Charman & Baron-Cohen, 1993; Eames & Cox, 1994; Lewis & Boucher, 1991). However, those who are good at drawing may owe their success to applying their capacity for iconic thought to the task (cf. Selfe, 1983). Putting it another way, it might be that clinically normal people have considerable difficulty in drawing perspective because their symbolic classification of the item as belonging to a given category of thing then contaminates their ability to draw it precisely as it appears. However, to date the evidence seems to suggest that artistically gifted people with autism are inclined to categorise objects according to meaning rather than shape (Pring & Hermelin, 1993). Nonetheless, it might be that the semantics of objects do not contaminate perception of shape in people with autism to the same extent as in people without autism.

To expand, domes, spheres, and circles are notoriously difficult to draw as viewed from an oblique perspective (Thouless, 1931). Pirenne (1970) documents this difficulty even from the perspective errors evident in Renaissance paintings. Yet Stephen Wiltshire takes this challenge in his stride in tackling perhaps the most difficult of all, the concave of a domed building viewed obliquely from underneath. Stephen's depiction of perspective might not be perfect, but it is remarkably good, and in a way that eerily seems to capture the whole ambience and space of the chamber. It would not be surprising if people with decades of practice in life and architectural drawing compared unfavourably with the teenage Stephen.

It seems that as far as clinically normal people are concerned, encoding the object as a circle, dome, or sphere is sufficient to contaminate their judgement of how it appears, which in this case is reflected in their drawing. Specifically, they proceed to draw the thing as more prototypically circular, spherical, or domed than it actually appears. It might be that children with autism are inclined not to symbolise and categorise in this way. A minority might be able to use this to their advantage in drawing more accurately what they see.

Accordingly, we can make a prediction about the potentially good performance of people with autism on a related task. Taylor and Mitchell

(1996) found that under one condition clinically normal people tended to exaggerate the circularity of an ellipse they viewed in a darkened chamber, when trying to match the seen shape on a computer screen. This condition was when the participants knew that the elliptical shape was produced by a circle viewed obliquely. All perceptual cues were eliminated, so they were purely being contaminated by the prior knowledge that the thing was a circle. Under another condition, participants were not informed that the thing was really a circle, and participants' judgements were accurate in this case. It might be that people with autism are able to give accurate judgements under both conditions. This would occur if their thought was predominantly iconic, meaning that their judgement could not be contaminated by encoding or classifying the viewed object as a circle. This is awaiting investigation.

CONCLUSION

It might be the case that, on some primitive level, the child begins with an incipient ability to handle referential opacity that allows early joint-attention and pretence. In return, the emerging communicative competence, especially on a verbal level, may promote an understanding of the particulars of the psychology of those around us. Early in life, it might be that we do not make the most of these competencies due to a realist bias.

In autistic development, perhaps the capacity for referential opacity is limited. This would result from a lack of imaginative abilities that in normal development serves as an essential supporting feature of cognition. Consequently, whereas in normal development there is progression toward symbolic thinking, autistic thought may remain largely iconic. However, some understanding of referential opacity and more general understanding of mind could develop belatedly in autism. But this might be insufficient to allow the individual to treat speech as a window on mind. Hence, individuals would be denied a deep understanding of the particular psychology of the people around them. They could therefore remain manifestly autistic, though some adaptation is possible. In contrast, in normal development children will experience an incessant flow of information from and about other minds principally via the channel of verbal communication. Accordingly, humans benefit from a life-long education on the mind, with the consequence that, all things equal, mature adults almost certainly will have greater insight into mind than younger people.

References

Ackerman, B.P. (1979). Children's understanding of definite descriptions: Pragmatic inferences to the speaker's intent. *Journal of Experimental Child Psychology, 28*, 1–15.

Ackerman, B.P. (1981). Performative bias in children's interpretations of ambiguous referential communications. *Child Development, 52*, 1224–1230.

Avis, J., & Harris, P. (1991). Belief-desire reasoning among Baka children: Evidence for a universal conception of mind. *Child Development, 62*, 460–467.

Baldwin, D.A. (1991). Infants' contribution to the achievement of joint reference. *Child Development, 63*, 875–890.

Baldwin, D.A. (1993a) Infants' ability to consult the speaker for clues to word reference. *Journal of Child Language, 20*, 395–418.

Baldwin, D.A. (1993b). Early referential understanding: Infants' ability to recognise referential acts for what they are. *Developmental Psychology, 29*, 832–843.

Baldwin, D.A., & Moses, L.J. (1994). Early understanding of referential intent and attentional focus: Evidence from language and emotion. In C. Lewis & P. Mitchell (Eds.), *Children's early understanding of mind: Origins and development* (pp.133–156). Hove: Lawrence Erlbaum Associates Ltd.

Baron-Cohen, S. (1987). Autism and symbolic play. *British Journal of Developmental Psychology, 5*, 139–148.

Baron-Cohen, S. (1988). Social and pragmatic deficits in autism: Cognitive or affective? *Journal of Autism and Developmental Disorders, 18*, 379–402.

Baron-Cohen, S. (1989a). Are autistic children "behaviourists"? An examination of their mental-physical and appearance-reality distinctions. *Journal of Autism and Developmental Disorders, 19*, 579–600.

Baron-Cohen, S. (1989b). The autistic child's theory of mind: A case of specific developmental delay. *Journal of Child Psychology and Psychiatry, 30,* 285–297.

Baron-Cohen, S. (1989c). Perceptual role taking and protodeclarative pointing in autism. *British Journal of Developmental Psychology, 7,* 113–127.

Baron-Cohen, S. (1991). Do children with autism understand what causes emotion? *Child Development, 62,* 385–395.

Baron-Cohen, S., Leslie, A.M., & Frith, U. (1985). Does the autistic child have a 'theory of mind'? *Cognition, 21,* 37–46.

Bartsch, K., & Wellman, H. (1989). Young children's attribution of action to beliefs and desires. *Child Development, 60,* 946–964.

Beal, C.R. (1988). Children's knowledge about representations of intended meaning. In J.W. Astington, P.L. Harris, & D.R. Olson (Eds.), *Developing theories of mind* (pp.315–325). Cambridge: Cambridge University Press.

Bonitatibus, G. (1988). What is said and what is meant in referential communication. In J.W. Astington, P.L. Harris, & D.R. Olson (Eds.), *Developing theories of mind* (pp.326–338). Cambridge: Cambridge University Press.

Bonitatibus, G., & Flavell, J.H. (1985). The effect of presenting a message in written form on young children's ability to evaluate its communicative adequacy. *Developmental Psychology, 21,* 455–461.

Boucher, J. (1989). The theory of mind hypothesis of autism: Explanation, evidence and assessment. *British Journal of Disorders of Communication, 24,* 181–198.

Bowler, D.M. (1992). "Theory of mind" in Asperger's syndrome. *Journal of Child Psychology and Psychiatry, 33,* 877–893.

Boysen, S.T. (1993). Counting in chimpanzees: Nonhuman principles and emergent properties of number. In S.T. Boysen & E.J. Capaldi (Eds.), *The development of numerical competence: Animal and human models* (pp.39–59). Hove: Lawrence Erlbaum Associates Ltd.

Bruner, J.S. (1964). The course of cognitive growth. *American Psychologist, 19,* 1–15.

Bruner, J.S. (1983). *Child's talk: Learning to use language.* New York: W.W. Norton.

Bruner, J.S., Olver, R.R., & Greenfield, P.M. (1966). *Studies in cognitive growth.* New York: John Wiley.

Butterworth, G. (1994). Theory of mind and the facts of embodiment. In C. Lewis & P. Mitchell (Eds.), *Children's early understanding of mind: Origins and development* (pp.115–132). Hove: Lawrence Erlbaum Associates Ltd.

Butterworth, G., & Cochran, E. (1980). Towards a mechanism of joint visual attention in human infancy. *International Journal of Behavioural Development, 3,* 253–272.

Butterworth, G., & Jarrett, N.L.M. (1991). What minds have in common is space: Spatial mechanisms serving joint visual attention in infancy. *British Journal of Developmental Psychology, 9,* 55–72.

Chandler, M., & Boyes, M. (1982). Social-cognitive development. In B. Wolman (Ed.), *Handbook of developmental psychology* (pp.387–402). Englewood Cliffs, NJ: Prentice-Hall.

Chandler, M., Fritz, A.S., & Hala, S. (1989). Small scale deceit: Deception as a marker of 2-, 3-, and 4-year-olds' early theories of mind. *Child Development, 60,* 1263–1277.

Chandler, M., & Hala, S. (1994). The role of personal involvement in the assessment of early false belief skills. In C. Lewis & P. Mitchell (Eds.), *Children's early understanding of mind: Origins and development* (pp.403–425). Hove: Lawrence Erlbaum Associates Ltd.

Chandler, M., & Helm, D. (1984). Developmental changes in the contribution of shared experience to social role taking competence. *International Journal of Behavioural Development, 7,* 145–156.

Charman, T., & Baron-Cohen, S. (1992). Understanding drawings and beliefs: A further test of the metarepresentation theory of autism. *Journal of Child Psychology and Psychiatry, 33,* 1105–1112.

Charman, T., & Baron-Cohen, S. (1993). Drawing development in autism: The intellectual to visual realism shift. *British Journal of Developmental Psychology, 11,* 171–185.

Charman, T., & Lynggaard, H. (1995). *Facilitating false belief performance in autism.* Unpublished manuscript, University College London.

Clements, W.A., & Perner, J. (1994). Implicit understanding of belief. *Cognitive Development, 9,* 377–395.

Connolly, J.A., & Doyle, A. (1984). Relation of social fantasy play to social competence in preschoolers. *Developmental Psychology, 20,* 797–806.

deGelder, B. (1987). On not having a theory of mind. *Cognition, 27,* 285–290.

Demorest, A., Meyer, C., Phelps, E., Gardner, H., & Winner, E. (1984). Words speak louder than actions: Understanding deliberately false words. *Child Development, 55,* 1537–1554.

Dennett, D.C. (1978). Beliefs about beliefs. *Behavioural and Brain Sciences, 1,* 568–570.

Donaldson, M. (1978). *Children's minds.* Glasgow: Fontana/Collins.

Dunn, J. (1994).Changing minds and changing relationships. In C. Lewis & P. Mitchell (Eds.), *Children's early understanding of mind: Origins and development* (pp.297–310). Hove: Lawrence Erlbaum Associates Ltd.

Dunn, J., Brown, J., Slomkowski, C., Tesla, C., & Youngblade, L. (1991). Young children's understanding of other people's feelings and beliefs: Individual differences and their antecedents. *Child Development, 62,* 1352–1366.

Eames, K., & Cox, M.V. (1994). Visual realism in the drawing of autistic, Down's syndrome and normal children. *British Journal of Developmental Psychology, 12,* 235–239.

Eisenmajer, R., & Prior, M. (1991). Cognitive linguistic correlates of "theory of mind" ability in autistic children. *British Journal of Developmental Psychology, 9,* 351–364.

Estes, D., Wellman, H.M., & Woolley, J.D. (1989). Children's understanding of mental phenomena. In H.W. Reese (Ed.), *Advances in child development and behaviour* (pp.41–87). New York: Academic Press.

Fischhoff, B. (1975). Hindsight is not equal to foresight: The effect of outcome knowledge on judgement under uncertainty. *Journal of Experimental Psychology: Human Perception and Performance, 1,* 288–299.

Fischhoff, B., & Beyth, R. (1975). "I knew it would happen": Remembered probabilities of once-future things. *Organisational Behaviour and Human Performance, 13,* 1–16.

Flavell, J.H. (1988). The development of children's knowledge about the mind: From cognitive connections to mental representations. In J.W. Astington, P.L. Harris, & D.R. Olson (Eds.), *Developing theories of mind* (pp.244–267). Cambridge: Cambridge University Press.

Flavell, J.H., Flavell, E.R., & Green, F.L. (1983). Development of the appearance-reality distinction. *Cognitive Psychology, 15*, 95–120.

Flavell, J.H., Flavell, E.R., & Green, F.L. (1987). Young children's knowledge about the apparent-real and pretend-real distinctions. *Developmental Psychology, 23*, 816–822.

Flavell, J.H., Green, F.L., & Flavell, J.H. (1993). Children's understanding of the stream of consciousness. *Child Development, 64*, 387–398.

Flavell, J.H., Green, F.L., & Flavell, J.H. (1995). Young children's knowledge about thinking. *Monographs of the Society for Research in Child Development, 60*, Serial number 243.

Fodor, J.A. (1992). A theory of the child's theory of mind. *Cognition, 44*, 283–296.

Fox, T., & Thomas, G.V. (1989). Children's drawings of an anxiety eliciting topic: Effect on the size of drawing. *British Journal of Clinical Psychology, 29*, 71–81.

Fraiberg, S., & Adelson, E. (1977). Self representation in language and play. In S. Fraiberg (Ed.), *Insights from the blind* (pp.248–270). London: Souvenir.

Freeman, N.H. (1994). Associations and dissociations in theories of mind. In C. Lewis & P. Mitchell (Eds.), *Children's early understanding of mind: Origins and development* (pp.95–111). Hove: Lawrence Erlbaum Associates Ltd.

Freeman, N.H., & Lacohee, H. (1995). Making explicit 3-year-olds' implicit competence with their own false beliefs, *Cognition, 56*, 31–60.

Freeman, N.H., Lacohee, H., & Coulton, S. (1995). Cued recall approach to 3–year-olds' memory for an honest mistake. *Journal of Experimental Child Psychology, 60*, 102–115.

Frith, U. (1989). *Autism: Explaining the enigma*. Oxford: Blackwell.

Frith, U., Happe, F.G.E., & Siddons, F. (1994). Autism and theory of mind in everyday life. *Social Development, 3*, 108–124.

German, T.P. (1995). *Children's explanation of action: Desires versus beliefs in theory of mind*. PhD Thesis, University of London.

Golinkoff, R.M. (1986). "I beg your pardon?": The preverbal negotiation of failed messages. *Journal of Child Language, 13*, 455–476.

Gopnik, A. (1993). How we know our minds: The illusion of first person knowledge of intentionality. *Behavioural and Brain Sciences, 16*, 1–14.

Gopnik, A., & Astington, J.W. (1988). Children's understanding of representational change, and its relation to the understanding of false belief and the appearance-reality distinction. *Child Development, 59*, 26–37.

Gopnik, A., & Graf, P. (1988). Knowing how you know: Young children's ability to identify and remember the sources of their beliefs. *Child Development, 59*, 1366–1371.

Gopnik, A., & Slaughter, V. (1991). Young children's understanding of changes in their mental states. *Child Development, 62*, 98–110.

Guralnik, M.J., & Paul-Brown, D. (1977). The nature of verbal interactions among handicapped and nonhandicapped preschool children. *Child Development, 48*, 254–260.

Hadwin, J., & Perner, J. (1991). Pleased and surprised: Children's cognitive theory of emotion. *British Journal of Developmental Psychology, 9*, 215–234.

Hala, S., Chandler, M., & Fritz, A.S. (1991). Fledgling theories of mind: Deception as a marker of 3-year-olds' understanding of false belief. *Child Development, 61*, 83–97.

Happe, F.G.E. (1993). Communicative competence and theory of mind in autism: A test of Relevance Theory. *Cognition, 48*, 101–119.

Happe, F.G.E. (1994). Current psychological theories of autism: The "theory of mind" account and rival theories. *Journal of Child Psychology and Psychiatry, 35*, 215–229.

Happe, F.G.E. (1995). The role of age and verbal ability in the theory of mind task performance of subjects with autism. *Child Development, 66*, 843–855.

Harris, M. (1992). *Language experience and early language development.* Hove: Lawrence Erlbaum Associates Ltd.

Harris, P.L. (1989). *Children and emotion: The development of psychological understanding.* Oxford: Basil Blackwell.

Harris, P.L. (1991). The work of the imagination. In A. Whiten (Ed.), *Natural theories of mind* (pp.283–304). Oxford: Basil Blackwell.

Harris, P.L., Brown, E., Marriott, C., Whittall, S., & Harmer, S. (1991). Monsters, ghosts and witches: Testing the limits of the fantasy-reality distinction in young children. *British Journal of Developmental Psychology, 9*, 105–123.

Harris, P.L., & Gross, D. (1988). Children's understanding of real and apparent emotion. In J.W. Astington, P.L. Harris, & D.R. Olson (Eds.), *Developing theories of mind* (pp.295–314). Cambridge: Cambridge University Press.

Harris, P.L., Johnson, C.N., Hutton, D. Andrews, G., & Cooke, T. (1989). Young children's theory of mind and emotion. *Cognition and Emotion, 3*, 379–400.

Harris, P.L., & Kavanaugh, R.D. (1993). Young children's understanding of pretence. *Monographs of the Society for Research in Child Development, 58*, Serial No. 231.

Heyes, C.M. (1993). Anecdotes, training, trapping and triangulating: Do animals attribute mental states? *Animal Behaviour, 46*, 177–188.

Hobson, R.P. (1990). On acquiring knowledge about people and the capacity to pretend: Response to Leslie. *Psychological Review, 97*, 114–121.

Hobson, R.P. (1993). *Autism and the development of mind.* Hove: Lawrence Erlbaum Associates Ltd.

Hobson, R.P. (1994). Perceiving attitudes, conceiving minds. In C. Lewis & P. Mitchell (Eds.), *Children's early understanding of mind: Origins and development* (pp.71–93). Hove: Lawrence Erlbaum Associates Ltd.

Hobson, R.P., & Minter, M. (1995). *Blindness and psychological development 0–10 years.* Paper presented at the Mary Kitzinger Trust Symposium: September, 1995, University of Warwick.

Hobson, R.P., Ouston, J., & Lee, A. (1988). What's in a face? The case of autism. *British Journal of Psychology, 79*, 441–453.

Hobson, R.P., Ouston, J., & Lee, A. (1989). Naming emotion in faces and voices: Abilities and disabilities in autism and mental retardation. *British Journal of Developmental Psychology, 7*, 237–250.

Howes, C., Unger, O., & Matheson, C.C. (1992). *The collaborative construction of pretend.* Albany, NY: SUNY Press.

Humphrey, N.K. (1992). *A history of the mind.* London: Vintage Books.

Jarrold, C., Boucher, J., & Smith, P.K. (1994). Executive function deficits and the pretend play of children with autism: A research note. *Journal of Child Psychology and Psychiatry, 35*, 1473–1482.

Jarrold, C., Carruthers, P., Smith, P.K., & Boucher, J. (1994a). Pretend play: Is it metarepresentational? *Mind and Language, 9*, 445–468.

Jarrold, C., Smith, P.K., Boucher, J., & Harris, P.L. (1994b). Comprehension of pretence in children with autism. *Journal of Autism and Developmental Disorders, 24*, 433–455.

Johnson, C.N., & Maratsos, M.P. (1977). Early comprehension of mental verbs: Think and know. *Child Development, 48,* 1743–1747.

Johnson, C.N., & Wellman, H.M. (1982). Children's developing conceptions of the mind and brain. *Child Development, 53,* 222–234.

Kanner, L. (1943). Autistic disturbances of affective contact. *Nervous Child, 12,* 17–50.

Kasari, C., Sigman, M., Mundy, P., & Yirmiya, N. (1990). Affective sharing in the context of joint attention interaction of normal, autistic and mentally retarded children. *Journal of Autism and Developmental Disorders, 20,* 87–100.

Keating, C.F., & Heltman, K.R. (1994). Dominance and deception in children and adults: Are leaders the best misleaders? *Personality and Social Psychology Bulletin, 20,* 312–321.

Klin, A. Volkmar, F.R., & Sparrow, S.S. (1992). Autistic social dysfunction: Some limitations of the theory of mind hypothesis. *Journal of Child Psychology and Psychiatry, 33,* 861–876.

Krauss, R.M., & Glucksberg, S. (1969). The development of communication: Competence as a function of age. *Child Development, 40,* 255–266.

Leekam, S.R., & Perner, J. (1991). Does the autistic child have a metarepresentational deficit? *Cognition, 40,* 203–218.

Leekam, S.R., & Prior, M. (1994). Can autistic children distinguish lies from jokes? *Journal of Child Psychology and Psychiatry, 35,* 901–915.

Leslie, A.M. (1987). Pretence and representation: The origins of "theory of mind." *Psychological Review, 94,* 412–426.

Leslie, A.M. (1994). Pretending and believing: Issues in the theory of ToMM. *Cognition, 50,* 211–238.

Leslie, A.M., & Frith, U. (1988). Autistic children's understanding of seeing, knowing and believing. *British Journal of Developmental Psychology, 6,* 315–324.

Leslie, A.M., & Frith, U. (1990). Prospects for a cognitive neuropsychology of autism: Hobson's choice. *Psychological Review, 97,* 122–131.

Leslie, A.M., & Thaiss, L. (1992). Domain specificity in conceptual development: Neuropsychological evidence from autism. *Cognition, 43,* 225–251.

Lewis, C., Freeman, N.H., Hagestadt, C., & Douglas, H. (1994). Narrative access and production in preschoolers' false belief reasoning. *Cognitive Development, 9,* 397–424.

Lewis, C., & Osborne, A. (1990). Three-year-olds' problems with false belief: Conceptual deficit or linguistic artefact? *Child Development, 61,* 1514–1519.

Lewis, M., Stanger, C., & Sullivan, M.W. (1989). Deception in 3-year-olds. *Developmental Psychology, 25,* 439–443.

Lewis, V., & Boucher, J. (1991). Skill, content and generative strategies in autistic children's drawings. *British Journal of Developmental Psychology, 9,* 393–416.

Lillard, A.S. (1993a). Pretend play skills and the child's theory of mind. *Child Development, 64,* 348–371.

Lillard, A.S. (1993b). Young children's conceptualisation of pretence: Action or mental representational state? *Child Development, 64,* 372–386.

Lillard, A.S., & Flavell, J.H. (1992). Young children's understanding of different mental verbs. *Developmental Psychology, 28,* 626–634.

Luria, A.R. (1960). Verbal regulation of behaviour. In J. Brazier (Ed.), *The central nervous system and behavior* (pp.359–423). New York: Josiah Macy Foundation.

Maratos, M.P. (1973). Nonegocentric communication abilities in preschool children. *Child Development, 44,* 697–700.

Markman, E. M. (1976). Children's difficulty with word-referent differentiation. *Child Development, 47,* 742–749.

Menig-Peterson, C.L. (1975). The modification of communicative behaviour in preschool-aged children as a function of the listener's perspective. *Child Development, 46,* 1015–1018.

Mitchell, P. (1992). Réalité et représentation du monde, une distinction innée? *La Recherche, 23,* 1332–1333.

Mitchell, P. (1994). Realism and early conception of mind: A synthesis of phylogenetic and ontogenetic issues. In C. Lewis & P. Mitchell (Eds.), *Children's early understanding of mind: Origins and development* (pp.19–45). Hove: Lawrence Erlbaum Associates Ltd.

Mitchell, P., & Isaacs, J.E. (1994). Understanding of verbal representation in children with autism: The case of referential opacity. *British Journal of Developmental Psychology, 12,* 439–454.

Mitchell, P., & Lacohée, H. (1991). Children's early understanding of false belief. *Cognition, 39,* 107–127.

Mitchell, P., Munno, A., & Russell, J. (1991). Children's understanding of the communicative value of discrepant verbal messages. *Cognitive Development, 6,* 279–299.

Mitchell, P., & Robinson, E.J. (1990). What determines the accuracy of children's judgements of their own knowledge? *Journal of Experimental Child Psychology, 50,* 81–101.

Mitchell, P., & Robinson, E.J. (1992). Children's understanding of the evidential connotation of "know" in relation to overestimation of their own knowledge. *Journal of Child Language, 19,* 167–182.

Mitchell, P., & Robinson, E.J. (1994). Discrepant utterances resulting from a false belief: Children's evaluations. *Child Development, 65,* 1214–1227.

Mitchell, P., & Robinson, E.J. (in prep.). *Children's early understanding of referential opacity.* University of Birmingham.

Mitchell, P., Robinson, E.J., Isaacs, J.E., & Nye, R.M. (1996). Contamination in reasoning about false belief: An instance of realist bias in adults but not children. *Cognition, 59,* 1–21.

Mitchell, P., Robinson, E.J., Nye, R.M., & Isaacs, J.E. (in press). When speech conflicts with seeing: Young children's understanding of informational priority. *Journal of Experimental Child Psychology.*

Mitchell, P., & Russell, J. (1989). Young children's understanding of the say-mean distinction in referential speech. *Journal of Experimental Child Psychology, 47,* 467–490.

Mitchell. P., & Russell, J. (1991). Children's judgements of whether slightly and grossly discrepant objects were intended by a speaker. *British Journal of Developmental Psychology, 9,* 271–280.

Mitchell, P., & Saltmarsh, R. (1994). Communicating, reading one's own mind and resisting reality. *Cahiers de Psychologie Cognitive, 13,* 652–660.

Mitchell, P., Saltmarsh, R., & Russell, H. (in press). Overly literal interpretations of speech in autism: Understanding that messages arise from minds. *Journal of Child Psychology and Psychiatry.*

Moore, C., & Corkum, V. (1994). Social understanding at the end of the first year of life. *Developmental Review, 14*, 349–372.

Moore, C., Pure, K., & Furrow, D. (1990). Children's understanding of the modal expression of speaker certainty and uncertainty and its relation to the development of a representational theory of mind. *Child Development, 61*, 722–730.

Moses, L.J. (1993). Young children's understanding of belief constraints on intention. *Cognitive Development, 8*, 1–25.

Moses, L.J., & Flavell, J.H. (1990). Inferring false beliefs from actions and reactions. *Child Development, 61*, 929–945.

Mundy, P., Kasari, C., & Sigman, M. (1992). Nonverbal communication, affective sharing, and intersubjectivity. *Infant Behaviour and Development, 15*, 377–382.

Mundy, P., Sigman, M., & Kasari, C. (1993). The theory of mind and joint attention deficits in autism. In S. Baron-Cohen, H. Tager-Flusberg, & D. Cohen (Eds.), *Understanding other minds: Perspectives from autism* (pp.181–203). Oxford: Oxford University Press.

Olson, D.R., & Torrance, N.G. (1983). Literacy and cognitive development: A conceptual transformation in the early school years. In S. Meadows (Ed.), *Developing thinking: Approaches to children's cognitive development* (pp.142–160). London: Methuen.

O'Neill, D.K., Astington, J.W., & Flavell, J.H. (1992). Young children's understanding of the role that sensory experiences play in knowledge acquisition. *Child Development, 63*, 474–490.

O'Neill, D.K., & Gopnik, A. (1991). Young children's ability to identify the sources of their beliefs. *Developmental Psychology, 27*, 390–397.

Ozonoff, S., Pennington, B.F., & Rogers, S.J. (1991). Executive function deficits in high-functioning autistic individuals: Relationship to theory of mind. *Journal of Child Psychology and Psychiatry, 32*, 1081–1105.

Perner, J. (1988). Developing semantics for theories of mind: From propositional attitudes to mental representation. In J.W. Astington, P.L. Harris, & D.R. Olson (Eds.), *Developing theories of mind* (pp.141–172). Cambridge: Cambridge University Press.

Perner, J. (1991). *Understanding the representational mind*. London: MIT Press.

Perner, J., Baker, S., & Hutton, D. (1994). Prelief: The conceptual origins of belief and pretence. In C. Lewis & P. Mitchell (Eds.), *Children's early understanding of mind: Origins and development* (pp.261–286). Hove: Lawrence Erlbaum Associates Ltd.

Perner, J., & Davies, G. (1991). Understanding the mind as an active information processor: Do young children have a "Copy theory of mind"? *Cognition, 39*, 51–69.

Perner, J., Frith, U., Leslie, A.M., & Leekam, S.R. (1989). Exploration of the autistic child's theory of mind: Knowledge, belief and communication. *Child Development, 60*, 689–700.

Perner, J., Leekam, S., & Wimmer, H. (1987). Three-year-olds' difficulty with false belief: The case for a conceptual deficit. *British Journal of Developmental Psychology, 5*, 125–137.

Perner, J., & Ogden, J.E. (1988). Knowledge for hunger: Children's problem with representation in imputing mental states. *Cognition, 29*, 47–61.

Perner, J., Ruffman, T., & Leekam, S.R. (1994). Theory of mind is contagious: You catch it from your sibs. *Child Development, 65*, 1228–1238.

Perner, J., & Wimmer, H. (1985). "John thinks that Mary thinks that ..." Attribution of second-order beliefs by 5–10-year-old children. *Journal of Experimental Child Psychology, 39*, 437–471.

Peskin, J. (1992). Ruse and representations: On children's ability to conceal information. *Developmental Psychology, 28*, 84–89.

Peterson, C.C., & Siegal, M. (1995). Deafness, conversation and theory of mind. *Journal of Child Psychology and Psychiatry, 36*, 459–474.

Pillow, B.H. (1989). Early understanding of perception as a source of knowledge. *Journal of Experimental Child Psychology, 47*, 116–129.

Pillow, B.H. (1993) Preschool children's understanding of the relationship between modality of perceptual access and knowledge of perceptual properties. *British Journal of Developmental Psychology, 11*, 371–390.

Pirenne, M.H. (1970). *Optics, painting and photography.* Cambridge: Cambridge University Press.

Povinelli, D.J. (1993). Reconstructing the evolution of mind. *American Psychologist, 48*, 493–509.

Povinelli, D.J., & Deblois, S. (1992). Young children's (*Homo sapiens*) understanding of knowledge formation in themselves and others. *Journal of Comparative Psychology, 106*, 228–238.

Povinelli, D.J., & Eddy, T.J. (in press). What young chimpanzees know about seeing. *Monographs of the Society for Research in Child Development.*

Power, D.J., Wood, D.J., & Wood, H.A. (1990). Conversational strategies of teachers using three methods of communication with deaf children. *American Annals of the Deaf, 135*, 9–13.

Pratt, C., & Bryant, P. (1990). Young children understand that looking leads to knowing (so long as they are looking into a single barrel). *Child Development, 61*, 973–982.

Preisler, G. (1995). *Blindness and psychological development 0–10 years.* Paper presented at the Mary Kitzinger Trust Symposium, September 1995, University of Warwick.

Premack, D., & Woodruff, G. (1978). Does the chimpanzee have a theory of mind? *Behavioural and Brain Sciences, 4*, 515–526.

Pring, L., & Hermelin, B. (1993). Bottle, tulip and wineglass: Semantic and structural picture processing by savant artists. *Journal of Child Psychology and Psychiatry, 34*, 1365–1385.

Pylyshyn, Z.W. (1978). When is attribution of beliefs justified? *Behavioural and Brain Sciences, 1*, 592–593.

Quine, W.V.O. (1961). *From a logical point of view.* Cambridge, MA: Harvard University Press.

Reiss, A.L., Feinstein, C., & Rosenbaum, K.N. (1986). Autism and genetic disorders. *Schizophrenia Bulletin, 12*, 724–738.

Riggs, K.J., Peterson, D.M., Robinson, E.J., & Mitchell, P. (1996). *Are realist errors in false belief tasks due to difficulty with counterfactual reasoning?* Unpublished manuscript, University of Birmingham.

Riggs, K.J., & Robinson, E.J. (1995a). What people say and what they think: Children's judgements of false belief in relation to their recall of false messages. *British Journal of Developmental Psychology, 13*, 271–284.

Riggs, K.J., & Robinson, E.J. (1995b). Children's memory for actions based on a false belief. *Journal of Experimental Child Psychology, 60*, 229–244.

Robinson, E.J. (1994). What people say, what they think and what is really the case: Children's understanding of utterances as sources of knowledge. In C. Lewis & P. Mitchell (Eds.), *Children's early understanding of mind: Origins and development* (pp.355–381). Hove: Lawrence Erlbaum Associates Ltd.

Robinson, E.J., Goelman, H., & Olson, D.R. (1983). Children's understanding of the relation between expressions (what was said) and intentions (what was meant). *British Journal of Developmental Psychology, 1,* 75–86.

Robinson, E.J., & Goold, J. (1992). *Young children's ability to report their own superseded beliefs: Facilitation via physical embodiment.* Unpublished manuscript, University of Birmingham.

Robinson, E.J., & Mitchell, P. (1990). Children's judgements of undecidability when they are ignorant. *International Journal of Behavioural Development, 13,* 467–488.

Robinson, E.J., & Mitchell, P. (1992). Children's interpretation of messages from a speaker with a false belief. *Child Development, 63,* 639–652.

Robinson, E.J., & Mitchell, P. (1994a). Young children's false belief reasoning: Interpretation of messages is no easier than the classic task. *Developmental Psychology, 30,* 67–72.

Robinson, E.J., & Mitchell, P. (1994b). Children's judgements of ignorance on the basis of absence of experience. *British Journal of Developmental Psychology, 12,* 113–129.

Robinson, E.J., & Mitchell, P. (1995). Masking of children's early understanding of the representational mind: Backwards explanation versus prediction. *Child Development, 66,* 1022–1039.

Robinson, E.J., Mitchell, P., & Nye, R.M. (1995). Young children's treating of utterances as unreliable sources of knowledge. *Journal of Child Language, 22,* 663–685.

Robinson, E.J., Riggs, K.J., & Samuel, J. (in press). Children's memory for drawings based on false belief. *Developmental Psychology.*

Robinson, E.J., & Whittaker, S.J. (1987). Children's conceptions of relations between messages, meanings and reality. *British Journal of Developmental Psychology, 5,* 81–90.

Rosenberg, M. (1979). *Conceiving the self.* New York: Basic Books.

Rozin, P. Millman, L., & Nemeroff, C. (1986). Operation of the laws of sympathetic magic in disgust and other domains. *Journal of Personality and Social Psychology, 50,* 703–712.

Ruffman, T., Olson, D.R., Ash, T., & Keenan, T. (1993). The ABCs of deception: Do young children understand deception in the same way as adults? *Developmental Psychology, 29,* 74–87.

Russell, J. (1982). Propositional attitudes. In M. Beveridge (Ed.), *Children thinking through language* (pp.75–98). London: Edward Arnold.

Russell, J. (1987). "Can we say...?" Children's understanding of intensionality. *Cognition, 25,* 289–308.

Russell, J., Jarrold, C., & Potel, D. (1994). What makes strategic deception difficult for young children — the deception or the strategy? *British Journal of Developmental Psychology, 12,* 301–314.

Russell, J., Mauthner, N., Sharpe, S., & Tidswell, T. (1991). The "windows task" as a measure of strategic deception in preschoolers and autistic subjects. *British Journal of Developmental Psychology, 9,* 331–350.

Saltmarsh, R. (1995). *Realism and representation in children's early conception of mind.* PhD, University of Wales.

Saltmarsh, R., & Mitchell, P. (1996). *Young children's acknowledgment of false belief when confronted with the evidence.* Unpublished manuscript, University College Swansea.

Saltmarsh, R., Mitchell, P., & Robinson, E.J. (1995). Realism and children's early grasp of mental representation: Belief-based judgements in the state change task. *Cognition, 57*, 297–325.

Samuels, M., Brooks, P., & Frye, D. (1996). Strategic game playing in children through the "windows task". *British Journal of Developmental Psychology, 14*, 159–172.

Savage-Rumbaugh, E.S., Murphy, J., Sevcik, R.A., Brakke, K.E., Williams, S.L., & Rumbaugh, D.M. (1993). Language comprehension in ape and child. *Monographs of the Society for Research in Child Development, 58*, No. 3–4.

Selfe, L. (1983). *Normal and anomalous representational drawing ability in children.* London: Academic Press.

Shatz, M. (1994). Theory of mind and the development of social-linguistic intelligence in early childhood. In C. Lewis & P. Mitchell (Eds.), *Children's early understanding of mind: Origins and development* (pp.311–329). Hove: Lawrence Erlbaum Associates Ltd.

Shatz, M., & Gelman, R. (1973). The development of communication skills: Modifications in the speech of young children as a function of listener. *Monographs of the Society for Research in Child Development, 38* (5, Serial No. 152).

Shatz, M., & O'Reilly, A.W. (1990). Conversational or communicative skill? A reassessment of two-year-olds' behaviour in miscommunication episodes. *Journal of Child Language, 17*, 131–146.

Shatz, M., Wellman, H.M., & Silber, S. (1983). The acquisition of mental terms: A systematic investigation of the first reference to mental state. *Cognition, 14*, 301–321.

Siegal, M., & Beattie, K. (1991). Where to look first for children's knowledge of false beliefs. *Cognition, 38*, 1–12.

Sodian, B. (1991). The development of deception in young children. *British Journal of Developmental Psychology, 9*, 173–188.

Sodian, B., & Frith, U. (1992). Deception and sabotage in autistic, retarded and normal children. *Journal of Child Psychology and Psychiatry, 33*, 591–605.

Sodian, B., & Schneider, W. (1991). Children's understanding of cognitive cueing: How to manipulate cues to fool a competitor. *Child Development, 61*, 697–704.

Sodian, B., Taylor, C., Harris, P.L., & Perner, J. (1991). Early deception and the child's theory of mind: False trails and genuine markers. *Child Development, 62*, 468–483.

Sodian, B., & Wimmer, H. (1987). Children's understanding of inference as a source of knowledge. *Child Development, 58*, 424–433.

Sorce, J.F., Emde, R.N., Campos, J., & Klinnert, M.D. (1985). Maternal emotional signalling: Its effect on the visual cliff behaviour of infants and young children. *Journal of Experimental Child Psychology, 35*, 369–390.

Sparrevohn, R., & Howie, P.M. (1995). Theory of mind in children with autistic disorder: Evidence of developmental progression and the role of verbal ability. *Journal of Child Psychology and Psychiatry, 36*, 249–263.

Sparrow, S., Balla, D., & Cichetti, D. (1984). *Vineland Adaptive Behavior Scales (survey form).* Circle Pines, MN: American Guidance Services.

Steverson, E.J. (1995). *The malleability of the developing representational mind.* PhD, University of Wales.

Steverson, E.J., & Mitchell, P. (1995a). *The suggestibility of children's early acknowledgment of false belief.* Unpublished manuscript, University College Swansea.

Steverson, E.J., & Mitchell, P. (1995b). *Reversion to realism in a false belief test following suggestion.* Unpublished manuscript, University College Swansea.

Sullivan, K., & Winner, E. (1993). Three-year-olds' understanding of mental states: The influence of trickery. *Journal of Experimental Child Psychology, 56,* 135–148.

Tager-Flusberg, H. (1981). Sentence comprehension in autistic children. *Applied Psycholinguistics, 2,* 5–24.

Tager-Flusberg, H. (1993). What language reveals about the understanding of minds in children with autism. In S. Baron-Cohen, H. Tager-Flusberg, & D. Cohen (Eds.), *Understanding other minds: Perspectives from autism* (pp.138–157). Oxford: Oxford University Press.

Tager-Flusberg, H., & Sullivan, K. (1994). Predicting and explaining behaviour: A comparison of autistic, mentally retarded and normal children. *Journal of Child Psychology and Psychiatry, 35,* 1059–1075.

Taylor, L.M., & Mitchell, P. (in press). Judgements of apparent shape contaminated by knowledge of reality. *British Journal of Psychology.*

Thomas, G.V., Chaigne, E., & Fox, T. (1989). Children's drawings of topics differing in significance. *British Journal of Developmental Psychology, 7,* 321–332.

Thouless, R.H. (1931). Phenomenal regression to the real object, II. *British Journal of Psychology, 22,* 1–30.

Valentine, T., & Bruce, V. (1986). The effect of race, inversion and encoding activity upon face recognition. *Acta Psychologica, 61,* 259–273.

Vygotsky, L.S. (1978). *Mind in society: The development of higher mental processes.* Cambridge, MA: Harvard University Press.

Wellman, H.M. (1990). *The child's theory of mind.* Cambridge, MA: MIT Press.

Wellman, H.M., & Bartsch, K. (1988). Young children's reasoning about beliefs. *Cognition, 30,* 239–277.

Wellman, H.M., & Bartsch, K. (1994). Before belief: Children's early psychological theory. In C. Lewis & P. Mitchell (Eds.), *Children's early understanding of mind: Origins and development* (pp.331–354). Hove: Lawrence Erlbaum Associates Ltd.

Wellman, H.M., & Estes, D. (1986). Early understanding of mental entities: A re-examination of childhood realism. *Child Development, 57,* 910–923.

Wellman, H.M., Hollander, M., & Schult, C.A. (1995). *Young children's understanding of thought bubbles and of thoughts.* Unpublished manuscript, University of Michigan.

Wellman, H.M., & Woolley, J.D. (1990). From simple desires to ordinary beliefs: The early development of everyday psychology. *Cognition, 35,* 245–275.

Welsh, M.C., Pennington, B.F., Ozonoff, S., Rouse, B., & McCabe, E.R.B. (1990). Neuropsychology of early-treated phenylketonuria: Specific executive function deficits. *Child Development, 61,* 1697–1713.

Wimmer, H., & Hartl, M. (1991). Against the Cartesian view on mind: Young children's difficulty with own false beliefs. *British Journal of Developmental Psychology, 9,* 125–138.

Wimmer, H., Hogrefe, G.-J., & Perner, J. (1988). Children's understanding of informational access as a source of knowledge. *Child Development, 59*, 386–396.

Wimmer, H., & Perner, J. (1983). Beliefs about beliefs: Representation and constraining function of wrong beliefs in young children's understanding of deception. *Cognition, 13*, 103–128.

Wimmer, H., & Weichbold, V. (1994). Children's theory of mind: Fodor's heuristics examined. *Cognition, 53*, 45–57.

Wing, L. (1988). The continuum of autistic characteristics. In E. Schopler & G.B. Mesibov (Eds.), *Diagnosis and assessment in autism* (pp.91–110). New York: Plenum Press.

Wing, L., & Gould, J. (1979). Severe impairments of social interaction and associated abnormalities in children: Epidemiology and classification. *Journal of Autism and Developmental Disorders, 9*, 11–29.

Winner, E., Rosentiel, A.K., & Gardner, H. (1976). The development of metaphoric understanding. *Developmental Psychology, 12*, 289–297.

Woolley, J.D., & Wellman, H.M. (1993). Origin and truth: Young children's understanding of imaginary mental representations. *Child Development, 64*, 1–17.

Wozniak, R.H. (1972). Verbal regulation of motor behaviour: Soviet research and non-Soviet replications. *Human Development, 15*, 13–57.

Zaitchik, D. (1990). When representations conflict with reality: The preschoolers' problem with false belief and "false" photographs. *Cognition, 35*, 41–68.

Zaitchik, D. (1991). Is only seeing really believing? Sources of the true belief in the false belief task. *Cognitive Development, 6*, 91–103.

Zajonc, R.B. (1983). Validating the confluence model. *Psychological Bulletin, 93*, 457–480.

Author index

Subject index